At the outset of the industrial revolu⟨   ⟩ancashire labor market was a model of thoroughgoing competition. Wages adjusted quickly and smoothly to changes in the demand for and supply of labor. Within two generations, however, workers and firms had retreated from the market. Instead of busting wages, firms paid fixed rates; instead of breaking ties on short notice, workers sought longer-term associations. Social norms – doing the right thing – protected and preserved the new labor-market arrangements. This book explains the causes and effects of changes in the labor market in the context of new developments in labor economics and new research in social and economic history.

Escape from the market

Escape from the market

Negotiating work in Lancashire

MICHAEL HUBERMAN

Université de Montréal
Centre interuniversitaire de recherche
en analyse des organisations (CIRANO)

CAMBRIDGE
UNIVERSITY PRESS

CAMBRIDGE UNIVERSITY PRESS
Cambridge, New York, Melbourne, Madrid, Cape Town, Singapore,
São Paulo, Delhi, Dubai, Tokyo

Cambridge University Press
The Edinburgh Building, Cambridge CB2 8RU, UK

Published in the United States of America by Cambridge University Press, New York

www.cambridge.org
Information on this title: www.cambridge.org/9780521142663

© Cambridge University Press 1996

First published 1996
This digitally printed version 2010

A catalogue record for this publication is available from the British Library

Library of Congress Cataloguing in Publication data

Huberman, A. M.
    Escape from the market : negotiating work in Lancashire / Michael
Huberman.
        p.   cm.
    Includes bibliographical references (p.   ).
    ISBN 0 521 56151 5 (hardcover)
    1. Textile workers – England – Lancashire – History – 19th century.
    2. Labor market – England – Lancashire – History – 19th century.
    3. Collective bargaining – England – Lancashire – History – 19th
    century.   4. Labor movement – England – Lancashire – History – 19th
    century.   I. Title.
    HD8039.T42G755   1996
    338.7'677'0094276 – dc20   95-48268   CIP

ISBN 978-0-521-56151-8 Hardback
ISBN 978-0-521-14266-3 Paperback

To Bella and Sam and Sal

The Lord above gave man an arm of iron,
So he could do his work and never shirk,
But with a little bit of luck,
Someone else will do the blinkin' work.

Alan Jay Lerner
My Fair Lady

Contents

Figures

Tables

Preface

Another book on the cotton-textile industry? The wealth of studies on the industry is legendary. From its inception as the first factory industry, the cotton-textile industry in Lancashire has been the source of scholarly attention and controversy. Debates on the standard of living of workers during the critical years of industrialization, entrepreneurial failure, the decline of the British economy, and on the nature and contributions of capital formation and technical change to economic growth have all been fought on the Lancashire battleground. Inspired by these contributions, and motivated by revisions in historical scholarship and new approaches in economic theory, economic historians have retained interest in the industry.

In this book, I look at one neglected corner of the industry – the development of the cotton-spinning labor market. In earlier treatments economists and historians concurred that labor markets of the period worked smoothly and efficiently and that firms found the workers they wanted at little cost. Relying on the insights of new contributions in labor economics and social history, this book challenges the received view.

My initial aim was to apply a basic efficiency wage model which, according to Robert J. Gordon, was the rage of the 1980s. The basic problem for Lancashire firms was how to elicit effort from workers, and for workers, how to smooth income flows before the advent of the "safety net." The economist's approach to the problem is to specify the information environment and the degree of risk aversion of workers and employers. In one variant of the basic efficiency wage model, firms pay a fixed wage that is set at a fair level in order to raise levels of effort. It became apparent, however, that the study of wage determination in Lancashire was incomplete without taking into account the origins of the efficiency wage itself.

This issue is at the heart of recent research by labor and social historians. To some analysts, key groups of workers in the period of industrialization, like cotton spinners, controlled the organization and pace of work and bargained over the relation between effort and pay. Other studies have concentrated on individual firms or regional histories. Together these studies emphasize the diversity of experiences; they are less concerned with explaining how the labor market actually operated and developed as a market.

The union of labor economics and history is not made in heaven, but it is more than a marriage of convenience. Whereas the achievement of labor economics is in deriving market outcomes from a given environment, the contribution of social and labor history lies in describing this environment and its structure. And whereas economists model the appropriate labor contract, historians describe how contracts are enforced and reproduced. Finally, the need to combine economics and history is ever more pressing when there are multiple equilibria, as in wage bargaining, because present and future choices are dependent on past decisions. I believe that the exchange between the disciplines leaves each approach stronger and that, combined, the two approaches make for a more convincing and complete interpretation of labor-market development.

Portions of this book have appeared elsewhere. Parts of chapters 2 and 7 appeared as "Invisible Handshakes in Lancashire: Cotton Spinning in the First Half of the Nineteenth Century," *Journal of Economic History*, vol. 46, no. 4 (December 1986), 987–98, copyright Economic History Association (reprinted with the permission of Cambridge University Press). Parts of chapters 2 and 3 appeared in "Industrial Relations and the Industrial Revolution: Evidence from M'Connel and Kennedy, 1810–40," *Business History Review*, vol. 65, no. 2 (Summer 1991), 345–78, copyright 1991 by the Presidents and Fellows of Harvard College. Parts of chapters 5 and 8 are from "Piece Rates Reconsidered: The Case of Cotton," *Journal of Interdisciplinary History*, vol. 26, no. 3 (Winter 1996), 393–417, copyright 1995 by the Massachusetts Institute of Technology and the editors of the *Journal of Interdisciplinary History* (reprinted with the permission of the editors of the journal and The MIT Press, Cambridge, Massachusetts). Portions of chapter 6 appeared in "How Did Labor Markets Work in Lancashire? Some Further Evidence on Prices and Quantities," *Explorations in Economic History*, vol. 28, no. 1 (January 1991), 87–120 (reprinted with permission of Academic Press). Finally, portions of chapter 7 appeared in "Some Early Evidence of Worksharing: Lancashire Before 1850," *Business History Review*, vol. 37, no. 4 (October 1995), 1–25 (reprinted with permission of Frank Cass and Co. Ltd. 1995). I wish to thank the editors and publishers of these journals.

I have many colleagues to thank, but I would especially like to acknowl- edge the comments and criticism of Gregory Clark, Jon S. Cohen,

Leonard Dudley, Barry Eichengreen, Eric L. Jones, William Lazonick, John Lyons, W. Bentley MacLeod, Douglas McCalla, John Munro, and anonymous referees. I would also like to thank seminar participants at McMaster University, Queen's University, Stanford University, University of California – Berkeley and Davis, Université de Montréal, and University of Toronto. A first version of this book was completed at the Agricultural History Center and the Institute of Governmental Affairs at UCD, and I wish to thank Peter H. Lindert and Alan Olmstead for their assistance. André Poulin provided excellent research assistance at the last moment. At Cambridge University Press, I benefited greatly from the attention of Karen Anderson Howes. All errors are my own. The Social Sciences and Humanities Research Council of Canada funded this project. Sally Cooper Cole and our children gave more and I have dedicated this book to them.

Glossary of technical terms

Blowing machine: Machine that blows apart and loosens cotton before carding.

Cambric: A plain cotton fabric from medium-count yarns.

Carding: The process of scrubbing cotton to clean the raw material and then forming long fibers into a thick rope in readiness for roving and spinning.

Carriage: The wheeled frame carrying the spindles.

Cop: The cylindrical yarn package formed in spinning.

Count: The degree of fineness of yarn. More precisely, the number of counts is equal to the number of hanks per pound of yarn, where one hank equals 840 yards. Hence one pound of no. 40 yarn contains 40 x 840 = 33,600 yards.

Doffing: Removing full bobbins and replacing them with empty ones.

Faller wire: The guide wire running across the yarns just before they reach the spindles; used to build cops.

Hank: Single strand of cotton 840 yards long.

Mule or common mule: Invented by Samuel Crompton, a machine that spun yarn intermittently. The spinning process consisted of three parts: drawing, backing-off, and winding. In the first stage the mule carriage moves outward from the spindles and the yarn is twisted by spindle rotation; in the second stage the spindles are reversed to release a few turns of yarn, enabling the faller wire to be lowered; in the final stage the carriage is returned toward the spindles and yarn is wound onto the spindles. Initially, all three stages were manually controlled.

Nose peg: Adjustment to insure that yarn was firmly wound without snarls onto the nose of the cop.

Number: See count.

Quadrant nut: The mechanism adjusting the speed of the spindles in inverse proportion to the diameter of the cop of yarn.

Rovings: Coarse loose thread produced on roving frame prior to spinning.

Self-acting mule or self-actor: A mule in which all parts of the spinning cycle (drawing, backing-off, and winding) are mechanically powered.

Sources: David Jeremy, *Transatlantic Industrial Revolution: The Diffusion of Textile Technologies Between Britain and America, 1790–1830s* (Cambridge, Mass.: MIT Press, 1981); William Lazonick, *Competitive Advantage on the Shop Floor* (Cambridge, Mass.: Harvard University Press, 1990); C. H. Lee, *A Cotton Enterprise, 1795–1840: A History of M'Connel and Kennedy, Fine Cotton Spinners* (Manchester: Manchester University Press, 1972).

Abbreviations

1 Introduction: the myth of the Lancashire labor market

Q. Do not wages essentially depend on supply and demand?
A. Yes, I admit the principle, but only question whether any regulation left to the parties or otherwise is not better.
Q. You mean by an agreement taking place between the masters and the men?
A. Yes.[1]

Economists and historians and the origins of the myth

Consider a simple economy in which all workers are identical and the skill requirements of jobs are the same, information and search costs are low, and issues of worker motivation and risk shifting are unimportant. There likewise exist no legal or institutional constraints that impede labor-market decisions. In this economy wages adjust freely to changes in the demand for and supply of labor. The flow of labor quickly accommodates any demand disturbances and long-run labor-market equilibrium would be characterized by identical wages for all workers and little unemployment. There would be little reason for workers to form long-term attachments to specific firms.[2]

Economists have found that the spot or auction model performs poorly for the period after 1945. Hard-pressed to reconcile the model with the existence of stubborn levels of unemployment, analysts initially invoked the Keynesian idea of sticky money wages. But because this approach did not explain why wages are sticky in the first place, there remained general unease about the solution. Economic agents should be able to write contracts that would eliminate the losses associated with fixed money wages. Motivated by this concern, a new research agenda on the frontiers of micro- and macroeconomics has attempted to specify under what conditions both real and money wages are rigid.[3] A variety of models has been proposed: implicit contract, insider–outsider, and efficiency wage theories,

1

among others. Although there are often sharp differences between them, a consensus has emerged – which Keynes himself shared – that sticky wages are a modern phenomenon, and that a Golden Age existed when neither institutional constraints nor information shortages impeded labor-market operations.

Many analysts have turned to the labor market during the industrial revolution in Lancashire as the prototypical representation of the auction market. Many consider that specific types of labor were homogeneous, abundant, and prepared to work for the going wage. "Markets did clear in the long run by changes in wages and prices," Jeffrey G. Williamson wrote, and "economists' assumption of perfect competition came about as close to being satisfied as one will ever get."[4] Labor-market attachments were casual, unemployment spells brief, and firms did not hesitate to cut money wages if demand for their output declined. Even Robert Solow concluded that "perhaps in nineteenth-century Manchester labor was bought and sold by thoroughgoing competition."[5] More than a case study, the Lancashire labor market has become, to borrow a hackneyed phrase, a stylized fact.

Two intellectual developments after 1945 led to the invention of the Lancashire model. The landmark study of A. W. Phillips gave credibility to the belief that sometime in this century there was a structural break in the relation between wages and unemployment.[6] A free and competitive labor market was swept aside by its opposite, an inflexible institution restricting individual movement and choice. Phillips observed the break for Britain sometime before 1913 and surmised that the "extension of collective bargaining and particularly the growth of arbitration and conciliation procedures" made wages less responsive to changes in unemployment. Similarly, using evidence for the United States, Paul Samuelson and Robert Solow speculated that after 1945 increased unionization altered the relation between wages and unemployment, although they did refer to the institutional changes of the New Deal as possible determinants as well.[7] Wage rigidity is now commonly attributed to institutional impediments. Robert J. Gordon, in a recent survey of wage and employment fluctuations in Britain, Japan, and the United States, commented without qualification that "the chief institutional features of British labour-market institutions are class consciousness, class conflict, labour militancy, and weak management."[8]

A second and distinct intellectual path to the Lancashire model can be traced to the work of Karl Polanyi. In his classic, *The Great Transformation*, Polanyi described the freeing up of land, capital, and labor markets over the course of the modern period. It was the introduction of the New Poor Law of 1834 that in his view established a competitive labor market in England. "The mechanism of the market was asserting itself and clamoring for its completion: human labor had to be made a commodity. Out of the horrors of Speenhamland [the Old Poor Law] men rushed blindly for the shelter of a utopian market economy."[9] But no sooner had the gates been opened than protective action like factory laws and social legislation closed them. Without rejecting this line of reasoning, T. S. Ashton argued that the labor market operated as a market for a longer period. At least in the industrial north, certainly by the 1830s if not earlier, a regional and imperfect labor market had been replaced by a "single, increasingly sensitive market for labor."[10] Polanyi's and Ashton's interpretations of the Lancashire model contrast with the view originating with Phillips in their periodization, and in suggesting alternative sources of institutional rigidities; but the bottom line is that all versions share the strong belief that structure in the labor market originated outside the firm.

To historians, the period of industrialization was more complex. In their accounts, two systems were at work simultaneously. Eric Hobsbawm believed that workers based their wages on a "customary not a market calculation" which fixed relative wages and assumed a standard day of work and effort. Firms got their skilled workers "at less than market cost."[11] Workers demanded and received their share of the gains of factory work only after they learned the "rules of the game," sometime after 1850, when the excess supply of labor tapered off and unionization took hold. The midcentury watershed in industrial relations was accepted by a generation of historians as evidence of a dichotomy between "custom" and the "market." In these accounts, as in the versions of Phillips, Solow, Polanyi, and Ashton, the market ultimately prevailed before 1850.[12] Patrick Joyce in *Work, Society, and Politics* adopted the midcentury split in industrial relations in his study of the relation between work and politics in the cotton-textile districts.[13] In his interpretation, as in others, the first factory workers were unprepared to meet the demands and pace of the new work routine. Their only defense was their customary habit of mutuality and fairness, but they were no match for the forces of market competition. "The sons and daughters of fathers who had known the violent and transforming power of mechanisation were often a *tabula rasa* on which the factory impressed its mighty stamp from childhood on."

Two snapshots of the labor market: 1800 and 1850

How well does the auction market view perform for the Golden Age? Consider the labor market for Lancashire cotton spinners in 1800 and 1850. In 1800 the market exhibited high turnover, short attachments, and contingent earnings and rates of pay, exactly what we expect to see in a

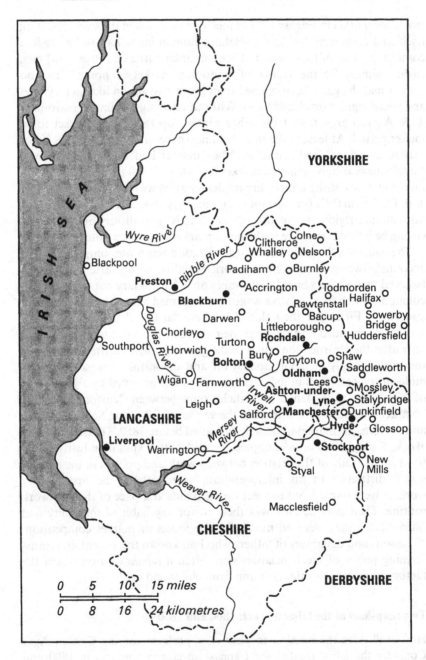

1.1   The cotton-textile district of Lancashire

spot market. This picture would seem to suggest that firms did rely on the market to supply an adequate workforce. But the picture for 1850 is in sharp contrast, with the labor market deviating from its textbook model in at least five ways:

- Piece rates for cotton spinners were relatively fixed.[14] In a competitive model with complete information, earnings and output record accurately the productivity of individual workers, and firms would have easily adjusted piece rates to changes in the demand for and supply of labor, and to changes in technology. Where earnings of piece-rate workers are greater than workers paid by the hour or week, the competitive model attributes this gap to compensating differentials due to the increased effort and ability of piece-rate workers.
- Despite the size and geographic concentration of the industry, piece rates were codified in regional piece-rate lists that imposed a rigid structure of remuneration. In 1840 about 900 spinning and integrated (spinning and weaving) firms in the industry employed roughly 18,000 spinners and 135,000 other workers. Most spinning firms were located in southeastern Lancashire, around Manchester (see figure 1.1). Despite their proximity and the apparent ease of worker mobility, there were well-established variations in earnings between regions. Piece-rate schedules also differed. In the textbook model, labor markets are loose and the law of one price prevails.
- During moderate recessions firms adjusted employment by working short hours. But the received wisdom is that, in the early stages of industrialization, changing the number of work hours was costly, and firms in all states of nature operated at full capacity and at full time. Besides, according to the standard model, firms could dictate hours because of the excess supply of labor.
- When forced to lay off workers, firms protected senior workers, just as they do in modern labor markets. But if the labor market in Lancashire approximated an auction market, firms would have instead kept their more productive workers, who were generally young. Moreover, there was an excess supply of young workers. In 1840 there were about 20,000 younger workers who had been trained to become spinners.
- Attachments between firms and workers averaged seven years, about the length of tenure of similar groups of manufacturing workers today. Again, in an auction model, arrangements would have been casual, especially if younger workers were more productive than older ones.

My explanation of the transition from the loose labor market of 1800 is that firms and workers initially attempted to rely on the market, but that both parties ultimately rejected it. *Structure was self-imposed.* Without well-developed capital markets and before the advent of unemployment insurance, workers needed some means to manage risk and stabilize income and consumption flows over changes in their life and work cycles. Firms rejected the market precisely because they faced a high level of competition and needed to secure a reliable and productive labor force. On this terrain of compromise, the two parties negotiated a compensation package that included relatively fixed piece rates – or what I will refer to as fair wages – and short time, seniority provisions, and lengthy tenure.[15]

In one respect the relation between firms and workers in the early factories had features of a classic principal–agent problem. The firm, as principal, required work to be done, but workers, the agents, were heterogeneous and information about their effort levels was unavailable to firms. To solve the incentive problem, theory suggests that firms and workers could settle on a form of compensation – like piece rates – advantageous to both parties. The problem, however, was more complex. It was and remains difficult to write contracts that cover all contingencies. Although output was measurable with little cost, the quality of output and the potential of new technology was not. Workers entered the factories with customary notions of a fair day's pay for a fair day's work and would expend optimal effort only if they were assured of this rate. The standard rate, they claimed, insured them against work- and life-cycle changes, and in response to piece-rate cuts and the introduction of new technology they collectively withheld effort. Hence, workers engaged in hidden actions, and because of the ensuing dynamic effects, the principal–agent approach is ill suited to explain labor-market strategies and outcomes.

Cooperation between firms and workers was not immediate. Pressed by competitive forces, firms initially challenged workers' control. But changes in work organization and constant attempts to cut rates of pay only raised unit costs. It took one generation for firms and workers to recognize the benefits of cooperation and negotiate a fair wage. The standard varied according to differences in technologies and labor forces, and to different histories of labor–management relations. In some regions, like Bolton, firms and workers came to recognize as early as 1810 the benefits of cooperation, but in other districts, like Preston, the tradition of ratebusting was more firmly entrenched. In all regions, firms and workers needed to demonstrate their commitment to fixed piece rates and to self-enforced contracts. To this end, firms designed layoff strategies that accommodated workers' life-cycle concerns. Firms working short time and providing older workers with employment security earned reputations as good employers, because these practices smoothed income and consumption flows. If firms failed to adopt this strategy they would not be ensured of a steady and productive workforce.

Until reputations were firmly established, cooperation was not complete, which meant that the fair wage itself and other labor-market arrangements needed to be enforced. To reduce noncompliance, labor-market rules were established on a regional basis. Some of these rules, such as the lists, were explicitly specified; others, such as short-hour working, were mere "rules of thumb." Whether implicit or explicit, workers and firms who broke the rules were stigmatized. Over time, sanctioning declined because the rules led to recurring behavior patterns and helped coordinate economic decisions by constraining the range of available choices. In this sense the rules had evolved into social institutions that were valued for themselves as fundamentally fair or just. Labor-market arrangements had transformed into a social norm and the escape from the market was complete.

Recent challenges: theory and history

The explanation of labor development offered here draws on and extends the recent literature in economics and history. The basic market clearing model that underlies the received view of the Lancashire labor market no longer retains the popular position it once held. Beginning in the 1970s or so, economists began to abandon the notion that there was an invisible hand that guided markets, and in its place started to focus on the difficulties involved in monitoring and enforcing the actual process of market exchange. In Walrasian economics information is free, but the new literature recognizes the possibility that information is not shared equally between market participants.[16] Consumers may not know the quality of the products they wish to buy; lenders of capital may have difficulty perceiving who is a trustworthy borrower; firms may not know who is a good worker. In these cases and others, market participants need to acquire information, and this may imply, for example, altering the method of pay or firms' organizational or governing structures. Information asymmetries and the like also leave open the possibility that markets are not as "thick" as those in a competitive environment, and that participants engaging in transactions do not take prices as given, but instead have some negotiating power over them. This type of approach generates multiple solutions. Confronted with this open-endedness, progress and relevance in economic theory necessitates a closer relationship with economic history, experimental studies, and econometric testing.[17]

Parallel to these theoretical developments, economic historians began challenging the concept of a Golden Age of unfettered market forces. The first traces of wage rigidity have been progressively pushed further and further back into the past. Based on research on US labor markets, Anthony O'Brien dated it as occurring in the 1920s; but Steve Allen and

Christopher Hanes found no significant change in the cyclical sensitivity
of US manufacturing wages since the 1890s.[18] It is now clear that at least
for the United States the roots of wage stickiness lie in the nineteenth
century, that is, during the period of industrialization itself and long before
the periodization of Solow, Samuelson, and others.

From a different perspective and using different techniques, British economic and social historians, and historians of industrial relations, have
also begun to challenge the division between custom and the market, and
the dominant role of the latter. Joyce's study has proved to be controversial, and there is growing evidence that in Lancashire as elsewhere workers
were better prepared to meet the demands of factory life than he suggests.[19] In a new study of the coal industry, James Jaffe concluded that
workers implicitly rejected the dichotomy between the anachronistic
customs of the pre-industrial economy and the "hegemony of the
market."[20] "Bargaining was accepted as the principal terrain of industrial
relations," or, put differently, the market became the miners' "industrial
culture." For Lancashire, William Lazonick has convincingly shown that
male spinners were able to control the organization of work and its supervision, forcing employers to maintain the tried and true methods of labor
management.[21] Lancashire spinners were engaged in bargaining over
wages and effort norms, and well before 1850, Lazonick concluded,
workers and employers were jointly responsible for making the rules of the
game. Even Joyce, in his recent work, *Visions of the People*, is less sanguine
about the triumph of the market. "We find" in the experience of cotton-
factory workers the "intertwining of custom and the market, and the continuing dominance of the former, albeit often in much reworked forms,
right down to . . . the early twentieth century."[22]

The contributions of this literature notwithstanding, there remains no
full-length treatment of the development of the Lancashire labor market.
This book seeks to close this gap. My aim is to determine under what conditions workers were able to negotiate for fair or customary wages, when
and where they were established, how labor-market rules evolved into
community standards, and how these standards were self-enforced. By
focusing on the method of pay, I hope to better understand when and why
labor markets become rigid over time. To set the stage I need to describe
the role of custom before the factory.

Labor supply and workplace traditions in the pre-factory age

The cotton-textile industry was well established in Lancashire by 1750.
Before the advent of modern technology, fustians were the main type of
cotton manufacture.[23] The manufacture of these cotton goods was orga-

nized on the putting-out system, and goods were sold mainly to the home market. A merchant, usually resident in Manchester, constructed a network of local agents in smaller towns like Bolton and Oldham who distributed raw cotton and linen to domestic spinners and weavers. Outworkers and their families drew some support from farming activities, but agricultural holdings were small and outworkers became increasingly dependent on wages from manufacturing for support.[24]

In the putting-out system, the household was the nexus of income generation, consumption, and production decisions.[25] As regional specialization intensified and the size of agricultural holdings diminished, households needed some mechanism to stabilize income flows. Tasks were allocated according to the productivity of individual family members, which often meant shifting work loads between generations. Under these circumstances, rural industry tended to encourage high rates of natural increase; from a life-cycle perspective, this provided aging parents some assurance that they would be taken care of in the case of sickness or infirmity. It would also smooth out consumption streams. Because markets for financial and liquid physical assets did not exist or were unreliable, intertemporal reallocations of income were accomplished by relying upon reciprocity and implicit contracting with household members. Nonetheless, underlying tensions between generations and genders were always present. The control of production and technology went to men, whereas women were relegated to subordinate positions.[26] Owing as much to this control as to the ability of the household in the putting-out era to coordinate production and allocate tasks, bonds among its members were preserved. It was in the factory period – when individuals, mainly fathers, lost their ability to employ children and control production – that kinship ties were strained and workers were forced to seek alternative means to manage risk.

For outworkers, the divisions between manufacturing and other activities and between leisure and work were blurred. The year was punctuated by a seasonal round of interruptions, and the workday itself mixed bouts of intense labor and idleness. According to tradition, on Monday and Tuesday the "hand-loom went to the slow chant of Plen-ty of Time, Plen-ty of Time; on Thursday and Friday, A day t'lat, A day t'lat."[27] Workers in all trades were known for upholding Saint Monday and often Holy Tuesday. The bucolic rituals of Sunday were extended an extra day or two and it was expected that workers would make up the lost income by working harder at week's end.

It would be inaccurate, however, to characterize the pattern of work and customs of the putting-out system as haphazard or undisciplined.[28] Embodying the natural and customary rights of artisans, habits like Saint

Monday gave domestic workers protection from the forces of market competition. By taking leisure off and on the job, workers found they could
exercise, albeit at times to a limited degree, control over the workday and
the relation between effort, time on the job, and the pay they received.
They wanted to maintain the stable and fixed parameters that regulated
their position and defined their relationships within the domestic system.
To this end, they collectively fashioned notions of what constituted a fair
or normal day's work and the related pay that would preserve their status.
In his excellent study on the transition to factory work in the woolen
industry, Adrian Randall situated the role of custom in the eighteenth
century:

Attempts to pin down the components of custom in a precise way are fruitless since
custom was not static but evolutionary, encompassing both long-standing practices and recent gains or compromises . . . Custom was . . . a potent and conservative force, a framework which sought to provide and safeguard stability and
security in an unstable, insecure, and unpredictable world.[29]

If merchants or employers encroached on their standards, workers
would respond. If the weaver was given longer warps or less credit for
waste, or if standard procedures for measuring and weighing yarn were
altered in the merchant's favor, or if employers cut piece rates, workers
were incited to embezzle to maintain the normal ratio between effort and
pay. Workers would try to increase the weight of the finished product by
throwing wool on wet stones and steaming yarn over a boiling pot.
Alternatively, spinners would return reels of yarn shorter than what was
demanded, or include in each hank a smaller number of threads. By the
last quarter of the eighteenth century a black market in wool and yarn had
become an organized business, and many a cotton manufacturer was said
to have begun his career by buying materials from this source.[30] Inevitably,
as merchants recognized their inability to control embezzlement, it became
an accepted part of the wage packet itself.

In the putting-out system, it was customary that women spun and men
wove, and this division of labor was observed in cottage production with
jennies. Mimicking the motions of hand spinning, the jenny (introduced in
1765) had a drawing action that drew and twisted simultaneously, spinning
yarn intermittently. In the cottages, where the jenny remained a small
machine chiefly operated by women, the evidence available suggests that
traditional work habits persisted.[31]

Building on the gender division of labor, the Arkwright mills attempted
to break traditional workplace behavior. The water frame (1768) was at
least five times as productive as the jenny; beginning in 1781, when
Arkwright's patents were successfully challenged, there was a proliferation

of mill building. By 1795 there were about 300 mills using Arkwright machines.[32] Andrew Ure attributed Arkwright's personal success to his administrative powers. The new factory system required "a man of Napoleon nerve and ambition to subdue the refractory tempers of workpeople accustomed to irregular paroxysms of diligence . . . Such was Arkwright."[33] An Arkwright-type mill employed between 200 and 250 people and, like the cottage industry, relied almost exclusively on women and children to spin yarn. The water frame used rollers which drew the roving out and then imparted twist in a continuous process. The technology required little skill and women and children in a centralized operation proved fairly easy to train and manage.[34]

A major technical breakthrough undermined the brief success of the Arkwright system. The water frame could not produce fine counts and was used primarily for the production of warps. On the other hand, the jenny was limited to weft yarn. For some time the two complemented each other, but Crompton's mule (1779) superseded both techniques, spinning high counts of warp and weft of a consistent quality. Investment in the new technique was rapid, and by 1812 there were 673 mule factories in operation.[35]

The characteristic feature of mule – so called because it combined the drawing action of the jenny and the roller principles of the water frame – was the placement of spindles on a wheeled carriage. Yarn was spun in an intermittent process.[36] Moving the carriage away from the rollers drew and twisted the yarn; pushing the carriage backward wound the yarn. Initially, neither the outward nor the inward run was mechanized and although the former was a simple process, the latter required great care. As the yarn was coiled onto the spindle, the carriage had to be pushed back with a constant speed, proportional to that of the rotating spindles. With the left hand the spinner regulated the winding of the thread into a cone-shaped package called a cop, while the right hand turned the handle of a fly-wheel and varied the speed of the rotating spindles. At the same time the body pushed the carriage back toward the frame. If the carriage was pushed too slowly, yarns would break; if it was pushed too quickly, the cop would be badly formed. Although there were technical improvements in common-mule spinning (and later self-actor spinning, which was an attempt to automate the spinning process completely), textile operatives retained manual control of the speed and pace of operation.[37] If there were multiple breakages of yarn on the larger machines, the mule had to come to a complete stop to piece the broken threads. There was also doffing: when the reels were full of spun cotton, the mule had to be stopped and the reels removed. Finally, there was cleaning. At all these times, spinners could expend effort as they were motivated to, and without proper supervision or incentives they could disguise how hard they could in fact work.

Mule spinning had its origins in the putting-out system and women and men operated the first generation of hand-powered mules.[38] Upon its introduction, mules of a dozen or so spindles were housed in the garrets of cottages and later in sheds (which were mostly converted corn mills). On these small mules, spinners mended the broken threads themselves or with the assistance of piecers, who commonly were family members. In these locations traditional work patterns persisted. Some women continued to spin on mules, even after they were fitted to a Boulton and Watt engine in the first factories, and competition between men and women for spinning positions would later become a key variable in managerial strategies to get work out. But by 1795, as Frances Collier observed, "men were in undisputed possession of the occupation."[39]

Beginning in the 1780s and lasting into the next century, a stream of hatters, shoemakers, smiths, tailors, handloom weavers, and other journeymen left their trades for the marginally higher wages of mule spinning.[40] The inflow was associated with men's redefinition of spinning. Men claimed that women could not push the mule carriage on its backward run, and that they did not have the skill to wind the yarn onto the spindle. Moreover, on the extended mules introduced in the first factories, spinning involved the supervision and recruiting of large numbers of young assistants who pieced threads, scavenged for waste which fell below the machine, removed the full reels, and cleaned the machines. Male spinners claimed that they were more capable than women of overseeing the production team.

Past experience informed how workers behaved in the new factories. Most migrants came from the surrounding rural areas in which the putting-out system was firmly implanted. Census sampling reveals that the first generation of operatives traveled short distances to find work in the sheds and early factories located in urban centers. For Preston in 1851, Michael Anderson found that only 13 percent of all residents who were migrants came from villages in which most adult males were engaged in agriculture.[41] The new male workers adopted the status of artisans, bringing with them the institutions and standards of eighteenth-century craft. Lacking a formal apprenticeship system and a tramping network, spinners formed clubs and friendly societies. Like similar associations in other trades, these societies offered protection, although incomplete, against hardships arising from accident, illness, and old age. They also provided spinners with a base to defend popular customs both in and out of the factory.

The steady flows of workers, in conjunction with a high natural birth rate and migration from Ireland, have given support to the view that the labor supply was highly elastic. Phyllis Deane referred to the "fact that it [the cotton industry] enjoyed an almost inexhaustible low-price labour supply"; Sidney Pollard concluded that "Manchester never had a real labour shortage"; H. J. Habakkuk concurred: "from 1815–50 the English manufacturer had a very elastic supply of labour at the ruling wage . . . and any shortages that did arise were local and temporary."[42]

But here is where the auction market approach begins to break down. Employers were concerned not only about availability of labor, but about whether an adequate labor supply today would be inadequate tomorrow. The sheer quantity of labor did not ensure that workers would be reliable and productive – labor purchased at a given wage did not necessarily translate into labor actually supplied. Arthur Okun wrote:

What a firm wants when it hires a worker is productive performance, which is not readily ascertainable in advance. A firm wishes to buy quality of work rather than merely time on the job spent by interchangeable people.[43]

Firms had to deal with issues of labor-force instability, quality, and productivity, and this meant devising ways to deal with the background and attitude of workers. The challenge to the owners of the early mule factories was therefore twofold. They had both to recruit a factory workforce and to break its standards of behavior. The ensuing conflict between workers and firms sets the background for this study of how labor markets developed.

The organization of the book

The first part of this book explores the transition of the cotton-spinning industry from the countryside to the factory. Because employers could not continuously recruit new workers, and workers could not endure endlessly the high costs of quits, it would at first appear that both parties had an incentive to come to some agreement over earnings and work conditions. But agreement was not immediate. Firms attempted to replace men with women and to bust rates of pay; spinners responded by restricting effort.

Throughout the century the piece rate was the primary source of tension between workers and firms, and in Part II, I examine the benefits and costs of this form of remuneration. Although in principle workers should cooperate with management when payment is by the piece, cooperation is rare, because firms have a strong incentive to cut rates whenever workers' earnings rise. Why then did firms like those in Lancashire stick with paying by the piece? I argue that piece rates can work when firms are committed to fixing rates. But how can workers and firms circumvent the market, and how are fixed rates established? How can firms commit to these rates? How is defection prevented?

Part III addresses these issues. Fair wages took hold in large firms in the

14   **Introduction**

leading industrial centers of Manchester and Bolton. By 1850, firms in other areas adopted these policies, although there were important exceptions. Firms needed to show their commitment to the fair wage, and to this end they introduced worksharing and a layoff strategy that protected senior workers. These arrangements were initially rules of thumb, but standard piece rates themselves became codified in written lists. Why did some rules get written down while others were more loosely adhered to? Written rules such as the lists impacted on future decisions since no one believed they would change. Yet all rules, whether formally stipulated or not, were governed by community standards of what was just and fair.

The concluding part summarizes the findings and their contribution to recent controversies in British economic history, and more generally to labor history and labor economics.

Part I

Labor-market failure?

2 Custom against the market: the early labor market

One thing you may depend upon, that the important question, whether the workmen shall be slaves of the master-spinners, or whether they shall have fair wages and due consideration in the scale of society, will shortly be at rest.[1]

Labor economics and labor history: some problems in approach

In 1795 M'Connel and Kennedy of Manchester succeeded in applying a Boulton and Watt steam engine to the outward run of the mule. In some economic histories, this completed the prerequisite or early stages of the industrial revolution and ushered in its model labor market. Although the backward run or winding phase still required physical exertion, on the power-assisted or common mule all manual skill in the actual spinning of yarn was superseded. Compared to the water frame and the jenny, the common mule spun a wider range of counts of uniform quality, and it was more economical in the use of power. It was quickly adopted by the giant firms in the industry as well as new entrants, marking a shift in the locus of the industry from rural to urban centers, such as Manchester, Bolton, and Preston. M'Connel and Kennedy participated actively in the construction boom. The firm built two new factories between 1797 and 1805 and the number of common mules it owned increased from 38 to 192.[2]

It is axiomatic that if firms were to realize financial returns on their new investments in plant and machinery, they had to recruit a supply of reliable and productive workers. In the simple labor market model, these are second-order concerns. At the market clearing or going wage employers can fill the number of openings they have and all workers who want jobs in this market can find them. For their part, historians of labor markets have shown more interest in recruitment, and on the basis of the availability of labor, the presumption is that firms recruited a workforce without much cost. The rural employer, according to the Hammonds, "had only to step on the ground to turn an empty village into swarming hives of workpeople"; and C. H. Lee, the historian of M'Connel and Kennedy, concluded unambiguously that the firm "had no difficulty in finding labor."[3]

The chief difficulty with the spot model and historians' emphasis on the quantity of labor available is that both approaches obscure how in fact the labor market developed as a market. The relevant economic question is what was the quality of labor that was attracted by the wages and working conditions firms offered. Did the market provide them with full information about labor types? Was the quality and quantity of labor adequate to get work out, or did firms have to alter their strategies to get the labor force they wanted? How did workers react? As for historians, they are bound to find scant evidence of "labor shortage" simply because these situations will not persist.[4] A temporary excess demand for labor may leave a residue of high wages, but over time firms adapt recruiting tactics or production technologies. Otherwise they will fail; the geographic scope of the market may itself contract or expand. There are, as well, strong feedback mechanisms between the choice of technology and the type of labor supply attracted.

Workers respond to the risk environment and opportunities available to them. Where workers have alternative sources of income or access to capital markets, or are insured to some degree from unemployment, their strategic behavior will differ from workers who are left to manage risk and uncertainty by themselves. Moreover, both workers and firms learn from their own behavior and each others'. Once in place, a wage package sends out a signal in the labor market that may be difficult to adjust.[5]

The task confronting students of labor markets, therefore, is to go beyond static descriptions of availability and analyze changes in market outcomes – wage and employment packages – in response to different sets of risk and information environments faced by both sides of the market. In light of these observations, in this chapter I reassess the strategies pursued by urban and rural firms to recruit a labor force and displace traditional workplace habits. I begin with a description of the customs the first generation of spinners brought to the factory.

Labor supply and risk management

The labor supply standing outside the urban factory may have been sufficient, but it contained a range of worker types.[6] There were the reliable spinners who showed up to work and gave full effort, but there were others who showed their "love of liberty" and, as they had done in the putting-out age, took Monday off anticipating that they could make up lost income by working harder at the end of the week.[7] Sports, races, fairs, and

animal fights drew spinners away from their mules; leisure was also consumed on the job. Still others would quit without notice or stay away and
send for their wages at week's end. Many of these transient workers were
employed by more than twenty firms in the first two decades of the nineteenth century.[8]

Along with labor-supply choices, technical factors broke the nexus of
income, consumption, and production decisions that families had controlled in the putting-out stage. Over the first twenty years of factory work
in urban centers it became increasingly uncommon for families to work
together. It was impossible for spinners whose average age was between
thirty and thirty-five to hire enough of their own children to piece broken
threads and scavenge loose cotton under the spinning machine.[9] The
problem intensified as more spindles were added and there was greater
demand for assistants on each pair of mules. Thus, spinners had to go
outside the immediate family to find the young assistants required in the
work team.

The decline in the family work unit reinforced changes in the household
that arose during industrialization. Comparing the family in the putting-
out stage and under the factory regime, Angus Reach observed in 1849
that its "cohesive powers" were diminished and the interests of individual
wage earners became stronger than the interests of the family as a whole,
because "the factory system tends to a speedier recurring break-up, and a
speedier recurring formation of families."[10] According to the sociologist
Michael Anderson, the underlying tension in the Lancashire factory-town
household lay in the ability of sons and daughters to quickly afford the
basic necessities of life, "a roof over one's head and the provision of food
and domestic assistance."[11] They no longer had to wait to inherit land.
Coinciding with changes in their own economic position, young men and
women had the ability to terminate and renew relationships with kin, and
evidence of their independence is that it was not customary for parent/
spinners to pass on pairs of spinning mules to their children/piecers. This
convention held throughout the century. Anderson also found that the
"loosely structured nets, fluid population, and weak hold of ideologies
minimized normative control" of the family.

The decline in the family work team, combined with pressures on traditional kinship networks, forced adults in the labor force to find new means
of managing critical life situations: old age, sickness, and unemployment.
To some analysts poor relief, if not meager, was at best supplementary – a
refuge of last resort; at any rate many workers loathed assistance because
they feared resettlement, or because of the stigma attached to going to
the authorities.[12] In his study of the 1847–48 recession, H. M. Boot found
that despite low levels of personal savings, only about 10 percent of the

workforce in Manchester went to the authorities for help.[13] Community institutions like charities were established, yet the amount of support they gave was limited; private markets to manage risk do not appear to have taken hold. It was natural that individual workers turned to family and household networks for support during crises, and Anderson argued that, with limited external sources of support, family ties were probably strengthened during periods of rapid economic change and critical life situations. Nevertheless, the support was fundamentally different from that which existed in the pre-factory period. Although families may not have been together in the same mills, most working members of the household found employment in the textile industry, and they could offer only limited support to each other when the industry was hit by a general decline in demand. In the putting-out stage, in contrast, there remained alternative non-manufacturing work for some members of the household. Moreover, individual decisions, Anderson suggested, were calculative and not reciprocal, and again in contrast to life-cycle patterns in the putting-out stage, decidedly short-term.[14]

Thus, family and household networks in factory towns, and options available to manage risk, differed markedly from those which had existed in the putting-out stage. The ease with which workers moved from job to job in this early period obviously tempered life- and work-cycle changes. But their principal means of defense against insecurity was the customary standard of a fair day's pay for a fair day's work that they inherited from the pre-factory era. Upholding the independence and natural-born rights of spinners, customary standards gave workers assurance that, as they aged, they would be able to keep on working at a piece rate which would maintain some acceptable level of earnings. If firms attempted to speed up work or squeeze more output and break conventional norms, spinners' response was to show that they could expend no more effort. If rate cuts went through, workers would embezzle to make up lost earnings. Into the 1830s there is evidence of workers in all stages of spinning who, like their precursors in the domestic system, sold cops of yarn on the black market.[15]

Although the elements of custom are difficult to pinpoint exactly, several aspects of the relation between pay and effort stand out. Fairness involved comparisons with well-specified reference groups both over and across time.[16] Male spinners wanted to preserve the custom that they would be rewarded for the output performance of the whole team and that they would be responsible for supervision of younger workers; they wanted to preserve the custom that they would be paid the same rate on old and new machinery; they wanted to be rewarded for the extra work they claimed was required to spin on mules with a larger number of spindles; they wanted assurance that the customary differential between different grades of yarn would remain intact, and that employers would not push them to work harder by giving them inferior qualities of cotton; finally, they wanted to preserve any type of earnings differentials that prevailed within firms and between the spinning areas of Lancashire.

Toward this end spinners organized themselves.[17] Many male spinners had come from crafts that already possessed rudimentary trade organizations that regulated apprenticeship, workplace customs, and piece rates. These spinners laid the foundation for the early trade clubs and societies of the 1790s and by the turn of the century, despite legislation against combination, their associations were leading the defense of standard levels of effort and pay. Women and piecers were barred from these associations and an entrance fee was imposed on migrant spinners. In the early strikes, spinners demanded regional piece-rate lists that would standardize earnings for equal work, regardless of the size of mule used. A related issue was the attempts by firms to alter the organization of production and introduce longer mules that threatened their craft status and standard rates. Spinners would hold to these basic demands throughout the century. Because labor-market decisions, however, have different degrees of reversibility, employers' initial response to these demands had implications for the direction in which the labor market would later evolve.

Employers' response: market reliance

The problem facing employers appears to have been trivial. It would be expected that firms were able to distinguish reliable and irregular workers by paying by the piece and by sub-contracting work. But firms did not rely exclusively on positive incentives, an indication – a recurrent theme in this book – that the method of pay was insufficient in eliciting full information about workers' abilities as it should have been in theory. Using the testimony of employers before factory inquiries, Pollard found that in the early period deterrents were more commonly used than positive rewards.[18] Corporal punishment, fines, and deductions were used to deter lateness, talking with fellow workers, or unnecessary waste. These harsh practices, excessive when compared to the actual cost of the misdemeanor, are lasting images of the first industrial revolution.

By all accounts the most widely used deterrent was dismissal. Given a footloose labor supply, high turnover offered the path of least resistance. Turnover was neither gender- nor age-specific, and was found in all stages of production, from the carding, cleaning, and drawing rooms to the spinning departments. A. & G. Murray, a concern generally regarded as being one of the best employers, had an annual labor turnover rate of almost 42 percent. This figure was probably not atypical of the industry as a whole.[19]

By 1815 or so, observed a Manchester doctor, it was the "general practice that workpeople are engaged from week to week, and they may leave at the end of every week." Some employers were clearly indifferent to high turnover; many firms did not keep payrolls. "We have never taken the least notice" of the number of workers who turn over, commented the manager of John Kennedy's factory.[20] This meant relying on the market to supply the steady flow of workers. "Perhaps it may not be generally known," said G. A. Lee, owner of a large Manchester establishment, "that there is really a place for hiring children; that is, on a particular Monday morning, there are a number of children that you can find at a particular place; their parents may perhaps attend, but it is rare." Such was the available supply that urban firms rejected the use of parish apprentices. Since they could not be threatened with dismissal, they had little inducement to work properly.[21] Low earnings complemented high turnover. Between 1810 and 1820 earnings of fine spinners fell by 33 percent; those of medium-count spinners by 18 percent.[22]

At first glance, the package of high turnover and low earnings appears to have matched labor-supply decisions. But unpacking the bundle reveals that urban firms were actively engaged in a high turnover policy to break pre-factory standards. Following Arkwright's example, the goal was to build a new workforce that had little past experience. Turnover kept factories filled with children, young adults, and women; if these conditions had held, it would have been unlikely that workforces would have matured as the industry established itself, thereby eliminating any likelihood of the steady accumulation of skills. It may be speculated that, at this juncture, employers perceived that the gains of turnover offset those related to experience. In 1818, 60 percent of all workers were below nineteen years of age.[23] These figures varied between regions. In Preston, for example, about 11 percent of workers were below nine years of age; the corresponding figure in Manchester was about half that, but in the same year about 50 percent of factory workers in the town were female.[24] Earnings evidence for Lancashire's main hub confirms that women replaced men. In comparison with the decline in pay of male fine and coarse spinners, the earnings of women fell by a smaller amount. Firms' hostile reaction to government legislation regarding hours of work of women and children is a further sign of the strategy to replace men.[25] If firms were limited in the number of men they could replace, or if they were prevented from replacing men at all, they would have been forced to seek alternative and costlier means to break down pre-industrial work habits. Those regions, like Preston, that were more reliant on women and children found themselves most exposed.

Turnover: an evaluation

The received wisdom is that in conjunction with high turnover, the stick and the carrot broke down pre-industrial work habits. Although there is heated disagreement about the origins of the new factories, the leading protagonists in the debate share the view that the early mule factories transplanted Arkwright's techniques successfully and surmounted problems of organizing, disciplining, and motivating their workforces. Stephen Marglin claimed that the triumph of the factory system itself and the motivation behind it lay in the use of discipline and supervision to elicit effort from workers, generating a more easily captured surplus for "bosses."[26] David Landes linked the rise and success of the factory system to the introduction of a new set of technologies, and although he acknowledged that firms had difficulty in extracting "full" labor for wages, he concluded, along with Marglin, that new methods of discipline and remuneration were introduced to deal with these problems.[27]

Despite the weight of these claims, there has been no thorough investigation of the high turnover policy. Moreover, any attempt must consider the industry's composition and organization. In the countryside there were mostly coarse mills, the Ashworth's fine-spinning mill outside Bolton being an important exception; many rural mills were small, although the Ashworth's and the Gregs' mills were among the industry's largest enterprises.[28] The urban sector was more heterogeneous. There were large, if not giant, fine-spinning mills in Manchester and Bolton; dominating Preston, and also present in Manchester, were large and medium-sized integrated mills (combining spinning and weaving activities), generally producing coarse and medium-quality goods; finally, coarse-spinning firms of various sizes, and some of the smaller ones, notably in Oldham, rented space and steam power in larger establishments.

The labor-market strategies of rural firms will be discussed later in this chapter. In the present discussion of urban firms, I will make a distinction between fine and coarse mills only. This breakdown can be justified because *at this stage* of the industry's development, the critical factor in assessing employers' responses in the labor market was the cost of cotton waste associated with high turnover of spinners.

Many coarse-spinning mills relied on throstles. A variant of the water frame, throstles automatically and continuously performed the drawing, twisting, and winding of yarn. The only intervention in the spinning process required from operatives was to piece up yarns when they broke and to replace bobbins, tasks which could be easily learned in a few days of training. As in the Arkwright mills, throstles were tended typically by women and children.[29] In some throstle factories, overlookers supervised operations and workers were frequently paid day wages. Whether spinning by throstle or mule, coarse mills comprised the majority in the industry, and since their policy of high turnover continued into the 1820s and 1830s, there is no reason to believe that it was ineffective in eliciting high levels of effort. Because the cotton they used was of the cheaper varieties, firms in this sector were not concerned with the waste and damaged yarn that often resulted when workers were replaced.

Fine-spinning firms were almost exclusively reliant on the common mule. Although these firms were a distinct minority, they were at the forefront of the industry in designing technology and expanding markets. But because of the large fixed costs associated with new investments in machinery and plant, and the quality of cotton used, they were hard-pressed to find a strategy of breaking down customary work habits. Indeed fine mills were at the vanguard in devising a strategy to deal with workers, and through a learning process all firms in the industry shared in their successes and failures. For these mills there is evidence that the high turnover policy had severe drawbacks.

I have collected data from the business records of M'Connel and Kennedy (M&K), the leading Manchester cotton-spinning enterprise, to evaluate the managerial strategies of the early fine-spinning factories.[30] How representative was M&K? Certainly the firm was no flyspeck. It spun the *finest* yarn in Lancashire and in 1816 it was the second-largest firm in the industry, employing 1,020 hands.[31] Of course, we would like to know more about other urban firms, especially small and medium-sized coarse spinners which approximated the median size of firms in the industry, but their records do not exist or are fragmentary at best. The firm may have been atypical not solely because of its size or product, but also because its record books survived. But primary source materials, including newspaper reports and evidence before parliamentary commissions, suggest that at least at this stage of the industry's development, the labor-market problems faced by M&K were not different in kind, but only in degree. At the turn of the century, M&K shared with other spinning concerns a similar technology and labor force. Although the firm was an innovator in the application of power to the mule, the new technology quickly spread among fine and medium-count spinners in the major urban centers of Lancashire. Located in the hub of Manchester's industrial zone, the Ancoats district, the industrial relations environment at the firm was representative. Finally, the age and gender mix of its labor force was comparable to the composition of workers at other firms, including coarse and integrated mills.[32]

Established in 1795, M&K met with early success.[33] The ability of the firm in its formative years to combine machine making, principally mules, and the spinning of fine yarns gave it an initial advantage over its rivals. Although it continued to make its own equipment, around the turn of the century the firm stopped selling machinery. The firm could not depend on the Lancashire yarn market for its survival, and by the early 1800s it had established contacts with buyers in Scotland and Ireland, the hosier and lace manufacturers of Nottingham, and producers on the Continent. Markets expanded and in the first two decades of the century, with prices inflated by the French Wars, M&K, like the entire spinning industry, enjoyed some years of high rates of profit. Capacity at the firm grew. One estimate is that the ratio of fixed to total capital at the firm averaged over 50 percent for the first quarter of the century.[34] Between 1802 and 1818 alone the labor force rose from 312 to 1,125, and spindleage increased from 21,840 to 79,020, representing an increase in the number of mules from 80 to 269.[35]

The earliest years for which records on industrial relations at M&K are available are for 1809 to 1818. At the outset of the period the firm relied on male spinners to hire piecers and supervise work on pairs of common mules, 180–300 spindles in length. But with the expansion of the industry, male workers increased their demands to preserve the customary relation between effort and pay, and organized lengthy stoppages in work. The first sign of intensified demand for higher pay was in 1810.[36] Piece rates were cut in 1811 after a four-month dispute, but according to M'Connel the rate cut that went through was smaller than he and other employers had desired. Another strike in 1813 was followed by a "great advance in wages."[37] Employers successfully reduced rates in 1816, but two years later there was a widespread turnout lasting three months for a return to the high earnings of 1814.

To protect itself from the growing number of competitors, reduce costs, and exercise its control over the mill-floor, the firm began to replace men with women spinners. "He [M'Connel] wanted to drop our wages," one male spinner remarked, and "we wished them not to be dropped, and through these means he would not quarrel with us, but put women to our work, and has employed women ever since."[38] Female spinners, contemporaries observed, could have kept the mules operating at half the pay – although it was unclear at what level of efficiency.[39] In the putting-out system women had operated jennies and mules, and although it is debatable whether women had the strength to move heavy mule carriages, this was not an issue on mules of fewer than 250 spindles like the ones at M&K.[40] Beginning in 1810 M&K began to hire women in place of men, and according to the firm's own history women in fact received half the wages of their male co-workers from 1812 on.[41] Because of the paucity of statistical documentation, it is impossible to report annual changes in the composition of the labor force, but the available records indicate that the proportion of female workers at the firm increased from an already high level of 48.7 to 62.3 percent between 1802 and 1818.[42]

The replacement of men by women not only reduced labor costs, but the threat of job loss may have had the added benefit of motivating all spinners to work hard, thereby reducing both unit variable and unit fixed costs. As at other mills, many adult male spinners at M&K lost their jobs during the turnouts and were replaced by younger hands.[43] For these spinners the cost of job loss was not insignificant. The expansion after 1810 was marked by years of frenzied activity and sudden contraction and, as we have seen, workers had little protection from cyclical fluctuations. Without alternative sources of income, spinners were driven hard by the specter of unemployment.

But the turnover strategy carried risks. In addition to leading spinning operations, male spinners were entrusted with the supervision and recruiting of their assistants. By hiring women, firms like M&K were gambling that the fall in labor costs would be greater than the unforeseen costs of changing the work organization.

The ledgers and record books of one of the firm's factories which are available for 1809 to 1817 can be used to evaluate the combined strategies of hiring more women and the threat of job loss. No direct evidence is available but it is highly probable that because of the vintage and size of the mules, the factory employed both men and women. The factory was the first built by the firm, and the number of spindles per mule (283) was about the average for the entire firm.[44] It contained eighty-seven mules of 300 spindles and fourteen mules of 180 spindles, and although it remains uncertain whether women could work the larger mules, it is clear that they could operate the smaller ones.[45]

Using John Kennedy's index of hanks per spindle per day, the output figures in table 2.1 were corrected for count of yarn because it took longer to spin higher or finer counts. After correction, output performance per spindle showed an improvement of 10.09 percent between 1809 and 1817. This productivity improvement would appear consistent with a human capital model in which spinners, through learning-by-doing, were steadily accumulating firm- and mule-specific skills. But the high turnover of the period works against this hypothesis. That the corrected series reached its peak in 1816, a depression year by all accounts, provides some evidence that the high turnover had its intended impact on productivity. Threatened by the fear of job loss during the trade decline, workers increased output to prevent being laid off.

The output gains reduced unit fixed costs and the hiring of women lowered labor costs, reducing total unit costs by about 10 percent.[46] This

Table 2.1 *Average weekly production statistics, M'Connel and Kennedy:*
1809–1817

				Hanks per spindle		
Year	Count	Hanks	Spindles	Actual	Corrected[a]	Waste[b]
1809	137	173728	29538	5.91	5.08	7.08
1810	141	187474	29647	6.37	5.86	6.67
1811	162	131810	27019	4.53	4.80	6.11
1812	132	194111	29603	6.42	5.58	5.78
1813	161	158373	28305	5.25	5.57	8.71
1814	153	177966	28641	5.86	5.97	8.16
1815	156	170369	29035	5.62	5.90	7.66
1816	165	175461	29284	5.76	6.05	9.19
1817	174	155717	30552	5.09	5.65	11.54

Notes:
[a] Output corrected by John Kennedy's index of hanks per spindle per day in 1812.
Index: no. 100 = 1.4 hanks per spindle; no. 120 = 1.25; no. 150 = 1.00; no.
200 = 0.75. Kennedy's calculations are reprinted in Edward Baines, *History of the Cotton Manufacture of Great Britain* (London: Cass, 1835; reprinted in 1966), 353.
[b] Waste = (Rovings – Twist/Rovings) × 100%.
Source: M&K Yarn Output Book, 1808–1818.

gain was offset, however, by increased wastage costs. In fine spinning it was the usual practice to prepare the cotton in rovings before it was spun on mules. Waste comprised the broken ends in the spinning process and, measured as the difference between the weight of rovings and twist spun, it almost doubled between 1810 and 1817. At the spinning stage of production, waste was commonly associated with inferior or bad cotton. But M&K had to use the best Sea Island cotton to maintain the quality of its yarn. Waste could have also been the product of spinning higher counts of yarn which required fewer imperfections or end breakages. However, the increased waste was not a technical problem. Wastage rates differed by over 30 percent in 1811 and 1816, even though there was little change in count spun between the two years, and for the entire period the change in yarn counts explained less than 10 percent of the change in waste.[47]

The increased waste was the result of end breakages that were left uncollected and unmended.[48] Male spinners had recruited and supervised their piecers and scavengers, who, as long as mules remained small, were family members. Whether in the factory or at home, the adult male spinner was a disciplinarian. The mule spinners of Manchester, it was reported, "kept their straps hanging in view for all, piecers and scavengers alike."[49] However, when firms like M&K began to hire female spinners the incentive system altered. Women, unlike their male counterparts, did not pay their piecers. The task of driving young workers and paying them fell to their immediate supervisors, the spinning-room overlookers. But firms throughout Lancashire had difficulty in finding qualified overlookers, and as many of them were paid by the week, they did not have the incentive to see that work got done quickly.[50] Whether their belief was valid or not, contemporaries maintained that women supervisors were more prone than men to use positive and humane incentives, such as the offer of food or money. And they held an additional belief, again like any ideology difficult to prove or disprove, that given the long work hours of the early factory system these tactics were doomed to fail.[51] Summarizing the evidence contained in the reports of the commissions on factory conditions, Ivy Pinchbeck, an early historian of women's work, wrote that "women spinners could not be expected to keep their boys at work by the frequent lickings considered necessary six and eight times a day."[52] Thus, in the new work organization the evidence confirms the belief, without attesting to its veracity, that women spinners and overlookers failed to supervise piecers and scavengers as men had, and, as a result, waste at the firm increased.

Wastage costs offset the benefits of increased output. Between 1811 and 1818 both wastage rates and the cost of waste nearly doubled. Unit costs rose by about 12 percent, completely negating the reduction in labor and fixed costs.[53] Other costs were also associated with the policy of hiring women. The firm incurred search costs because women, unlike men, did not recruit their assistants.[54] If the high number of quits of young workers was indicative, these costs were not trivial. Referring to young workers, Thomas Scott, an overlooker at M&K, observed that "there [was] no person about the building who [was] employed beyond the week." Workers of all ages did not need to give a week's notice before leaving, and they frequently did not show up on Monday morning. In 1818 the rate of turnover of the firm reached 100 percent.[55] On balance, therefore, the increased waste and labor turnover costs may have outweighed the benefits associated with the rise in output.

Thus, the combined strategy of high turnover and wage cuts was not viable. Marglin was correct in his assertion that the first factories used work organization as a strategic variable to get more work out, but he underestimated, in cases like cotton spinning, the enforcement costs involved in changing from one organization to another. For M&K these costs were initially unknown; this is the ever-present risk in moving from one type of organization or institutional arrangement to another. The firm might have persevered with the policy if profits remained healthy for, like other firms, it saw the long-term benefit of getting rid of recalcitrant male workers and replacing them with women. However, after 1820 when the fall in margins signaled a squeeze on profits, the firm was compelled to find a way to reduce costs or to raise productivity by some means other than the hiring of women.

Labor demand and supply at rural mills

The locus of technical change shifted after 1800 to urban centers like Manchester and Bolton, but the industry had its origins in the countryside and some rural mills, like the Greg and Ashworth enterprises, retained their position in the industry throughout the first half of the century.[56] Naturally isolated because of their dependence on water, rural mills could not simply announce a wage and wait for workers.[57] In these circumstances turnover was costly and to recruit a stable workforce firms offered the possibility of long-term employment.

Initially, many rural mills relied on parish apprentices to tend their vacant machines. To fill Quarry Bank mill at Styal which was opened in 1784, Samuel Greg recruited children from all parts of the country: Newcastle-under-Lyme, Liverpool, London, and many Cheshire parishes.[58] The apprentices were bound to work for about seven years. They had little opportunity to acquire the customs of the domestic system and the factory itself, to use Arthur Redford's felicitous phrase, was regarded as a kind of workhouse.[59] Greg was in no hurry to establish a permanent community at Styal. Until the 1830s it experienced no labor shortage and its choice of technology suited its labor force. The firm specialized in extremely coarse yarn and at the outset used water frames exclusively – machines older children could operate easily.[60]

For many firms the apprenticeship system proved costly to maintain, and by the turn of the century it was breaking down.[61] Some firms were negotiating contracts for "free" children, but most mills became dependent on a local labor supply that was losing its resistance to factory work.[62] Using the enumeration books for the census of 1851, table 2.2 compares the birthplaces of male spinners at the Ashworth's New Eagley mill at Turton, located about ten miles from Bolton, with a sample of workers from Bolton itself. Ashworth's mill was built in 1793 and it specialized in fine yarn. Whereas most Bolton workers were born in the town, the Ashworths did not pay high enough wages to attract urban labor. Still, most of their workers came from Lancashire villages within ten miles of the mill. But in times of peak demand, the Ashworths, like the Gregs, relied as well upon overseers to put them in touch with suitable families from southern England. Although this scheme was short-lived, the upshot

Table 2.2 *Birthplaces of spinners in 1851*

| | Percentages of spinners in region | | | |
| | | Distance between birthplace and workplace | | |
Town	Working in birthplace	Under 5 miles	Between 5 and 10 miles	More than 10 miles
Bolton (N = 204)	72.1	6.2	10.1	11.7
Turton (N = 71)	10.1	33.3	28.9	27.7

Sources: Sample taken from PRO/HO 107/209–2212, 2208. Method of sampling is described in chapter 7.

was that rural mills expanded and contracted the geographic scope of their labor market to recruit an adequate labor force.

Whether or not they were locally recruited, families came to replace individuals as the basic unit of labor supply. Recall that at urban mills the application of steam power, the lengthening of mules, and the concomitant increase in demand for piecers loosened the connection between spinners/fathers and piecers/children. But at rural mills the family wage or contract persisted, even strengthened, in the workplace. Common mules at rural mills were powered mainly by water and as their size was generally smaller, the demand for piecers was not as great.[63] Where women spun on throstles and children did the preparatory work, men were employed as yard hands and general laborers; where men spun on common mules, women and children prepared cotton for spinning and mended the threads.[64]

It was expected that turnover rates of families (weighted by the number of individual members) would be less than the sum of the rates of members of the unit if they were hired separately. The migration decision of rural families was a function of urban wage levels and employment probabilities for all members of the household, and relocation and housing costs. In the city, in contrast, factory inspector Leonard Horner observed that the "danger of [an employer] losing his best workmen" was greatest because "there are several factories near each other, [and] the workers can readily go from one factory to another without changing their own dwellings."[65] Young and qualified spinners in Manchester could move easily from factory to factory, especially during the years of rapid expansion until 1825, but according to the historian of the Gregs, its rural mills were the

principal employers in their areas and there was no alternative employment.[66] There is evidence of individual young men and women moving to
the cities when they became independent of the household, and wages for
this cohort generally conform to the pattern found in the cities. In this
respect labor markets in the period were integrated, but for the most part
the employment of families succeeded in reducing turnover, at least in
comparison to the scale witnessed in urban centers.[67]

As for labor-market efficiency, in worker–firm relationships in which
exchanges are multifaceted, the balance is said to be cleared in the long
run.[68] Rural firms shaped their strategies in developing new standards of
work behavior around the family, giving them more margins to work at
than urban firms. They had the leverage to lower wages of selected
members of the family who were less mobile, and to raise rents, the cost of
provisions, or other charges. We know that fines appear to have been used
more frequently and were heavier at the Ashworth mill than in Bolton, but
that workers were not dismissed or were not incited to quit.[69]

From the workers' perspective, family ties raised the cost of exit. Under
these conditions, to invoke Albert Hirschman's terms, loyalty came to
dominate both voice and exit.[70] The isolation of rural mills helped preserve
a loyal workforce. Even though the Gregs' mill at Styal was only eleven
miles from Manchester, the "very isolation of many factory colonies,"
Mary Rose wrote, "meant that most rural millworkers rarely came into
contact with trade unions or even their literature."[71] Rhodes Boyson in his
history of the Ashworths reached a similar conclusion: "Henry Ashworth
always boasted that he found employment for all the children of his operatives and such continued family employment from children up to men . . .
undoubtedly created a stable and reliable labour force which was less likely
to be stirred by belligerent trade unionism."[72]

Without challenge to their authority, employers as patrons inculcated in
workers, or clients, their vision of factory life. In contrast to urban locations where paternalism's hold was loose, the isolated factory colonies
were an ideal environment for a close dependent relationship. The basis of
this relation was the notion that wealth carried with it certain obligations,
including attending the needs of subordinates.[73] The chapels, schools,
libraries, shops, recreational facilities, and housing provided directly by
employers in factory colonies defined workers' dependence. Patrons
believed that if they enriched the lives of their clients they would be more
productive, while the latter, without any viable alternative employment,
old-age security, or health insurance, "understood that the master's interest [was] their own."[74] Because paternalism permeated the mill wall, rural
workers were less likely to resist attempts by employers to extract more
effort.

Conclusion: an integrated labor market?

I have identified three areas or zones with different labor-market experiences in the early decades of the century: small urban concerns that spun on throstles or common mules; large urban firms using powered common mules and specializing in fine yarn; and rural firms that spun coarse yarn on older technology. Labor was mobile and although its supply appears to have been adequate everywhere, the emphasis on integration obscures important differences in recruiting and disciplining tactics among the areas. Three different market outcomes or solutions coexisted. To break down customary work habits in urban centers, firms relied on the threat of dismissal and the replacement of men, although as the M&K experience attests, this strategy was costly at large mills spinning fine yarn. Dismissal was probably more effective at small urban mills, because coarse yarn was cheaper and waste was not a constraint; deterrents were more effective as well in rural areas where labor markets were isolated and paternalistic relations were strong. Rural mills would continue with these practices throughout the century and, despite an older vintage of technology, they would remain a competitive threat until urban mills had developed an alternative way of eliciting effort.

3 Principals and agents: the labor market into the second generation

> The operators in my shop made noises like economic men. Their talk indicated that they were canny calculators and that the dollar sign fluttered at the masthead of every machine . . . It [was] precisely because they were alert to their economic interests . . . that the operators did not exceed their quota. It might be inferred from their talk that they did not turn in excess earnings because they felt that to do so would result in piece work price cuts.[1]

The effort problem and agency theory

In a model of the labor market in which firms have less than full information about the effort levels of workers, the parties design mutually beneficial or compatible incentive contracts. If the quantity and quality of output are measurable at little cost and if workers are risk-neutral, piece payoffs are the optimal contract.[2] And if team work makes it difficult to evaluate individual performance, according to Armen Alchian and Harold Demsetz, workers will elect their own monitors to ensure high levels of individual effort.[3] In one respect Alchian and Demsetz are correct. Workers in Lancashire did monitor each other; but as with workers elsewhere, it does not follow that their interests were always and everywhere compatible with those of the owners of machinery.

The flaw in this principal–agent model is that individual workers who are paid by the piece, or teams of workers who elect their own monitors, themselves have an incentive to restrict effort in order to maximize lifetime income.[4] Where the quality of output is uncertain and the potential of new technologies is unknown, individual workers or groups of workers can take hidden actions and disguise how quickly they in fact can work. Effort in these circumstances is uncontractable. "Of necessity," Oliver Williamson observed, "the employment contract is an incomplete agreement, and performance varies with the way in which it is executed."[5] The labor-market transaction is unique, in other words, because conflicts between buyers and sellers of labor time cannot be resolved through the market in the same fashion as the conflict between the buyer and seller of any other input:

Even after the contract terms are agreed, the employer has to deal with economic agents who still have their own interests (and indeed a conflict of interest) at stake, which is not the case with the purchase of other inputs. *Ceteris paribus*, employees, unlike other inputs to the production process, retain an interest in working less hard.[6]

My analysis of the principal–agent problem begins with a study of the confrontation between M&K and its spinners in the 1820s over the amount of effort required to operate the longer mules. The accounts of M&K, again subject to qualification, are the most extensive source available to study the incentive problem. The firm remains representative because payment by piece was universal and the hidden actions of workers were present at all firms, small and large, fine and coarse, alike.

The retention of men: an irreversible decision?

In 1818 M&K began construction of a new mill, Sedgwick Factory, which in full operation housed seventy-two mules each carrying 348 spindles.[7] For the firm, the investment represented an increase in the number of mules of 25 percent, of spindles 30 percent, and in the number of spindles per worker from 70.2 to 81.1 between 1811 and 1818. The long mules at M&K were typical of the new machinery being introduced in the fine-spinning sector. The steady improvement in spinning technology and the application of steam power had made it possible in the early decades of the century to spin fine counts of yarn on mules with over 300 spindles.[8] The introduction of long mules on a wide scale was delayed, however, until the early 1820s when, in the face of growing competition, heightened by the narrowing margins between prices and cotton costs, they became a necessity if firms like M&K were to realize a normal rate of profit.[9]

Men were hired to operate the long mules. At M&K the proportion of females fell from 62.3 percent in 1818 to 51.8 percent in 1838.[10] The secondary literature contains a number of competing explanations why women were not employed on long mules: the exclusionary rules and practices of male-dominated trade unions; the greater physical strength necessary to operate the long mules; the belief that men were more effective authoritarians and supervisors than women; and a general ideology of discrimination.[11] In the case of M&K it would appear that the supervisory role of men was paramount. The increase in the size of mules led to the hiring of additional piecers and scavengers – about one more per mule – so the supervisory functions of spinners expanded.[12] Although in narrow terms it may have been the case that at the outset women were indeed less effective supervisors then men, in another sense this view was a well-accepted ideology, whether in fact it was true or not. There were pressures both inside and outside the mill to give men better-paying jobs. As young workers in the factory, Wayne Lewchuk has written, boys learned the mysteries of the trade, appropriate attitudes toward employers, male codes of sexual conduct, and male social responsibility. Mutual recognition between workers and employers was viewed as a manly arrangement.[13]

Undoubtedly it is difficult to separate the relative influences of discrimination and pure abilities; we can, however, be more certain that technical change itself was more an effect than a cause of the substitution of men for women. To many economists the demand for skill or human capital is technologically determined. But the Lancashire case suggests that the choice of technique was endogenous in employer's labor-market strategy.[14] Once men were hired, firms were going to make the most of their physical and organizational capacities. At the point of installation, as Lazonick put it, the length of mule was a variable and the strength of the male worker was fixed.[15] The mule was then extended until it made more efficient use of the adult male worker's physical capacities. William Kelly, a builder of spinning machines, wrote that as "the size of mules rapidly increased to 300 spindles and upwards, the idea of saving by spinning with boys and girls [young men and women] was superseded."[16] With the addition of spindles not only did supervisory tasks increase, but so did repairs and it was widely believed that mechanical aptitude was a purely masculine trait.[17]

Along with technical change, exclusionary tactics of unions appear to have been more an effect than a cause of the retention of men. Union activity had retreated after 1818 when a bitter dispute in Manchester over wages and the hiring of female spinners ended with local authorities curbing the disturbance with force. Trade union organizations resurfaced as a voice of fine spinners in Manchester only after long mules were in place and with men in spinning positions. With their jobs safeguarded, male spinners rebuilt their trade unions. The exclusionary statements and policies of unions in the late 1820s and early 1830s responded to the introduction of the long mules. Spinners anticipated that the new technology would result in unemployment because of the increased number of piecers who picked up spinning skills. Although they could not control the number of piecers, they could restrict entry into the trade, albeit to a limited degree, by opposing the employment of women.[18]

Whatever the cause, firms like M&K were willing to go along with the

Table 3.1 *Estimates of spindles, spindles per mule pair, and number of mule spinners: 1788–1850*

Year	Total number of spindles (millions)	Estimates of mule spindles (millions)	Spindles per mule pair (hundreds)	Number of mule spinners	Proportion of self-actors
1788	1.94	0.49	90	550	
		or		or	
		0.15		1553	
1811	4.67	4.20	600	7016	
1817	6.65	5.90	600	9833	
1832	9.00	8.10	700	11571	
1834	12.00	10.80	700	15428	c. 3%
1841	15.70	14.10	750	18800	
1845	17.50	15.70	750	20933	
1850	20.40	18.40	1000	18400	c. 40%

Sources: Alan Fowler and Terry Wyke, eds., *The Barefoot Aristocrats: A History of the Amalgamated Association of Operative Cotton Spinners* (Littleborough: George Kelsall, 1987), 249. Numbers of spindles are from G. N. von Tunzelmann, *Steam Power and British Industrialization to 1860* (Oxford: Oxford University Press, 1978), 182; G. W. Daniels, "Samuel Crompton's Census of the Cotton Industry in 1811," *Economic Journal* (*Economic History Supplement*) 2 (1930), 107–10; number of mule spinners was estimated by dividing spindleage by an estimate of spindles per pair. The low estimate for 1788 is from G. W. Daniels, *The Early English Cotton Industry* (Manchester: Manchester University Press, 1920), 121; the higher figure from S. D. Chapman and S. Chassagne, *European Textile Printers in the Eighteenth Century* (London: Heinemann, 1981), 41. The estimate of self-actors in 1834 is from Andrew Ure, *The Philosophy of Manufacturers* (London: Charles Knight, 1835), 134.

boycott of women, since they believed they could not operate the long mules without men anyway. The countervailing factor was owners' belief that sufficient incentives were in place ensuring that male spinners on the new longer mules were motivated to work hard. By the 1820s workers and firms had accumulated a generation of factory experience, and there were now enough younger workers familiar with the machinery and its demands to replace spinners who became too old to work or had vacated their mules for other reasons. Table 3.1 presents estimates of the number of spinners in Lancashire.

Although their number doubled between 1811 and 1830, their position was tenuous, because more "piecers [were] produced in Lancashire than spinning mules."[19] For every spinner there were two to three piecers, and three to four young workers and women in the preparatory departments. In fact, the number of openings contracted at each successive stage in a spinning factory, from cleaning the raw cotton, through carding to spinning.[20] In 1833, roughly 10,000 young boys and about the same number of adolescent girls worked under the direct supervision of spinners or employers and at eighteen years old they could have moved easily into spinning operations. John Lyons has come to a similar conclusion, based on a detailed study of the census manuscripts. "The mills could offer new employment almost exclusively to the young, and continuing employment almost exclusively to those who had previous factory experience."[21] If they so desired, firms could have relied entirely on an internal hiring scheme, a type of tournament, in which at each stage of production they could have chosen from the best workers available while firing the rest. In this scheme older workers past their peak performance years could be replaced without much cost.

There was a risk, however. By ceding authority of the mill floor to men, employers were making a decision that would be difficult to reverse. It was not a coincidence that women were used in place of men during the first generation of factory work, given their role in domestic industry, but the situation had evolved. If women were removed from the workforce by a combination of government legislation restricting their hours of work, union sanctions, and deliberate employer strategies, it would be hard to recruit a trained and experienced supply of them when needed, even if all skills demanded were general. This is an elemental characteristic of labor-market development: different decisions have different degrees of reversibility. Labor markets can move in many directions, but not all directions at once. The gamble for Lancashire firms was whether they could make full use of the abilities of men, because once men were installed it would be difficult for firms to revert back to the policy of hiring women.

Piece-rate bargaining into the second generation

Before evaluating whether the gamble paid off, the decision making process of the suppliers of labor time needs to be elaborated. By the middle of the 1820s, the first generation of urban mule spinners probably had between fifteen to twenty years of factory experience, and as they were approaching thirty to thirty-five years of age, there were signs that they were recognizing that quits or exit was costly. Over the life cycle, the present value of spinning jobs was relatively high in comparison with mining and other urban occupations. Moreover, the costs of leaving spinning clearly rose with age. Not only were their physical skills deteriorating

– spinning required a dexterous touch – but older workers could no longer be assured of long-term kinship support if they lost their jobs. Faced by the uncertainty of the market, changes in technology, and the specter of unemployment, like other industrial workers during periods of rapid economic change, they sought a wage and employment bundle that provided them with some income support. This bundle could have included some combination of earnings' certainty and employment stability. This does not imply, however, that workers would have accepted an "implicit contract."[22] With this type of contract, relatively risk-averse workers pay insurance to their employers in favorable states of nature and receive indemnities in unfavorable states. Although this contract guarantees a fixed income, it is open in the sense that the rate of pay itself is not specified, and it is precisely the piece rate itself that was a dominant concern of workers in the early factories.

Modern analysts assume that workers generally prefer a fixed income to fixed rates of pay, and it is management that is solely concerned about the effort–pay link. But revealing an aversion to risk or exhibiting low rates of time preference would have weakened workers' bargaining position.[23] During the rapid social and economic change of the industrial revolution, workers wanted to exercise control over effort to preserve the standard rates they had brought with them into the factories. Custom was their chief safeguard in an uncertain world. By accepting contracts of fixed incomes, workers would have given up control of the piece rate, and this would have implied abandoning the relation between effort and pay. The standard rate gave workers some protection that as they aged they would not have to work harder to maintain their levels of income; it also regulated the degree of competition between firms by fixing labor costs, which in spinners' view protected them against technological unemployment. Indeed, as evidenced by their defense of piece work, textile operatives, like pottery workers and coal miners, saw piece-rate bargaining as a means to share in the growth of productivity.

If they accepted a fixed income, moreover, workers had no guarantee that firms would not intermittently announce that the state of trade was bad and use this as an excuse to cut or ratchet down the piece rate; similarly, firms could have claimed unilaterally that technology had improved and cut rates.[24] Relinquishing control of the piece rate would be an open invitation to further cuts, unleashing Hobbesian competitive forces that factory workers and earlier generations of domestic workers fought long and hard to cushion themselves against. "If we quietly succumbed to this [piece-rate] reduction," a Manchester operative declared in the middle of the 1850s, "other reductions would follow . . . until we reached the utmost limit of bare existence."[25] In other words, an implicit contract which stabilized earnings could not prevent unemployed workers from bidding down the wage rate. Hence, spinners demanded contracts fixing rates of pay. The concerns of the first factory spinners, as we shall see, became the lessons for subsequent generations.

Did piece-rate earnings represent compensating differentials?

The stage was set: workers' desire to control the piece rate was pitted against firms' concern to get effort out and reduce unit costs. It was anticipated that the constant threat of replacement would force spinners to use their authority over the work team to get them to mend threads more quickly and reduce waste. Spinners at M&K did drive their piecers hard. There is anecdotal and quantitative evidence that more spinners beat piecers at M&K than at other mills.[26] The standard labor market model would support this evidence. Workers paid by the piece are usually found to have higher earnings, everything else given, than workers paid on a day or weekly basis. Their higher earnings are said to represent a compensating differential for their increased effort.[27] However, in Lancashire, the overall strategy of raising effort and reducing unit costs hinged on whether the firm could break down customary work habits and ensure that male spinners themselves had the incentive to operate the longer mules to their maximum physical abilities. The data I have collected indicates that incentives in place were ineffective in eliciting high levels of effort.

For Sedgwick Factory, a mill which was built by M&K to house longer mules, there exists a weekly account of hanks per spindle for the years 1822 to 1827 (table 3.2). The retention of men spinners clearly reduced the output loss associated with high wastage.[28] However, these gains were offset by the lack of any trend in output. Since there was little turnover in this period, it would be expected that output would increase steadily as spinners became more familiar with the new long mules. Indeed Lee suggested that technical change of this sort was the principal source of productivity gain at the firm.[29] For the entire industry Landes took a similar position, maintaining that on the new technology the steady accumulation of specialized skills, a byproduct of the division of labor, translated into ever higher levels of output.[30] However, Lee's and Landes' claims about productivity trends are not supported by the evidence. Although hanks per spindle were higher at Sedgwick Factory than for the old mill between 1809 and 1817, after correcting for count spun, productivity showed great fluctuations, reaching a peak in 1822 and a nadir in 1825.

The fall in output per spindle could have been the outcome of changes in capacity utilization, but this was not the case. In periods of declining

Table 3.2 *Average weekly production statistics, M'Connel and Kennedy's Sedgwick Factory: 1821–1826*

| | | | Hanks per spindle | | |
| | | | Actual | Corrected[b] | Waste[c] |
Year	Count[a]	Hanks	Actual	Corrected[b]	Waste[c]
1821[d]	120.0	362332	8.23	6.58	9.87
1822	119.3	233124	9.05	7.24	13.25
1823	116.5	279992	8.74	6.90	9.31
1824	118.5	261004	8.46	6.77	10.69
1825	115.1	318773	7.81	6.24	8.90
1826	121.0	295390	6.89	6.77	3.72

Notes:
[a] Average count over year.
[b] Output corrected by Kennedy's index of hanks per spindle per day, using no. 150 as a base.
[c] Waste = ((Rovings – Twists)/Rovings) × 100%.
[d] Factory began operation in April 1821.
Source: M&K Sedgwick Factory Ledger.

trade, like the last months of 1825, it was the firm's policy to work at full capacity and reduce its unit fixed costs.[31] There was limited short-time working in 1826, about one month of working five days instead of six a week, but the number of hanks per spindle was falling even before the reduction in capacity utilization. Other hypotheses could explain the output reduction: high absentee rates, lengthy strikes, machine repairs, the spinning of higher counts, or changes in cotton inputs. But the ledgers and letter books of the firm, and its inventory and cash books, contain no evidence in support of these hypotheses. In fact the record books are silent on the causes of the output decline.[32]

Picasso in Lancashire: reputations and negotiations

An alternative hypothesis which is consistent with the lack of documentation is that M&K was unable to elicit maximum effort from its workers. The firm attempted to cut wages in 1823, late 1825, and 1826, and spinners responded to the challenge by reducing effort. Wherever payment is by the piece, the restriction of output has been and remains a common response to the threat of wage cuts.[33] Along with exiting, workers can impose significant damage costs on their employers by reducing output; this tactic is a potent weapon in bargaining.

In analyzing restriction-of-output campaigns two issues need to be resolved: why rational economic agents reduce effort and output, and why these campaigns persist. These issues will be dealt with in more detail in chapter 5, but to better evaluate the empirical evidence some preliminary observations need to be made. Robert Gibbons formally models a single worker interacting with a single employer to explain the incentives of withholding effort.[34] Where information is hidden and the worker can engage in hidden action, and "if neither the firm nor worker can commit to future behavior, then no compensation scheme, piece-rate or otherwise, can induce the worker not to restrict output." Consider two tasks, one easy, the other hard. Firms only see high or low output and use this to categorize the nature of the job. If workers produce high output, the firm believes the task is easy and will bust piece rates. Because firms cannot commit to hold rates constant, a worker in an easy job has an incentive to produce the same amount as if the job were more difficult – that is, to restrict output.

Although calculating payoffs is beyond the scope of this chapter, game theory provides a useful framework in which to organize and interpret the historical record. Consider a game with incomplete information played by labor and capital. Labor and capital are trying to maximize their individual payoffs, but no mechanism exists for enforcing agreements which would allow them to cooperate and seek the optimum joint payoff and effort levels. In this scenario, workers have information about their effort and utility functions which are not observable to capital; capital has unique access to information about market forces and technical change. Neither labor nor capital can calculate fully the other party's payoff.

Under these conditions, the best each coalition can do is to make inferences based on past information. After each round, the parties reestimate their payoffs based on the new information they have received. This is a sequential bargaining model and the solution concept commonly used is one of sequential equilibria.[35] In models with incomplete information, it is probable that each coalition will base its next move on the reputations and credibility of the other.[36] Labor expects capital to keep introducing newer technology, and capital expects labor to restrict effort. For both coalitions, once a reputation is established, it is costly to deviate from it. Thus, if workers stop restricting effort, they will lose the benefits accruing to their reputation.

Labor's reputation for restricting effort originated in the putting-out stage and the renewal of unionization in the 1820s gave their threats credibility. I have no direct evidence that output restriction became more widespread with the introduction of the new longer mules, but, according to some social and labor historians, the years after the French Wars saw the heightened polarization of capital and labor.[37] In the putting-out system, there was always the chance, however fleeting, that spinners and weavers could aspire to the position of merchant or manufacturer; and for obvious reasons it was also difficult to organize collective responses before the factory.[38] But with the increasing capital requirements of new spinning mules and the concentration of workers in the early large factories, output restriction became a more pressing and viable alternative. For employers, the increased burden of fixed costs made work stoppages more costly, and from the workers' perspective the new investments highlighted their dependent status in the new factory order. In this environment, technical change and piece-rate cuts were met by concerted attempts both inside and outside the factory to preserve customary levels of effort and pay.

The environment at M&K in the middle of the 1820s was ripe for an attempt by labor to reduce output. Technology at Sedgwick was new and the firm had yet to put in place a list of piece rates for different counts of yarn spun on the new machines. Spinners claimed that to maintain output on long mules they had to give as least as much effort as on small mules. If employers succeeded in reducing piece rates, spinners would have had to work harder to maintain their standard level of earnings.[39] By reducing output and observing standard rates of effort, spinners would show their employers that they were unwilling to work harder.

Firms could have prevented output restriction if they had information on the quality and quantity of production levels. Although employers knew the long mules would increase output, engineers and their own manuals could not provide them with exact amounts. Moreover, as will be discussed in detail in chapter 4, firms failed to invest in new methods of supervision. The setting and regulating of mule speeds, the winding of cops, and the pushing back of the carriage were left to the discretion of labor, providing them the opportunity to hide how hard they could in fact work.[40] Testimony of employers, overlookers, and spinners before the parliamentary commissions on factory employment describes the ability of workers to control and maintain standard rates of effort. These responses of a Manchester textile worker were typical:

Q. Does not the engine in any particular factory, when a certain number is spinning, always go at the same speed?
A. Yes.
Q. Then it generally turns off the same quantity of work in the same time?
A. Yes, in general it does; but that depends more on the overlooker than the spinner, because let the engine go what it will, he can always alter the wheels to any swiftness.
Q. When the overlooker is spinning any particular number, forty for instance, does he ever vary the speed?
A. No. For any particular number it always remains at the same speed.

Q. Then how can a spinner increase the quantity of work by working harder?
A. By putting the stretches quicker up, he can get off more work.

Using a game theory framework, labor's production decision is a version of the Picasso problem.[41] Consider that the artist wants to maximize lifetime income and that the price for his work depends on the total supply that exists when he dies. Picasso would like to select an optimal quantity to produce during his lifetime. In a world of certainty, collectors realize that regardless of what he produced previously, each year Picasso will reconsider the problem and attempt to maximize his income for the remainder of his life. Collectors would therefore expect the artist to increase his output late in life, and knowing the rate of his output they are willing to pay only the low price corresponding to his large lifetime output, even when Picasso is young. However, consider the problem if collectors are uncertain about whether Picasso's rate is high or low. If he begins at a low rate, then later randomizes between high and low rates, collectors will be unable to estimate lifetime output. Picasso will realize a greater portion of his monopoly power.[42]

Collective action: output restriction as a public good

Standard economic analysis maintains that restriction-of-output campaigns are temporary at best because labor's coalition is unstable. Picasso is an individual, while restriction of output is a public good and may be unsustainable. Each spinner would benefit by working to his maximum ability and gain the benefit of the additional output. The coalition would be broken.

It is also possible, however, that sellers of labor time concerned about the stigma of breaking rank would be constrained by some target or standard rate of output. If there is any loss of utility for those who deviate from norms, then groups of workers would restrict output when faced with piece-rate revision.[43] In some situations, like in a professional sports team, where all members of a group can benefit from an individual's effort, reputation is an increasing function of effort and the penalty for breaking output norms is trivial. But on the mill floor in the early stages of industrialization the effects of increased output were uncertain. They could include lower wages for all, higher effort norms for all, or even job loss if the increase in production outstripped demand. Since the cost of breaking rank could have been high, it would be expected that workers would collude to protect the standard rate or effort norm.

In their classic studies of industrial workers in the middle of the twentieth century in the United States, Melville Dalton and Donald Roy found that effort norms were upheld where workers shared common backgrounds, attended the same churches, read the same newspapers, and the like.[44] Lancashire was no different. The sanctions applied to strike breakers, or knobsticks, is evidence of the use of codes of behavior. Individuals who worked above or below group norms would be stigmatized, finding it difficult to secure employment elsewhere, to get relief during crises, or simply to enjoy the company of workmates. For ratebusting to succeed, the utility gain from defection had to exceed the punishment of non-conforming. Ratebusters would have had to maintain separate spheres of activities and social networks from the majority of workers.[45] What we know of the high degree of socialization in Lancashire towns and particularly among its spinners indicates that this would have been very difficult. Lancashire communities had long memories. Forty years after the great Preston strike of 1854, Thomas Banks, the secretary of the town's spinners' union, claimed defiantly "that we are in possession of the records of every man who r[a]n the blockade, and earned himself the name of knobstick."[46] Workers participated in sanctioning other workers in the fear of being sanctioned themselves.

Output-restriction campaigns would have succeeded even in cases of hypocritical cooperation, that is, where spinners enforced effort norms on others, but did not themselves comply to rules of behavior. Douglas Heckathorn showed that actions of this nature raise the total amount of cooperation, increasing the marginal gains from adhering to codes of behavior.[47] The result is a positive feedback system in which each new actor's decision to cooperate strengthens the regulatory interests of that actor and others. Thus, Heckathorn concluded, hypocritical cooperation can potentially serve as a bridge spanning the chasm from collective inaction to full cooperation, in which actors comply and sanction others who fail to.

Testing for the "conscientious withdrawal of efficiency"[48]

The weekly production statistics I have collected from the Sedgwick Factory ledger of M&K can be used to assess the number of spinners holding to effort norms and the degree of output restriction and its timing. My approach here emulates the pioneering studies of piece-rate workers of Dalton and Roy.[49] As evidence of conformism and the tendency of piece workers to restrict output, they found the majority of workers produced in a narrow range around a standard level of output; those producing 25–50 percent or more above the norm were considered ratebusters; those producing about 25 percent or so less were goldbrickers (they believed their rates were too low); finally, there was a small group of learners who produced at 40–50 percent less than the output norm.

Ten pairs of mules were randomly selected and their output recorded on three occasions during each year (the last weeks of April, July, and October) between 1822 and 1826. I assume that each spinner retained his pair of mules throughout the period.[50] After correcting for count spun, figure 3.1 graphs the output of five of the ten mules sampled, taking the average of all ten mules from 1822 to 1826 as the base or output norm (= 100). The number of mules is restricted for purposes of presentation only. There were no learners in the sample. The output of most mules rise and fall together within the range of 10–20 percent of the standard level of output.

There are two periods when most workers are below the output norm: early 1823, and early and mid-1826. In these years, paraphrasing Dalton and Roy, spinners were goldbricking. The timing meshes with evidence from contemporary sources on the response of spinners to attempts to lower their pay. In 1823 firms in Bolton cut piece rates on longer mules; workers in Manchester had good reason to fear that their employers would do likewise, and spinners like those at M&K responded by reducing output to protect the standard relation between effort and pay. In late 1825 and early 1826 when trade slowed down, local newspapers reported renewed attempts by firms to cut rates. Again they were met by workers reducing effort. Note that mule 6 is an exception in the first period, but his performance falls in place with other mules in 1825 and 1826.

Multivariate analysis confirms this pattern of activity. To save degrees of freedom I restricted the estimation to mules 6 through 10. In the estimations reported in table 3.3, the log of output for each pair of mules was regressed on year, seasonal, and mule dummies. In the simple regression of column 1 the coefficients for 1823 and 1826 were significantly different than 1822, the benchmark year. When mule and dummy variables are added similar results hold, with the exception of mules 7 and 9 whose performance was significantly different. This effect disappears in the more complicated model reported in column 3 which includes interaction terms. The results clearly show the significance of output restriction in 1823 and 1826.[51]

Conclusion: incomplete contracts

In Manchester in the 1820s the piece rate did not work as it should in theory. Although it is difficult to assess the degree of hidden actions in Lancashire, the conditions were right for workers to defend effort norms. For adult male spinners, payment was everywhere by the piece, and there were high degrees of socialization. We also know from modern studies that output restriction is a ubiquitous feature of payment by piece.

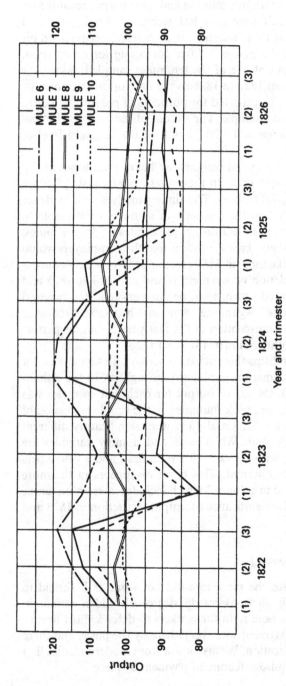

Note: The output norm (= 100) is the average of ten mules sampled.

3.1 Individual mule output at M'Connel and Kennedy, 1822–1826

Table 3.3 *The determinants of output restriction, 1822–1826*

	Dependent variable:[a] log of output		
Dummy variables	(1)	(2)	(3)[b]
1823	−0.1367 (−2.785)*	−0.1367 (−3.066)*	−0.2860 (−4.313)*
1824	−0.0842 (−0.042)	−0.0412 (−0.936)	−0.0076 (0.114)
1825	−0.1021 (−1.432)	−0.0921 (−1.234)	0.0365 (0.551)
1826	−0.3329 (−6.719)*	−0.3329 (−7.469)*	−0.1606 (−2.422)*
T2		0.0751 (1.123)	0.0833 (0.579)
T3		0.0308 (0.901)	0.0249 (0.434)
M6		−0.0235 (−0.834)	−0.0067 (−0.082)
M7		−0.2706 (−4.236)*	−0.0570 (−0.070)
M8		−0.0808 (−1.238)	−0.0239 (−0.295)
M9		−0.2060 (−3.266)*	−0.0351 (−0.443)
M10		−0.0661 (−1.010)	−0.0071 (0.876)
M6x1823			−0.6412 (−0.558)
M7x1823			−0.0096 (−0.084)
M8x1823			−0.1220 (−1.066)
M9x1823			0.0983 (0.856)
M10x1823			0.0844 (0.734)
M6x1824			0.0938 (0.082)
M7x1824			−0.3152 (−0.274)
M8x1824			−0.1679 (−0.146)
M9x1824			0.0485 (0.423)
M10x1824			0.0441 (0.384)
M6x1825			−0.1555 (−1.356)
M7x1825			−0.4205 (−3.661)*
M8x1825			−0.1771 (−1.548)
M9x1825			−0.3331 (−2.901)*
M10x1825			−0.1286 (−1.253)
M6x1826			−0.2117 (−1.843)
M7x1826			−0.4439 (−3.865)*
M8x1826			−0.4468 (−3.891)*
M9x1826			−0.5288 (−4.604)*
M10x1826			−0.5288 (−4.604)*
Constant	10.3522 (170.115)	8.8852 (155.991)	8.766 (186.972)
R^2	0.273	0.456	0.753
Degrees of freedom	145	134	110
t-test[c]	8.356	9.212	10.115

Notes:

* $p<0.05$ (two-tailed test); t-statistics in parentheses.

[a] The benchmarks for estimates in all equations are: 1822; T1 (first trimester); M5 (mule 5).

[b] The estimated results are from a regression that includes interaction effects between trimester and year. All (8) effects were insignificant.

[c] Tests the hypothesis that the coefficients on the 1823 and 1826 variables (including interaction terms) are not different from zero. The hypothesis is strongly rejected in all models.

Source: M&K Sedgwick Factory Ledger.

Through workers' hidden actions, the damage imposed by goldbricking workers at M&K was not trivial. By 1820, fixed costs represented about 35 percent of unit costs. At a time when margins and profits were falling, reducing output by 25 percent raised unit costs by almost 9 percent. These calculations do not include costs to the firm of failing to adjust piece rates downward. In his classic essay, "Custom, Wages, and Workload," Hobsbawm argued that workers could not impose such substantial costs, and that because of customary norms which they brought with them into the factories, firms paid them below market rates.[52] But at M&K the opposite in fact held. Effort norms did not weaken the bargaining position of workers, nor did they imply low market wages. Custom was anything but an anachronistic force; indeed the dichotomy between custom and the market, central to the approach of many labor and social historians, obscures their complementarities. It was in defense of the age-old standard between effort and pay that workers at M&K restricted output, and because they could impose significant damage costs, they succeeded in maintaining, even improving, their rates of pay and earnings.

4 Who's minding the mill? The supervision problem

Engineer: "Do you never put the nose peg on?"
Minder: "Oh yes, I always put it on when t'moon's on't full."[1]

The effort problem and industrial organization

If employers had difficulty in setting rates of pay on their new investments, they could have obtained additional information by expending more resources. Modern management when confronted by worker resistance has tended to increase levels of supervision.[2] These options were not taken up in Lancashire. Although economic historians have downwardly revised estimates of aggregate growth in Britain, the received view that the industrial revolution outran investments in new managerial structures remains unchallenged.

There were other avenues to control the effort problem. M&K was a large firm that had made major investments in new technology in the *expectation* of high rates of effort. It could have raised the amount of fines or meted them out arbitrarily, increasing the cost of withholding effort. Other firms learning from its example could have chosen to remain small; still others could have chosen alternate technologies, like the self-actor, which were intended to completely eliminate the manual attention of the spinner, thereby reducing monitoring costs and ensuring higher rates of output and better quality.

This chapter reveals that different approaches to the supervision problem varied by size of firm and region. With some important exceptions, notably the experience of Preston mills, I find that large urban firms regardless of specialty faced a supervision problem. Small firms and rural mills had alternative means to elicit high levels of effort. To set the background, I begin with a brief overview of the state of the art of mill management in the first half of the century.

Overseeing the overlookers

The average firm had at most one overlooker per spinning room, or one for every thirty spinners. Additional overlookers, or gaffers, could be hired to monitor performance, but employers commented frequently about their scarcity. When an overlooker at an Oldham mill migrated to the United States, the vacancy was unfilled until his return five years later; other employers were not so fortunate. Some were compelled to hire gaffers who could not keep books, or who showed no interest in administration, and still others who had little or no experience in cotton-spinning mills. One Manchester firm was even forced to hire a gaffer employed previously in twenty-seven other mills. It was inevitable that employers complained about the diligence of those hired, some of whom were paid by a fixed rate. "No I have nothing to do with quantity," one gaffer said, "I have my wages regular and nothing more, let the work come out as it will."[3]

Overlookers in the early period lacked the technical information neces- sary to monitor effort and set rates of pay. Charles Babbage proposed an early variant of a time and motion study, but most of what he wrote, Pollard concluded, remained on paper only.[4] Some enlightened employers, like Robert Owen and the Dundee flax spinner William Brown, also gave advice on mill management.[5] However, their approaches were idiosyn- cratic.

The principal sources available on mill management were technical manuals; my examination uncovered three genres.[6] Attesting to the impor- tant Scottish contribution to the cotton-textile industry, many of the first manuals were published in Glasgow. As the M&K experience revealed, however, this contribution lay in engineering and machine building, and not in managerial skills. The early manuals gave no information about speeds of machinery and their proper operation. Walter's tract – the copy I saw bears the signature of Henry M'Connel – contained basic tables that converted hanks of yarn into pounds spun for various counts. There was no discussion of how to manage a mill and it omitted how to calculate wages.[7]

The objective of the second generation of manuals was to make "the manager master of his own business."[8] Montgomery's 1832 volume is typical of this approach, but still he devoted only four pages to the prob- lems of labor management. Instead of antagonizing his workers, the "spin- ning master requires to act with prudence and caution . . . always on the alert to prevent rather than check faults, after they have taken place." Montgomery recommended a laissez-faire policy. Fines should not be excessive and spinners should be left in charge of their own work. Ever the economist, he wrote: "[They] are paid for what they do, and [are] responsi-

ble for both the quality and quantity of their work . . . Hence it is not necessary that a spinning master should always be present."[9]

The model mill of the period was based on a system of delegation and
demarcation; investments in new management skills were limited.[10] The
gaffer worked alongside the engineer who was responsible for the steam
engine and transmission system, the carder who controlled the preparatory processes, and the warehouseman. Each department of the mill was a
self-contained entity responsible only to the general manager. The system
depended on the application of detailed information by department heads,
and to this end the manuals contained a wealth of data on how to set and
regulate speeds and alter counts of yarn on the machines used in all
departments. However, the authors themselves raised serious reservations
about how much of this information was received and applied. "Having
been engaged in the different departments of the cotton business for many
years," one wrote in his introduction, "I have found a general deficiency in
theoretical knowledge amongst practical persons filling important situations in cotton and other factories."[11] Montgomery concurred in his 1850
edition of the *Cotton Spinners' Manual*.[12] By the middle of the century it
was accepted that overlookers would record output and waste; they would
assist spinners in making the necessary changes when altering counts
spun, but they did not and could not monitor effort. The system of managerial delegation implied that the setting and the regulating of mule
speeds rested in the hands of spinners.

Assuming the delegation of work, the third generation of manuals published after 1850 were addressed to both owners and operatives. They
reflected the bargaining over effort levels in the 1830s and 1840s that will
be discussed in chapter 6. It will suffice to note that in comparison with
earlier manuals, the later ones recognized the inexactness of spinning.
Skill, machinery, and cotton were "very elastic." Anticipating the general
adoption of established lists of piece rates after 1850, the manuals
implored that "only after limits" on machine speeds and the type of cotton
used "have been fixed" and agreed upon could firms realize steady levels of
effort and output.[13] Firms could not be assured that workers would give
maximum effort, because given the nature of technology the contract
between the parties was open-ended. I will return to these themes in the
third part of this book.

The effort problem unbound: large mills in Bolton and Manchester

The failure of the early manuals to provide an algorithm estimating how
hard spinners could work was most transparent in large and medium-sized
mills employing more than 150 to 200 workers.[14] A medium-sized firm

employed about twenty-five to thirty spinners in two or three spinning rooms, and about seventy-five piecers and scavengers. Contemporaries gave evidence of this size of mill not hiring sufficient numbers of gaffers to account for output, let alone to monitor effort. In these establishments the top level of management had the responsibility for monitoring and setting rates of pay, but at one large firm in Manchester management seldom ventured into the spinning rooms. The sheer size of large firms enabled workers to keep their employers "ignorant of what [was] passing in the . . . room."[15] Still, medium-sized and large firms could have applied fines even in random fashion. But as evidence of spinners' control of work organization, Montgomery found that they "are generally unwilling to submit to fines either for bad work or for improper conduct; it seems to be a general feeling amongst them that they would much rather have the master turn them away than fine them."[16] The problem was not restricted to spinning. One establishment in the Derby knitting trade reverted from a large shop to a decentralized type of production. In large shops, the owner explained, "the hands did more what they liked; they would not do this; nor would they do that."[17]

The monitoring problem was complex because of the association between size and technical change. In the early period of the industry's development, especially before 1825, most technically advanced firms were large and spun fine yarn.[18] G. N. von Tunzelmann referred to these firms' innovations as the "white heat of technology."[19] To supply the enlarged mules and mend the additional breakages of yarn these firms hired more workers in the preparatory stages and employed more piecers. By the early 1820s in Manchester many of the leading fine-spinning firms employed over 500 workers. In Bolton, another major fine-spinning center, the average firm employed about 200 workers in the early 1830s. Thereafter, markets stagnated and there was little new capacity added in fine spinning. Still, as late as 1841 the average fine-spinning mill employed about 200 workers, the size of firm which faced a managerial constraint.[20] Size by itself would not have been an issue if technical change was slow or if its impact was neutral. But the application of new technology in this sector was rapid and uneven. It would have been hard for firms to distinguish and separate shocks in output generated by new technology, new raw material requirements, or changes in worker effort; as a result, it was difficult for large firms to set rates of pay. In a more general context, John Pencavel identified the Manchester and Bolton employers' problem in his analysis of piece rates:

If the production technology and individuals' preferences and opportunities were constant over time, by trial and error the employer will grope toward the optimal piece rate; but such a stationary environment is not, of course, the one in which the employer operates.[21]

The effort problem confronted: the Preston example

Like the mills of Bolton and Manchester, Preston's factories also spun medium and fine counts of yarn, at least until the 1850s. In 1811 it ranked fourth in numbers of mule spinners in Lancashire, after Manchester, Bolton, and Ashton-under-Lyne; and in 1841, eighth.[22] Its leading firms at the middle of the century were well established, having grown in the years of high profits before and during the French Wars. The Ainsworth, Swainson, Birley, Paley, and Horrockses (later Horrockses, Miller and Co.; and Horrocks, Crewsden and Co.) mills dominated the town's industry throughout the period.

The history of Horrockses needs elaboration, because in some local histories "it was in fact the cotton industry in Preston."[23] John Horrocks built his first factory in 1792 and later added two other mills in 1796 and 1797. Unlike most Manchester and Bolton fine-spinning establishments, it was a fully integrated or combined firm. Its accomplishments were staggering. By 1811 the firm operated the greatest number of spindles in the world, and in 1825 it employed some 4,000 operatives in spinning, weaving, bleaching, and calico printing.[24] In the 1840s the firm employed about 2,000 operatives in spinning alone.[25] Anthony Howe estimated that the average fixed capital value at the firm between 1801 and 1829 was £203,122, or about five times that of M&K for 1798–1809.[26] In addition the firm retained market leadership in terms of both size and the quality of its product until the last quarter of the century.

With regard to its labor–management relations, Horrockses was well known for its harsh regime and it did not rely exclusively on the specter of high turnover to elicit effort. Bent on extirpating any nascent trade union formation, it regularly prosecuted operatives for quitting work without notice, for absenteeism, and for other acts of indiscipline.[27] Joyce observed that the firm translated its market power into political influence throughout the century, and many of the leading mills in the town shared its labor-market strategy.[28] The Ainsworth mill, which employed about 800 operatives in 1850, often took the lead in cutting rates of pay and provoking labor disputes.[29] Summarizing the town's industrial relations, one commentator in 1842 described that "the cotton lords of Preston are the greatest tyrants in the country. It is well known that they grind their workmen down more than any other persons getting their work done cheaper, and therefore they can undersell their neighbours."[30]

Preston firms succeeded in eliciting effort and supervising workers despite their size. In 1816 the average Preston firm employed 127 workers, about 15 percent fewer than in Bolton firms; but by 1841 the average firm had 287, about 24 percent more than found in Bolton.[31] Although after 1850 Preston became known for its large integrated concerns, earlier the relative size of this sector was similar to that of southern Lancashire towns. Even in 1841 many of Preston's firms, like those in Manchester and Bolton, specialized in spinning on common mules operated by men.[32] How then did large Preston firms escape the monitoring problem confronting their competition elsewhere?

A strand in the literature has suggested that the Preston labor market was looser than that found in southern Lancashire towns. Located on the edge of the Fylde, Lancashire's main agricultural district, the town and local manufacturers were provided with an abundant supply of local labor.[33] The abundant supply, James Lowe, a contemporary observer, wrote, gave "the employing class an immense power of control over the employed."[34] From the outset, Preston millowners tried to utilize younger and cheaper labor than millowners in other areas.[35] In the period after 1840 the number of alternative jobs in the town declined for men.[36] It was common for machine engineering firms to be located in the same towns as the mills for whom they were producing, and Preston was no exception. But after 1840 as mass-production engineering firms became dominant, particularly in the production of the new self-acting mules, much of this activity was shifted to Oldham, and all the Preston firms shut down.

There are problems with the loose labor market argument. Firms, as I described in chapter 2, were concerned not only with the quantity of workers standing outside the factory gate, but with their quality as well. It would be sheer speculation to suggest that Preston firms had better access to information; indeed, given the rapid population movement in the town, this type of information might have been harder to acquire.[37] Moreover, the distribution of jobs held by adult men did not differ significantly from that found elsewhere. From the census of 1851, table 4.1 breaks down the occupational distribution of males over twenty years of age.

The town did employ fewer machine makers than Bolton and Oldham, significantly fewer ironworkers than Bolton; the number of respondents who gave "agricultural laborer" as their occupation was greater than both southern Lancashire towns. Still, the number of construction workers, which includes some skilled occupations, was greater than elsewhere; there is no reason to believe that the category of laborers, which was considerably larger in Preston, but undefined in the census, consisted entirely of low-paid workers. Finally, the percentage of men in textile manufacture was only slightly less than that found in Bolton and Oldham. Reviewing this breakdown, Anderson, who undertook the most extensive social and

Table 4.1 *Occupational distribution in Bolton, Oldham, and Preston, 1851*

| Occupation | Male workers over 20 years old (percent of total in town) | | |
	Bolton	Oldham	Preston
Textile manufacture[a]	5529 (35.09)	6631 (35.35)	5428 (31.93)
Ironworkers[b]	1334 (8.47)	655 (3.49)	668 (3.43)
Construction[c]	1042 (6.60)	850 (4.53)	1271 (7.47)
Laborers[d]	582 (3.69)	867 (4.62)	1266 (7.45)
Machine makers[e]	581 (3.69)	1288 (6.87)	318 (1.87)
Shoemakers	392 (2.50)	368 (2.00)	586 (3.45)
Agricultural laborers	391 (2.49)	348 (1.85)	558 (3.28)
Coal mining	332 (2.10)	1393 (7.49)	16 (0.00)
Total males in occupations	10183 (64.46)	12400 (66.10)	10111 (59.50)
Total males over 20	15783	18759	16995

Notes:
[a] Includes fustian, calico, flax, and linen manufacture.
[b] Includes blacksmiths, nail manufacture, boiler makers, and ironmongers.
[c] Includes carpenters, joiners, plumbers, glaziers, and mason workers.
[d] Undefined in census.
[e] Includes tool makers.
Source: PP 1852–53 (1691) LXXXVIII, 648–51.

demographic study of Preston, concluded that "in general, the town's occupational structure was very similar to that of other urban areas of the county as a whole."[38]

A more compelling explanation of Preston's employers' effectiveness in eliciting effort is that compared to firms elsewhere they were better organized. Table 4.2 compares the degree to which large firms in Preston and Manchester dominated their local industries in 1815–16 and 1841.[39] While the importance of large firms (over 500 employees) declined in Manchester, in Preston in 1841 they employed almost one-half of the total workforce. Because of its size and the entry and exit in its industry, Manchester may not be a reliable benchmark; yet even in comparison with Bolton, where the family firm had an "hereditary monopoly of local industry under a separate caste of employers," Preston stands in contrast.[40] By 1841 the five largest mills in the town employed 40 percent of all the cotton-spinning hands in the town, whereas in Bolton the five largest mills had a little more than 30 percent of the total labor force; moreover, the

Table 4.2 *Concentration of workers in large and small firms: Manchester and Preston*

| | Percent of labor by size of firms (number of firms) | | | |
| | Manchester | | Preston | |
	1815	1841	1816	1841
Size of firms by number of workers				
1–150	28.48 (71)	12.50 (54)	55.70 (18)	18.41 (20)
151–500	27.29 (12)	55.81 (62)	44.30 (6)	33.61 (14)
500 and above	42.24 (7)	31.68 (12)		48.39 (7)
Total number of firms	90	128	24	41
Total number of employees	11471	31903	2772	10795

Sources: Manchester: Roger Lloyd-Jones and A. A. LeRoux, "The Size of Firms in the Cotton Industry: Manchester, 1815–41," *Economic History Review* 33 (February 1980), 75–76. Preston: PP 1816 (397) III, 499; PP 1842 (31) XXII.

concentration level may have fallen in Bolton from 1811 to 1841.[41] V. A. C. Gatrell, in his study of firm sizes, concluded that, for all of Lancashire, small firms "retained their numerical predominance."[42] In Preston the experience was different.

Buttressed by their smaller numbers, and led by Horrockses and other giant mills, Preston employers exhibited a relatively high degree of cohesion and continuity. The founding of the Masters' Association of Preston cannot be dated exactly, but unlike associations in other towns that were mainly defensive and appeared only in response to worker agitation, the Preston organization had a continuous existence, at least between the major confrontations of 1836 and 1853. Howe, in his study of these two disputes, wrote that the "organisation of the masters was impressive." In the 1836 dispute, "it almost completely united the employers, while deviant masters were expelled."[43] During the 1853 dispute, membership in the association comprised most major local millowners, united by a £5,000 bond and a levy of five shillings on each firm's horsepower. In addition, the association's members required a discharge note from all spinners seeking reemployment. Thomas Miller, the sole proprietor of Horrockses, was the chairman of the association, and William Ainsworth was its secretary. The 1853 association was not comprehensive, but deviant millowners were punished.[44] When Swainson's mill attempted to reopen in 1854 at the 1853 rate of pay, the association threatened the mill with forfeiture of its bond.[45] Swainson relented and reduced its wages to the level of other masters'. More than a defensive organization, the association unified employers who actively sought to destroy unionization. "The question of authority," Howe wrote, "was a collective one, that of the masters as a body, and an individual one, that of the master within his factory. The wage relationship was conceived as one between employer and hand, regulated by supply and demand, not by the medium of the union."[46]

The combined "tyranny" of the masters, to borrow a phrase from Dutton and King, was an effective means to elicit effort, and as a result, the industrial relations environment in Preston remained confrontational throughout the first half of the century. Under the leadership of Horrockses, the masters successfully defeated the spinners' union in 1837, reducing rates of pay by 10 percent; the 1853 dispute led to another defeat for the union. Preston workers were hard-pressed to organize either formally or informally against piece-rate cuts, and the relatively high degree of population movement in and out of the town exacerbated the problem of organizing. Unlike other towns' trade unions, into the second half of the century the Preston's spinners' union exercised no meaningful control of the labor market.[47]

The effort problem postponed: small and coarse-spinning mills

The position of fine spinners in the industry as technical leaders was not commensurate with their numbers. Although it is difficult to obtain precise numbers for the early period, about 15 to 20 percent of output can be classified as fine or medium-fine yarn above no. 60.[48] Using this benchmark, Horner in his exhaustive survey of 1841 found eighty fine-spinning mills in Lancashire, representing no more than 10 percent of the entire industry.[49] Coarse spinning, whether in the countryside or in town, was by far the dominant sector.

Initially, monitoring was less of a problem in the urban coarse-spinning sector because the average mill was small. In the 1820s and 1830s, many firms in Oldham rented or shared space in a factory with a single power source, and as late as 1841 the average coarse mill in Lancashire employed only 100 workers or about twelve to fifteen spinners.[50] In small mills over-lookers were not necessary even to account for output and spinners worked directly under their employers. The multiplicity of small firms did have a drawback. In contrast with the cotton lords of Preston, it was unlikely that employers could organize associations and develop common strategies in disciplining workers, like instituting written employment records.

Nevertheless, employers in the sector had little difficulty in setting rates of pay, because at both urban and rural mills a good deal of extremely coarse yarn was spun on throstles. Throstle spinners, who were mainly teenaged girls and young women, were unskilled operatives and they neither organized nor supervised production. Young boys or women also spun coarse weft yarn on small common mules. Moreover, trade union organization in the sector was initially weak.

Richard Roberts' self-acting mule, first patented in 1825, was intended to automate spinning completely. The impetus behind it was a request from some of the leading millowners for a machine to displace refractory male spinners with women and young adults and break down customary work habits.[51] Its diffusion was delayed until the fall in the price of coal in the 1840s, and according to S. D. Chapman, its spread coincided with "a leap forward in the optimum scale of production."[52] In fact, many of the original self-actors in use were slightly modified common mules, and up until the 1850s, the new machine could only spin yarn below no. 50. Extremely fine yarn was spun on the older technology into the 1880s.

In the initial period after the introduction of the self-actor, a larger proportion of younger people and women were employed than had been on the common mule. However, despite the claims of engineers and employers, men continued to dominate minding (spinning) positions and the workplace customs of the first generation of mule spinners persisted. As was the case in the rehiring of men on long mules, the preservation of spinning on self-actors as a male domain was, according to Lazonick, first and foremost due to the supervisory requirements of mule spinning, and more generally to the traditional management structures of the Lancashire spinning enterprise.[53] In comparison with his work on the common mule, the minder on the self-actor spent a good portion of his day piecing. But with the introduction of new technology, firms did not expend additional resources altering the organization of work. In Oldham, Joyce found that overlookers made their presence visible in spinning rooms only in the late 1870s.[54] The minder continued to lead the work team, which on longer mules consisted of a big piecer, an adult male over eighteen years of age, and a little piecer. It was a principal function of the minder to supervise and recruit his team, whom he continued to pay by time wages. Throughout the century, these tasks continued to be thought of as best done by men.

Given their authority on the mill floor, minders were in position to control the level of effort of the work team. Two problems plagued the complete automation of the self-actor.[55] First, the nosing motion required continuous manual attention. To compensate for the taper of the spindle so that yarn would be wound firmly and without snarls onto the nose of the cop, the minder had to manually delay the rise of the faller, the wire used to guide the thread, during the last stages of the inward run. The second and more serious problem was that Roberts' initial design of a quadrant nut (a quarter wheel which automatically synchronized the speed of the spindles in inverse proportion to the diameter of the cop and in direct proportion to the inward speed of the carriage) produced snarls in the yarn. To prevent snarls, the minder or the big piecer would turn the screw manually, about 1,500 to 3,000 times in the course of a day. Failure to perform the operation diligently could result in a sawney, a simultaneous breakage of hundreds of strands of yarn. Moreover, the minder was also responsible for monitoring the tightness of the straps and bands that drove the moving parts of the self-actor and for repairing any of the straps and bands that broke.

There are no coarse-mill records available comparable to those for M&K to assess whether minders as leaders of the work group restricted effort and output of the team. But the technical literature and other accounts confirm that they exercised their ability to control the type of cop formed, the quality of yarn, and the speed of machinery. During the initial stages of cop formation, snarls could usually be hidden by the minder and the inferior quality of his output would often go unnoticed as it was being checked in the spinning room.[56] Workers adapted themselves to the lack of supervision. In response to the truculent minder whose defiance I cited at the outset of this chapter, the engineer's admonition was mild: "We ought all do our best irrespectively of whether we see the manager coming or not."[57]

The problems faced by employers were compounded because minders had mule-specific skills. All textile workers accumulated general skills that could be transferred across firms, but the leaders of the work team were in position to make for themselves additional specific skills that were neither costlessly acquired nor exchanged. Peter Doeringer and Michael Piore found in their study of modern labor markets, that these types of skills arose precisely where "technology is unwritten." Skills derive from improvements the workforce itself introduces, and from workers' ability to perfect their "monopoly over the knowledge of the technology should there be an incentive to do so."[58] Using similar language, H. J. Catling, an historian of mule technology and who had experience on the mill floor, summarized the endogenous formation of spinning skills and the problem it presented for employers:

There was also the considerable practical difficulty that the operative spinner was firmly of the opinion that no two mules could ever be made alike. As a consequence he proceeded to tune and adjust each of his own particular pair of mules with little respect for the intentions of the maker or the principles of engineering. Before very long, no two mules ever were alike.[59]

The quandary for employers was how to channel workers' knowledge to meet the interests of the firm.

The effort problem solved: the rural sector

Technical change was slow in the rural sector. Many firms relied on throstles for a long period, and using this machine which spun yarn continuously, there was little opportunity for workers, who were mostly female, to hide levels of effort. But even in large rural mills that had made new investments in long common mules, like the Ashworth's mills, or in self-actors, like the Gregs', the effort problem was less severe. The multiple exchanges between patron and client over time and across goods and services reduced transaction costs, because the costs of information collection and contract enforcement were spread across all exchanges.[60] If workers were not observed at the point of production, rural managers had daily contact with them in the chapel, schools, clubs, and mill stores. The paternalistic bond generated information about worker behavior. Even if they could not monitor effort and set optimal rates of pay, firms had the alternative to cut at other margins, for example by raising rents or the cost of provisions. From the workers' perspective, because of the large number of transactions between the parties, the cost of restricting effort was greater than in urban settings. Workers caught restricting output would endanger a whole set of transactions for themselves and their families, and, as a result, they were less likely to retaliate against employers' attempts to cut wages. In many respects the situation in rural sites was not too dissimilar to that found in towns dominated by a large employer.[61] Like rural millowners, Horrockses of Preston as well as Ashtons' of Hyde rented out housing to their workers and could exercise control of its workers outside the factory gate.[62]

Conclusion: setting the stage

There was a spectrum of responses to the supervision problem. In the rural sector and towns like Preston, a viable strategy was in place to deter output restriction; in other urban coarse-spinning centers the effort crisis was postponed until the 1840s. But at large and specialized fine-spinning firms, the costs of relying on the market were realized as early as the 1820s. The new longer mules did not translate immediately into increased productivity, and firms' investments were squandered. The market neither supplied employers using the new technology with information on how much output could be produced and its quality, nor did it provide spinners with the incentive to work hard. As a result, large firms like those in Manchester and Bolton had to search for alternate ways to get effort out.

Part II

The economics of piece-rate bargaining

5   The fair wage model

The basis of the notion that there should be given "a fair day's wage for a fair day's work" is that every man who is up to the usual standard of efficiency of his trade in his own neighbourhood, and exerts himself honestly, ought to be paid for his work at the usual rate for his trade and neighbourhood; so that he may be able to live in that way to which he and his neighbours in his rank of life have been accustomed. And further, the popular notion of fairness demands that he should be paid this rate ungrudgingly; that his time should not be taken up in fighting for it; and that he should not be worried by constant attempts to screw his pay down by indirect means. This doctrine is modified by the admission that changes of circumstance may require changes of wages in one direction or another.[1]

Market alternatives to structure

There are four general types of labor compensation: time, salary, piece payoffs, and profit sharing. If the contents of labor economics textbooks in the 1970s and into the early 1980s are any indication, it had been widely believed that labor-market operations and dynamics were independent of the payment scheme. But in recent historical and theoretical work, the method of pay is the glue in the labor market, affecting and being affected by the choices and strategies of suppliers and demanders of labor time. All payment schemes are not identical and their effects are not neutral. In their exhaustive survey of labor contracts in agrarian economies, for example, Keijoru Otsuka and his coauthors concluded that payment schemes are identical only in cases where information about work effort is perfectly known, and enforceable, and where workers are risk-neutral. When markets are imperfect, complete contracts are difficult to write and the type of payment has implications for the quality of labor recruited, the level of effort elicited, how the benefits of technological change are shared, and how the labor market itself adjusts to shocks in aggregate demand.[2]

This chapter explains why Lancashire firms and workers opted for piece payoffs. If the labor market approximated an auction market, then there should have been more flexibility and variability in methods of pay and employment conditions. Spinners who were relatively more risk-averse would have found employment at firms offering time payoffs, whereas workers who were willing to shoulder the risks of the business cycle would have taken piece payments. Similarly, firms concerned about quality of output or capital depreciation would have preferred time payoffs; alternatively, those wanting to screen a heterogeneous labor pool would have paid by the piece. Through a self-selection process, groups of workers and firms would have in principle found each other. Workers with different preferences could have been pooled together in one firm, or separated in firms offering different contracts. The pertinent questions, therefore, are why did piece rates dominate, and why was there so much structure and uniformity in the payment scheme and in related employment conditions, such as hours of work?

The answer, in part, is that piece payoffs were the traditional method of pay and it was costly to change this type of arrangement. It was difficult to specify all possible contingencies and match the preferences of heterogeneous workers and firms. But no contract is fixed for ever, and the economist would say that if the costs offset the benefits a new payment scheme or contract would have been warranted. The problem with this line of reasoning is that it conflates the origins of contractual arrangements and their persistence. The piece rate may have been adopted in the putting-out stage because technological change was slow, output could be measured easily, and with limited capital expenses its benefits outweighed costs; from the workers' perspective, the piece rate embodied notions of fairness and customary earnings. It does not follow that it persisted for the same reasons. Over time the method of pay became a contractual arrangement that both parties adapted to. Although the form of payment did not cover all possible contingencies, and in this sense the contract remained incomplete, payment by piece persisted in Lancashire because over time it consolidated elements of fairness and it induced cooperation on both sides of the market.

This chapter develops a simple bargaining model in which firms and workers negotiate over fair wages. By paying a fair wage firms could put an end to restriction-of-output campaigns and workers would reciprocate by giving more effort. Moreover, in a piece rate model where firms abstain from ratebusting, technical change is worker-sponsored. Over time where bargaining is repeated, the fair wage coordinates the actions of individuals, and as long as both parties expect commitments to be upheld it may evolve into a rule or norm. In this way firms and workers adapt to the method of pay without changing it.

Piece rates: benefits and costs

The past decade has seen renewed interest among economists in explaining the existence of different methods of compensation. In general this approach sets out the technical conditions, preferences toward risk, the variability of worker types, and the availability of information that would give rise to different types of payment schemes. Edward Lazear, among others, showed that piece rates are likely to be used when output could be measured at low cost and with little error, when workers are heterogeneous in ability levels, and when the value of the alternative wage is high relative to average output at the firm.[3] The latter condition ensures that low-output workers are induced to leave. Workers would cooperate with management, revealing full information about the nature of their work, and sharing with management new ideas in return for higher earnings. Empirical studies for the post-1945 period have confirmed the relation between the cost of measuring output and the method of pay, and between earnings and piece rates.[4]

These conditions appear to fit the cotton-spinning industry as well. Referring to the first factories, Marx claimed that piece work was "the form of wage most appropriate to the capitalist mode of production."[5] The labor supply was heterogeneous and individual yarn output was easily measurable, with little error. Indeed one of the earliest and most wide-spread innovations in the textile industry was a counter to measure the length and fineness of the yarn spun. As for alternative employment, at least for younger workers in the urban sector, there was a wide range of opportunities. Under these conditions it appears that the choice of payment was optimal and the contract well specified.

The costs of piece-rate schemes, however, are not trivial. Machinery and other equipment may depreciate more rapidly when payment is by the piece, because workers in principle are motivated to speed up; the quality of output may suffer as well. These drawbacks can usually be offset by special tariffs.[6] In Lancashire there are examples of fines levied for bad workmanship, and in some cases spinners had to pay for oil used to lubricate their mules and the straps and bands broken during the backward and forward runs. But although in principle it is possible for agents to write complex arrangements, in practice it has proven difficult to implement such schemes. Hence, by the 1830s or so, in fine-spinning Manchester mills, fines, as I discussed previously, were small, if levied at all.

Perhaps the most complex problem is the determination of the optimal piece rate itself. In Lancashire the first and second generations of spinning manuals did not provide this type of information. And although Babbage drew up an early version of a time and motion study, the development of an algorithm for the setting of piece rates is generally associated with Frederick Taylor, the father of the American school of scientific management of the late nineteenth century.[7] In cotton textiles this approach was first tried out in the 1930s, but as in other sectors of British industry it was poorly received by both managers and workers.[8] Nonetheless, the nature of the calculation proposed gives an indication of the degree of complexity involved in setting piece rates.

Using time and motion studies, Taylor and his associates set a base time for the specified task.[9] This component usually represented about three-quarters to one-half of the total time allocated for the task. To the base was added first a percentage to cover fatigue, personal care, and machine breakdowns, and a second percentage to provide an incentive to the workers. Taylor claimed that these proportions and the initial base could be scientifically measured. In situations where technical change was rapid, work-study experts advocated that piece rates be abandoned temporarily in favor of time payoffs until management would have a better idea of how much could be produced on the new machinery. Observing this phenomenon, economists have hypothesized that in industries with ongoing technical change it would be rare to see payment by the piece.[10]

However, the setting of piece rates is not solely an engineering problem. Richard Edwards, in his richly detailed study of the contested terrain between labor and management in the United States in the late nineteenth century, found that piece-rate schemes failed frequently because they relied on workers to provide technical information:

Managers' ability to control soldiering resulted from their inadequate knowledge of the actual techniques of production. Most of the specific expertise – for example, knowledge of how quickly production tasks could be done – resided in workers . . . Piece rates always carried the allure of payment for actual labor done (rather than labor power), thus promising an automatic solution to the problem of translating labor power into labor . . . but as long as management depended on its workers for information about how fast the job could be done . . . there was no way to make the piece-rate method deliver its promise.[11]

This is a very different piece-rate regime than the one imagined by Lazear. Why do workers not cooperate as Lazear's model expects them to? Although analysts in the Marxist tradition have always recognized the difficulty of transforming the quantity of labor purchased into actual labor, mainstream economists have only recently turned their attention to this question.[12] According to Lorne Carmichael and Bentley MacLeod, the answer lies in the law of competition and the inability of firms to keep piece rates constant. Consider a firm that introduces new technology without adjusting rates. Workers gain experience in the new technology and their output and earnings rise. However, cooperation between firms and workers is short-lived because new technologies and skills spread from one firm to another. Other firms, sometimes started up by ex-employees of the first, can always undercut the innovating firm by starting up a new operation, teaching the new techniques, and setting a lower piece rate. Even if individual firms and workers wish to protect piece rates, the forces of competition overwhelm them.[13]

In response to rate cuts, workers often respond by restricting output, that is, hiding information from management. Surveying a variety of industries in Britain in the late nineteenth century, D. F. Schloss found workers participating in "ca'canny" in response to employers' "nibbling" and "chasing."[14] Similarly, Stanley Mathewson in his classic study of US industry in the 1930s observed workers restricting effort where they feared rate cuts or unemployment and where they wanted to express personal grievances. Mathewson also reported that

occasionally workers have an idea that they are worth more than management is willing to pay them. When they are not receiving the wage they think is *fair*, they adjust production to the pay received.[15]

Other studies have emphasized workers' response to technical change.[16] Upon the introduction of new technology, workers may construe that management is using the threat of a piece-rate cut to get them to work hard. In principle, adjustments to reflect the fact that new machinery has made the old piece rate too generous might be accepted, but in practice determining whether the reduction is fair is difficult. If workers feel threatened they may collude to restrict output, thereby signaling that they cannot work any harder. If they are successful, they will have undermined attempts to extract more effort and they will hoard from management the benefits of the new technology.

Output restriction in Lancashire is consistent with this body of research. To preserve their wage and employment conditions, as we have seen, workers like those at M&K reduced effort levels in the mid-1820s and prevented rate cuts on new technology. Workers in the period had good reason to collude because the impact of the new technology was uncertain, but as late as the 1920s, C. S. Myers gave examples of numerous situations in British industry where workers set "traditional" standards of output which they protected by restricting effort.[17] A legacy of the industrial revolution, these practices continued unabated in Britain in the post-1945 period.[18]

In summary, the costs incurred by paying by the piece may not be trivial. Firms appear to be incapable of abstaining from busting rates. This raises three related issues. First, there is the technical problem in setting the optimal piece rate. The second problem is that piece rates are difficult to set where technical change is rapid. There is no evidence, for Lancashire in the first half of the nineteenth century, of firms temporarily abandoning piece for time payoffs when new machinery was introduced.[19] The third problem is more general: how can the piece rate be set without antagonizing workers, especially in Lancashire – and elsewhere – where the workers have the ability to hide information and take hidden action about effort levels? Where piece-rate busting continues, workers are not motivated to cooperate and sponsor new technologies. It is not surprising that the number of workers paid by the piece in North America and in Britain has declined steadily since the late nineteenth century. If, as J. R. Hicks observed, time-rate contracts are more easy to set and adjust, why then do certain piece-rate schemes persist?[20]

Alternative models: bonding, human capital, and tournaments

To a large extent payment by piece was retained in cotton spinning because it was the traditional method of pay in the industry. Inherited from the putting-out system, along with sub-contracting, piece payment was the tried and true method of labor management. Its failure to elicit effort in the first factories like M&K gives credence to Pollard's claim that management was ineffective in solving the work-discipline problem; rather they evaded it.[21] However, there was some flexibility and alterations in the choice of pay. Gregory Clark found a variety of different payment schemes in the weaving factories of the early and the middle of the nineteenth century. In one mill the piece rate implicitly deducted a rental charge for looms and space; in other establishments a quota system was in place, setting minimum output schemes per machine while paying a fixed piece rate per unit of output.[22] Attempts were made to pay spinners by the time and to pay piecers directly, but they were short-lived. Compared to other industries, the basic piece-rate scheme in spinning remained intact – indeed, over the century, its coverage in textiles expanded.[23] The implication is that, in spinning, employers had found a way to adapt the traditional method of pay to factory conditions and put an end to output restriction. "Of all the industries investigated," Carroll D. Wright concluded in his survey of work stoppages in various countries, "this one [the British textile industry] alone is free from allegations of more or less conscious restriction."[24]

The economics literature suggests a number of approaches to solving the moral hazard and adverse selection problems faced by firms.[25] One solution to output restriction is bonding workers for more than one period or forcing them to pay an entrance fee. All or part of first-period compensation could be paid in the second period to be forfeited if workers fail to finish the task. Alternatively, bonding can be achieved by tilting the earnings curve.[26] There exist multi-tiered piece-rate schemes in which older workers receive higher rates and collect their entrance fee, thus compensating them for their low wages when they were young. In all these scenarios, the threat of losing the bond or entrance fee can create work incentives and enable the market for jobs to clear.

The problem with this solution is that it assumes that workers can borrow; even if this was likely in Lancashire, it is unsatisfactory because the information uncertainties making it difficult for firms to evaluate effort levels would also plague lenders.[27] Attempts to bind workers face other obstacles. They are incompatible with the prohibition of involuntary servitude; they give an incentive for an employer to make a layoff appear to be a quit, because the bond is then forfeited; and they are inconsistent with a strong preference for smooth income and consumption streams. While these considerations do not imply that bonding is impossible, they suggest that complete bonding may be difficult.

A variant of the bonding argument which gets around the capital market constraint is based on the well-known human capital model. Job applicants who cannot pay an entrance fee can offer to work in low-wage apprentice status for an initial period, thereby creating a wedge between productivity and earnings. The high rates paid to spinners could be seen as deferred income, a return on their investment in skills, to compensate for the low wages they received as piecers. It would be inaccurate to describe piecing as an apprenticeship. To be sure, piecers did pick up some specific and company skills, but there were two or three junior workers per spinning machine, or as one authority put it, "more piecers were produced in Lancashire than spinning mules."[28] Although it is hazardous to measure the balance between firm-specific and general skills, it would be difficult to imagine why firms would share in investments. There was in theory an active external market for trained spinners. If piecers did pay a bond, firms would have easily reneged on repayment, since they fired piecers as they came of age (usually eighteen or twenty-one years old); at any rate, they could have made layoffs appear to be quits. Why would workers take on the risks of apprenticeship if there was a low probability firms would retain them?[29]

Tournament models provide an alternative rationale why firms may pay supracompetitive wages to elicit effort from workers. In this type of model, workers who win a spinning position are rewarded by high pay.

The problems of incomplete contracting persist, however. Despite the selection process, the quality of output may suffer, and the possibility remains that once spinners obtain the prized position, the firm could not be assured that they would not hide information about how hard they could work.[30]

Alternative models: efficiency wages

The efficiency wage literature proposes an alternate means of eliciting high levels of effort. The basic approach assumes that there exists some positive relation between productivity and wages, and that by fixing wages at some level firms maximize profits. The wage acts as an incentive device, and because it is used for something other than the allocation of labor there remain unexploitable gains, a surplus, to be shared between the employed and firms.

The link between high wages and productivity has a long tradition in economics. Perhaps the first known statement of the relation can be traced to the mercantilist period, a position which was later echoed by Adam Smith.[31] However, the early literature did not always distinguish between more pay for more effort (which gives rise to an upward-sloping labor supply schedule), and more effort per unit of time. Be that as it may, these views were not popular. Merchants engaged in the putting-out system frequently remarked that higher wages, instead of eliciting more effort, served only to reduce the worker's dependence. One observer noted that the "best friend" of cotton manufacturers was "high provisions," and that "every one but an idiot knows that the lower classes must be kept poor, or they will never be industrious."[32] It was during the second generation of factory work that questions of efficiency received the attention of authorities like Charles Babbage and Andrew Ure. Summarizing the views of nineteenth-century commentators, Maxine Berg wrote: "Incentive devices like the piece rate united the interests of the worker to the output of the machinery, a combination encouraging greater efficiency."[33]

In economics the wage–productivity relation resurfaced in the late 1950s in development economics where the connection between wages and productivity was physiological: higher wages provided a better diet which in turn permitted greater effort and output.[34] More recently, under the label "efficiency wage theory," economists have turned to the wage–productivity relationship to explain why the labor market does not always operate as an auction or spot market, and why there are large fluctuations in output and employment that appear to be correlated with aggregate demand.[35] Unlike previous attempts in explaining large output adjustment, the efficiency wage model generates real wage rigidities. The wage–productivity relationship has also been used to develop theories of dual or segmented labor markets and for setting out policy proposals for higher minimum wages.[36]

Assume an economy with identical, perfectly competitive firms, each with a production function of the type $Q = F(e(w)N)$ where e is the effort or efficiency level of a worker, N is the number of employees, w is the real wage, and Q is output.[37] All workers are assumed to have identical wage–productivity relationships with $e' > 0$, $e(0) < 0$. The elasticity of $e(w)$ with respect to w declines as w increases. The profit-maximizing firm solves:

$$max \ F(e(w)N) - wN.^{38} \tag{1}$$

The solution yields the optimal wage w^*, known as the efficiency wage, which minimizes wage costs per efficiency unit of labor and satisfies the condition that the elasticity of effort with respect to the wage is unity. If at w^* there is an excess supply of labor, no firm has an incentive to lower its wage, unemployment occurs, and a surplus arises.

These results have been derived in a variety of models. Standards of nutrition, firm-specific capital, adverse selection, and monitoring problems are some of the factors that may give rise to efficiency wages. In the popular shirking model, workers have some knowledge of their productivity that is unavailable at low cost to firms, and under conditions of full employment workers have the power of exit that makes it difficult for employers to impose their effort norms. As a result, individual employers offer their workers higher wages to induce workers not to leave, but when all employers do so unemployment results. Assuming the costs incurred by firms in monitoring and the costs to workers if they are detected shirking, these models then seek to determine the equilibrium relation between effort and pay within each firm, and the equilibrium level of involuntary unemployment in the economy as a whole.

Despite their popularity, these types of models have their problems. To many it is unclear why even a small amount of expenditure on supervision would not eliminate shirking. To others, tournaments or piece-rate contracts would always dominate, because individual workers under these methods of pay have the incentive to increase output. This criticism gets at the nub of efficiency wage theory, which models one worker's reaction to a firm's wage offer. If a worker does not like the offer, she will not work; there is no strategic behavior on the part of individual groups of workers or firms. The upshot is that efficiency wage models assume that workers' sole response to unacceptable wage offers is exiting. There is no room for piece-rate bargaining, let alone efficiency piece rates. Workers accept or reject the equilibrium efficiency wage and there is no negotiation over the division of the economic surplus.[39] Hence, as a stylized approach, efficiency wage theory might explain the economy's response to a demand shock; it is less than satisfactory in addressing how groups of workers and firms negotiate wage and employment conditions.

Nonetheless, efficiency wage theory does offer important insights into the relation between effort and wages. The approach I describe below is similar in many respects to the efficiency wage model of George Akerlof and Janet Yellen.[40] In their approach, workers who are paid a fair wage will reciprocate by giving more effort, but when workers do not receive their just wage they react without calculation: "If people do not get what they think they deserve, they get angry." Thus, as with other efficiency wage models, their approach is weakened because it deemphasizes how groups of workers can behave strategically to a wage cut. The fair wage in their model is fixed by an ethical standard; it is not determined by bargaining. The theory also suffers because the reference groups are not well specified. The model in the next section builds on the Akerlof and Yellen approach, but it incorporates endogenous effort norms, strategic behavior, and suggests that the source of reference wages lies in community-developed and - enforced standards.

Fair wages as a solution to the piece-rate problem

Figure 5.1 summarizes the piece-rate problem as found in the early factories, like that of M&K, c. 1820.[41] The earnings of spinners had been increasing for some time, and it was uncertain whether firms would cut piece rates. Spinners had two initial options: to trust that their employers would not cut rates of pay and in return give full effort, or to distrust them and restrict output. Employers had the corresponding options of honoring the workers' trust or violating it and cutting piece rates. There were three possible outcomes to this quandary. 'Renege' meant that firms cut piece rates in spite of workers giving full effort; 'commit' meant that firms kept piece rates constant; and 'restrict' meant that workers initially reduced effort.

Spinners obviously preferred 'commit'; they would keep higher earnings at the same piece rate, the standard rate. On the other hand, because employers had incentive to 'renege', spinners were inclined to reduce their effort. This scenario harmed both parties, since workers and firms would have done better with 'commit'. Although it may not have seemed advantageous to the firms, 'commit' at least gained them the full effort of spinners and provided them with greater revenues than available at 'restrict'. The problem is that 'commit' was difficult to achieve. Faced by the threat of competition from new enterprises with the latest in technology, firms were inclined to bust the piece rate. Herein lies the failure of most piece-rate schemes.

Commitment is not improbable, however. 'Renege' is extremely costly

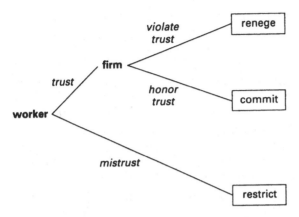

5.1 The piece-rate problem

for firms and workers who engage in repeated negotiations. One can imagine that workers and firms do not immediately arrive at a settlement or rule to divide the available rents or surplus where information is imperfect and where it is not known whether the other party is a tough or soft bargainer. Indeed it may be to the advantage of one or both parties to delay settlement in order to get this type of information. But cooperation often does emerge, and a low wage–low effort equilibrium can be transformed into a high wage–high effort state. Gary J. Miller in his excellent recent study of piece-rate bargaining suggested that cooperation is very likely to occur in very long-run organizations.[42] Even though cooperation is not necessarily the dominant strategy, cooperation is likely where each player has gained confidence that the other side is trustworthy. Cooperation in a repeated game need not be based on mutual altruism; it is based on the shared knowledge that each can punish the other if either fails to cooperate in this period. It must be reinforced that cooperation is one possible equilibrium position. More formally, both mutual cooperation and mutual defection are equilibrium points in a repeated prisoners' dilemma. Firms need to secure a reputation for upholding the wage and abstaining for busting rates; workers need to develop a reputation for not withdrawing effort. Only if commitments are kept repeatedly can cooperation evolve. "Negotiations," according to Robert Wilson, "are the evolution of the parties' reputations."[43]

How might cooperation evolve and what would it look like? One possibility is suggested by the industrial relations literature I have previously referred to. After 1850 and late in the century in response to Taylor's schemes, a prominent school of industrial relations in both Britain and the

United States continued to promote the policy of paying high and fair wages to eliminate output restriction and work stoppages. "Experience proves that if you want your men to do their level best," Schloss wrote, "you must rigorously abstain from nibbling their wages down, even if it be demonstrable that a mistake in their favour has been made in fixing prices."[44] Commenting on the problems inherent in Taylor's scheme of setting rates and its failure to put an end to restriction of output, the chairman of the American Management Association arrived at a similar conclusion. "As employers began to realize the economic principle of high production for a given overhead, they soon learned that rate cutting was equivalent to 'killing the goose that laid the golden egg.'"[45]

Fixing rates to ensure fair levels of earnings can be viewed as a "tit-for-tat" strategy in a coordination game. A tit-for-tat strategy in a multiperiod game is defined as playing the cooperative alternative, 'commit', in the first play of the game and mimicking the other player's response in subsequent moves. In the first round, employers agree not to cut piece rates, so long as workers agree to provide high levels of effort; but if employers break this commitment then workers will respond by defecting, that is, by choosing to 'restrict'. As Miller has written, the cooperative outcome would be an equilibrium if and only if each party perceived a long-term commitment; if either party is myopic or if the game is suspected to have ended, then each side would take the short-term gain of defecting.[46] The tit-for-tat solution is fragile, at best.

Since rational actors can reach outcomes ranging from mutual defection to mutual cooperation, theory alone cannot predict what the actual outcome will be. Fairness itself is by no means fixed or exogenous. William R. Leiserson, a leading figure in New Deal industrial relations in the 1930s, observed the range of fair outcomes:

The workman has constantly in his mind what is a fair and honest day's work, and you can't set wages by time study or by any other scientific method that does not take into consideration the worker's judgment of fairness in this thing . . . managers have their ideas of justice. A really scientific method of fixing wages is one that will put together the management's idea of a fair rate and the workman's idea of a fair rate, and I don't see any other method of doing that except through collective bargaining.[47]

Consider figure 5.2.[48] An individual spinner has an alternative wage, v, and at that wage he will give a level of effort $e(min)$ achieving a level of utility of $u(min)$ while the firm earns profits of π^*. However, both worker and firms can do better such that the firm remains in the isoprofit line through $(v, e(min))$. If the firm pays a higher wage, the spinner will give more effort, until the efficient outcome is reached (w^*, e^*) where the worker's indifference curve is just tangent to the firm's isoprofit curve.[49]

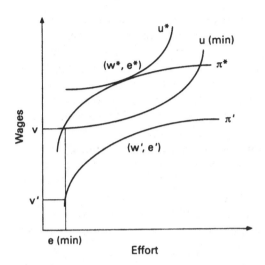

5.2   The fair wage model

As drawn, the worker gets all of the gains and the fair wage is completely preserved, but it is clear that the actual outcome is negotiated. There is a contract curve (not shown) of efficient points extending downwards from *(w*, e*)* to a point on the indifference curve through *(v, e(min))*. If the firm can enforce any level of effort and supervise workers completely so that they cannot restrict effort to protect their standard rates, thereby commanding a strong bargaining position, it can do no better than choose the point at the other end of the contract curve. But if monitoring and enforcement of effort are costly, then workers can bargain for higher and fairer wages. It is possible that firms and workers can decide on a fair division of the surplus and would want to stick to it, because it is costly for both sides to renegotiate.[50] The range of final outcomes underscores the complex interplay between the custom and the market, or, put differently, why workers' notion of a fair wage is not necessarily identical to their employers'.

Do the right thing: self-enforcing labor-market rules

The preceding section described the basis of cooperation and examined the process by which fair wages are negotiated; it remains to be considered how the fair wage itself is preserved and enforced. Why doesn't the pool of unemployed bid down the fair wage? Why don't workers compete against each other? I have previously introduced this issue in chapter 3 in discussing the free-rider problem associated with output restriction. Drawing on insights from game theory, Solow proposed an answer that seems relevant for workers wanting to manage risk and protect themselves from competitive or "Hobbesian" forces.[51] In a model in which workers and firms play an indefinitely repeated game, he showed that "sitting tight" can be an equilibrium strategy for an unemployed worker. The less workers fear the prospect of competition (and where there is little prospect of a reasonable and steady income stream), the less workers will undercut; the less they discount the future, the more likely it is that they will sit tight. It would be foolish for groups of workers to undercut if their unemployment spells were brief. If they did, firms would always use the strategy of cutting pay and everybody would be worse off as a result.

To be sure, for some individual workers and firms there are unexploited gains. Divisions between private and social gains always exist and fair wage arrangements need to be enforced and defection penalized. Especially after the introduction of agreements, when they are untested and fragile, too much conflict can cause the fair wage to be undercut; to insure compliance, firms and workers will need to take action against rate-busters and other defectors.[52] Those breaking norms will be stigmatized, ostracized, and blacklisted. Legislative intervention is another vehicle for enforcing codes of behavior. But even when legislation is impractical, over time there is a tendency for norms to become standardized, and workers and firms abide by them because they are the convention or the golden rule. A convention acquires a moral or just force when almost everyone in the community follows it and when it is in the interest of each individual to follow the rule, provided that all people she deals with, and her major rivals, do likewise.[53] Thus, social institutions provide information to each participant about the behavior of others.

There are economies in this process as well. The specific form of labor contracts may be less important than the standardization of wages and hours that reduce the number of parameters and options workers and firms have to evaluate. Moreover, in the absence of some mechanism of collective choice, it may be difficult to alter labor-market arrangements. "We do things," Solow wrote, "because they are the right thing to do, not because we have reckoned all the consequences." It is in this sense that the labor-market arrangements like the fair wage evolve into golden rules that coordinate the actions of individuals.[54]

Comparative statics: what lies ahead

Assume that the industry is composed of two sectors: a primary sector made up of large urban firms, like M&K, experiencing rapid technical change and a severe effort problem; and a secondary sector consisting of rural and small urban mills, where technical change was slow and supervision was not a problem. This segmentation highlights extremes, but it is useful in focusing on the determinants of wage and employment conditions. In both sectors workers desire to preserve standard piece rates and earnings, but only in the primary sector can they restrict effort and impose costs or damage on their employers. In the absence of effective bonding mechanisms, tournaments, and the like, large firms are compelled to pay fair wages. These are not strictly efficiency wages, because firms would prefer to pay lower piece rates if they could.

Our goal is not the calculation of the equilibrium payoffs, but to use this framework to interpret the historical record. Consider again figure 5.2. In the primary sector earnings would be higher up the contract curve; in the secondary sector the negotiated wage would be lower on the curve, tending close to the contingent or alternative wage. Small differences in initial monitoring and bargaining conditions may have large effects; the dispersion of fair wages can be substantial. Recall that, in the simple efficiency wage model, the elasticity of effort with respect to the wage rate is equal to unity. That is, labor and effort are multiplicative in the labor-augmenting production function, and withdrawing effort only reduces the efficiency of labor's own input and has no effect on other aspects of the production process, like the depreciation of machinery. If these assumptions are relaxed, it can be shown that the effort–wage elasticity is relatively low when production activities are particularly susceptible to damage from the actions of workers, especially those who act strategically; conversely, if damage is not an issue, the effort–wage elasticity is high. Under reasonable conditions, it follows that workers with a high "damage potential" – that is, the primary sector – are paid relatively higher earnings.[55] The wage gap between the two sectors persists, because workers will not undercut the fair wage and forego future benefits, and because if firms make a low offer, workers would have an incentive to restrict output anyway.

Initially, the primary sector is composed mainly of large fine spinners, but by 1850, with the introduction of the self-acting mule, large urban coarse spinners would also pay fair wages. In contrast to the competitive model, pay premia are not associated with the different levels of human capital investment workers bring into the mills. The effort problem differs markedly between urban and rural sectors. As long as the costs of maintaining schools, shops, and chapels are less than the alternative of paying high and fair wages, the bond between patron and client remains an effective means of eliciting effort. Firms in the rural sector after 1850, therefore, would continue to pay wages lower than those in urban regions. In the first part of chapter 6, I examine urban and rural wage data for fine- and coarse-spinning firms and assess whether they conform to this pattern.

The second half of chapter 6 compares the predictions of the fair wage and competitive models about piece-rate changes. The determination of piece rates and earnings has implications for labor-market adjustment. In terms of figure 5.2, a shock in demand lowers firms' isoprofit curve and worker's alternative wage to v'. The actual wage negotiated, however, need not fall proportionately. To demonstrate their commitment to workers, and to reveal that their actions are not opportunistic, firms may not want to cut piece rates. From the workers' perspective, the decline in outside opportunities increases the costs of being caught restricting effort, but workers may feel that firms are taking advantage of the decline in trade and that a piece-rate cut would not be restored, or that they will also be laid off, and they may meet a proposed pay cut by restricting effort. The result of these opposing effects could give rise to wage sluggishness and unemployment in the primary sector.[56] In the secondary sector firms can cut wages without fear of antagonizing workers. Some unemployed primary-sector workers might take jobs in the secondary sector, driving the wage even lower; others might prefer to wait out the recession.[57] In sum, wage declines would be larger and employment adjustment smaller in the secondary sector.

If wages are fixed, firms must adjust the quantity of employment. The composition of unemployment, or the division of the surplus, can be seen as a measure of firms' commitment to the fair wage. Firms that go on short time during trade declines preserve attachments with their workers, and when forced to lay off they usually will fire young workers first. At these firms, workers will anticipate smooth consumption streams and will respond by giving more effort. Although short time has declined in popularity since 1945, layoff rules that protect seniority are well observed in modern labor markets. The origins of these layoff patterns remain unclear. Chapter 7 describes the rationale and evolution of these patterns in Lancashire in the context of the fair wage model.

By working short time and offering seniority provisions, employers show their commitment to the fair wage; in response, workers should cease restricting output. In well-developed labor markets with secure commitments and with regularized communications and contacts between the parties, wage and employment packages tend to become standardized in implicit and explicit rules. In chapter 8, I describe the codification of the Lancashire fair wage in piece-rate lists and its effect on labor-market development.

Part III

How did labor markets really work?

6   Fair and unfair wages: 1825–1850

For the purely economic correspondence between the wage paid to a particular worker and his value to the employer is not a sufficient condition of efficiency; it is also necessary that there should not be strong feelings of injustice about the relative treatment of different employees (since these would diminish the efficiency of the team), and there should be some confidence about fair treatment over time (which is necessary in order that the individual worker should give his best). These requirements do not fit together at all easily with the result that wage rates are more uniform, both between workers, and over time, than they would be if the labour market worked like a commodity market. These tendencies are enhanced by unionisation, but even in the absence of formal unionisation they are likely to be present to some extent.[1]

Testing for fair wages: some drawbacks

How do economists reconcile evidence of "uniform" wage rates and the competitive model? Empirical work on testing efficiency and fair wage theories is in its early stages.[2] Because it is difficult econometrically to avoid the identification problem of whether high wages are the cause or the result of greater worker productivity or bargaining power, much of the recent work has resorted to examining wage differentials of identical groups of workers. The problem with this approach is that data sets are incomplete and it is hard to control, either separately or in combination, for compensating differentials, labor quality, or skill differences, or shifts in labor demand and supply across sectors. As ever, it is difficult to prove or disprove that labor markets are perfect.

Despite its inherent data limitations, research on the economic history of labor markets avoids many of these pitfalls. Historical studies of alternative wage theories are concerned about wage differentials and their effects, but they are interested as well in origins and causes.[3] In this class of work, the bottom line in evaluating competing models must be to ask, in a broad sense, whether the fair wage or another alternative wage theory predicts empirical relations that would be unobserved in its absence. In this chapter I will present evidence that a bargaining model uncovers features of early nineteenth-century labor markets that have previously been neglected or misunderstood.

My account begins with the Manchester strike of 1829. Emboldened by their control of production on long mules, fine spinners successfully resisted attempts to cut rates of pay. Piece rates and earnings in Manchester remained constant between 1821 and 1827, about 15 to 40 percent higher than the surrounding districts.[4] But in March 1829, seizing the opportunity presented by a slump in trade and in response to the challenge of unionization, the newly formed Masters' Association of fine spinners, which included M&K, announced a cut in piece rates, translating in some cases to a fall in earnings of 25 to 30 percent.[5] A long and bitter strike ensued and, according to the standard interpretation of the dispute, the masters prevailed. However, there were gains in the settlement for workers as well. Soon after its resolution, M'Connel expressed concern that the lengthy strike reduced its market share, and that, contrary to the objectives of the Masters' Association, the cut in rates was not sufficient to cover the advance in cotton prices.[6]

For fine-spinning firms like M&K the dispute was a watershed in industrial relations. Instead of antagonizing their spinners and bargaining over wages indeterminately, after 1829 large firms in Manchester and Bolton initiated a policy of paying fair wages. Herein lay the basis for cooperation. Faced by a decline in demand these concerns cut wages, but only hesitantly. On the other hand, at rural mills, at small urban establishments, and in Preston, employers continued to pay lower wages and cut them quickly and arbitrarily in response to changes in demand and supply. However, with the increase in size and proportion of urban firms, aggregate evidence suggests that after 1840 the strategy of paying fair wages gained wider currency.

The primary sector: large fine spinners

The piece-rate cuts in Manchester in 1829 were enforced by a city-wide list of prices. A town list had been in use in Bolton since 1813, but until 1829 most fine-spinning concerns in Manchester had paid by mill lists.[7] Under the old scheme, earnings were based on pounds of output spun, regardless of the length of mule, and spinners gained the entire benefits of the increased output of the new long mules like the ones installed at M&K in the early 1820s. In 1823, Bolton fine-spinning employers had successfully introduced the principle of discounting piece rates on longer mules to capture a return on their investments, and in the face of intense competition firms in Manchester demanded the same payment scheme.[8]

Workers fought the cut in ratès and the principle of discounting, but they did not dispute the adoption of the list itself. The list was based on the relation between pay and effort as it stood in 1829, thereby embedding elements of a fixed standard rate.[9] The standard incorporated many of the customary payment rules the first generation of workers had brought into the factory. Standards of reference remained intact. The list recognized that it took longer to spin higher counts of yarn and that workers would not find that their earnings fell if firms improved the quality of output; despite the introduction of discounting, it fixed rates of pay per pound of output for a mule of a given size, and spinners would capture the gains if employers attempted to speed up work or extract more effort. The list also addressed life-cycle concerns. The fixed standard provided older spinners with some insurance of stable earnings and all workers with protection against the unremunerated intensification of their labor. The list standardized the relation between effort and pay of *male* workers exclusively, putting up another barrier against the hiring of women, even though the latter could be hired at a lower wage. Finally, in accepting the list as a basis for negotiations, employers were explicitly recognizing the role, or at least the inevitability, of trade unions.

The list also put an end to ratebusting within and between mills. Because it was difficult to adjust one rate without changing the entire list, workers had little to fear that individual workers would undercut them. As for wage setting between mills, in the past, factories operating older and smaller vintages of machinery had frequently engaged in competitive rate cutting, undermining some leading firms' attempts to pay by a local list. The 1829 list, which was to a large extent restricted to the cotton lords of Manchester and its environs, was more easily enforced.[10] It was widely publicized and firms and workers who broke the standard would be stigmatized by both parties.

The district list did have benefits, at least potentially, for firms. By eliminating the cycle of competitive piece-rate cuts, the list would in principle reduce conflicts with workers and stoppages in production. It was anticipated that, if firms offered an established and known rate of pay, spinners would reciprocate and expend more effort. Stable rates would lead to higher earnings and this would raise the cost of job loss for workers, providing them with a further incentive to work hard. As a result, firms would gain some of the benefits of technical change and lower unit fixed costs. Recall that these costs were not trivial, amounting to about 35 percent of

Table 6.1 *Piece-rate changes: M'Connel and Kennedy, 1834–1841*
(percentages)

Variable[a]	1834–41	1834–36	1837–40
Earnings	28.43	15.61	31.89
Piece rate	10.30	6.97	12.24
Output	16.21	8.41	19.88

Notes:
[a] Monthly statistics.
Method: Piece-rate changes were calculated by taking the natural log of both sides of the equation: *earnings = piece rate per unit of output × output*; solving for log (piece rate); and then taking antilogs.
Sources: Earnings: M&K Cash Ledger; output: M&K Monthly Production Ledger.

unit costs at M&K, and that at Sedgwick Factory spinners could increase effort and output by as much as 25 percent.[11]

To realize the benefits of the list, however, firms had to convince workers that the relation between effort and pay would not deteriorate, and to this end they would not engage in opportunistic behavior and tamper with the structure of the list. Workers wanted assurance that when rates were cut during trade declines the old rate would be restored when trade recovered, and that firms would not attempt to raise their revenues by changing either the type of raw cotton or the quality of output without compensating them for any additional effort required to maintain their normal level of earnings. Spinners would work hard as long as they received pay for their effort. If firms kept their commitment about piece rates, they would realize the benefits of higher levels of output and lower unit fixed costs.

The ledgers of M&K reveal that the firm kept its commitment. In the first quarter of the century it was the firm's strategy to work at full capacity and, as prices fell, to make proportional cuts in piece rates, although as we have seen this strategy was met by worker resistance that made it difficult to actually cut rates. Using data on output and earnings from the monthly and weekly record books, I have estimated piece-rate changes for 1834 to 1841. (The method of calculation is described in a note to table 6.1.) The period covers good business years, 1834–36, and bad years, 1837–40. Piece-rate changes increased in bad years, but for the entire period they were less than output changes. Instead of antagonizing workers the firm resisted making large and arbitrary rate cuts. After the protracted dispute of 1829 and loss of market share, the firm realized that it was in its interest not to incur further stoppages.[12] M'Connel wrote that "in consequence of the exceedingly depressed state of the fine yarn market," it was the intention of his firm to produce less, "rather than reduce wages."[13] To be sure, in light of the discussion in chapter 5, the evidence suggests that workers and firms were still in the process of securing information about each other and trust was incomplete. At this stage neither side had established a fully credible reputation that commitments about effort norms and standard rates of pay would be fully honored; as a result disputes persisted, although not with the same level of intensity found in the 1829 strike.

Despite these drawbacks, the new policy kept the firm afloat during some difficult years. According to Lee, technical change was the principal means available to the firm to reduce costs. After 1825, however, when the firm stopped making investments in new technology, productivity stagnated and the fall in margins signaled a squeeze on profits. Lee claimed that the firm lost money in three consecutive years in the 1830s.[14] If firm and family funds were not inexhaustible, as is generally supposed, how did M&K survive the succession of bleak years of the 1830s and 1840s? One explanation is that the fall in profits in the 1830s was not dramatic. Lee's evidence on profits is taken from the accounts of the firm, but contemporary accounting statements of profit and loss did not use consistent and realistic depreciation rates and they therefore can be misleading or downright wrong.[15] This only underlines the question: how had the firm realized at least normal returns on its fixed capital after 1825?

I believe that the answer lies in the ability of the firm to harness the physical capabilities of male spinners operating long mules and raise productivity and profits by paying by an established list of prices. The list succeeded because it gave workers control over technical change, allowing them to gain the benefits of their increased effort. M&K's experience was representative of fine spinners. Although earlier statements on the correlation between high wages and productivity can be found, the view grew in popularity after the 1829 strike. Referring to Manchester, Andrew Ure reported that it was the custom in some of the largest and best firms in the early 1830s "to keep them [piece rates] as high as the mills could possibly afford, in order to be entitled to the best quality work."[16] Employers who paid fair wages earned favorable reputations as "plain, just, and honest," whereas "some factories," a textile worker reported, "have a bad character, and this clings to them."[17] The distinction between good and bad employers was not restricted to Manchester. "In our trade," testified the secretary of the Associated Cotton Spinners of Scotland in 1856, the "honourable employer" would always pay the "recognized rate" and "would never think of deviating from it."[18]

Table 6.2 *Weekly earnings of spinners in Manchester, 1806–1850 (in s)*

Year	Fine spinners	Medium-count spinners	Coarse spinners	Average
1806	33.25	28.00	22.00	25.83
1810	42.50	33.00	24.00	30.08
1814–22	32.00	28.00	24.00	26.00
1823				23.00
1824				21.00
1825				25.67
1827				22.50
1828				24.00
1829				25.25
1830				24.75
1831				26.16
1832				24.50
1833	33.25	28.00	22.00	25.83
1836	40.00	26.00	18.50	24.33
1839	42.00	21.50	19.50	23.25
1841	40.00	21.50	16.50	21.67
1845–46	42.00	23.50	18.00	23.50
1849–50	37.00	19.75	19.50	21.83

Source: George H. Wood, *The History of Wages in the Cotton Trade During the Past Hundred Years* (Manchester: Hughes, 1910), 28.

Wage evidence is consistent with these claims (table 6.2). Between 1833 and 1840 weekly earnings of Manchester fine spinners increased, recovering to levels that were first reached in the 1810s, about the time firms began implementing a high turnover policy.[19] The two periods were similar in that both saw queues of workers forming outside the mill wall. Peter Ewart, a Manchester millowner, observed that for every vacancy at his mill there were five or six applicants in the early 1830s.[20] But the similarities ended here. Unlike the earlier period, the unemployed in the 1830s could not or would not bid down wages. They could not because firms that paid lower wages would find their workers restricting effort; they would not because spinners and senior piecers who based their decisions on what was right and fair held to and observed output norms. That there existed gains for individuals to exploit is revealed in newspaper reports of workers and firms continuing to undercut the list of prices.[21] Nonetheless, high unemployment in the 1830s persisted and ratebusters and knobsticks were stigmatized. In Manchester after the costly 1829 dispute, large firms supported strikers at smaller firms in the region that refused to pay the standard.[22] Much of the violence of these disputes and those throughout the century was centered on the blackleg, "the transgressor of communal codes of honour, rather than the employer."[23] To invoke Solow, massive undercutting – by workers and firms – was evolving into a taboo.

Boot has recently suggested that the steady increase in earnings of textile workers during the period represented a return on their investment in human capital, and not a premium required to elicit effort.[24] The point I wish to advance is that the two arguments are not mutually exclusive, and that empirically they are difficult to distinguish between. The human capital argument views earnings across time; but at any one moment complete contracts are difficult to write and enforce. Even if earnings represented investments in skill, firms may have continued to pay premia to avoid output restriction.

A final point concerning the wages of spinners needs to be addressed. The persistence of high wages in the face of stubborn levels of unemployment in the 1830s begs the question of whether the extra effort of spinners resulted from a fear of job loss, or from the new industrial relations climate within firms. Undoubtedly, it is difficult to separate external and internal factors and in some respect they were one and the same thing. If all firms fixed earnings at fair (high) levels, unemployment would have resulted. But the change in firms' policies appears to have been independent of the excess supply of labor. This is consistent with the fair wage model, because in the shirking class of efficiency wage models, all discipline is assumed to occur via the threat of dismissal.

Here again the M&K experience was representative, even a leading example. Beginning in the 1830s it regularized its policy of hiring from within the ranks of the firm. M'Connel's boast that "we seldom if we can avoid it engage strangers" gave workers the commitment of lengthy tenure, putting an end to its use of the turnover threat.[25] In certain respects the possibility of long-term employment mitigated the premium needed to elicit effort from workers. Recall that not all young adults in the preparatory stages or piecers would become spinners. Given the ratio of spinners to other workers in the factory, the probability was in fact less than 20 percent. To rise to a well-paid spinning position workers had to demonstrate their commitment. Was this a fair wage or a reward for their hard work as in a tournament model? Again it is important to separate the determinants of labor-market decisions across and over time. Firms had to pay fair wages because they could not be assured that once junior workers became spinners, they would not resort to opportunistic behavior. That piece-rate changes failed to match improvements in technology is consistent with the change in employers' attitudes toward paying fair wages. In

1845 Henry Houldsworth, the Manchester millowner, replaced some of his older machinery with new jack frames, a preparatory machine, and although he estimated that productivity would increase by 10 percent, he insisted upon only a 3 percent decrease in piece rates, a reduction readily accepted by his workers.[26] Since no further reduction occurred until 1848, the relatively small adjustment to piece rates gave rise to wage drift.[27] This is precisely what one would expect where technical change is worker-sponsored. As Houldsworth explained some years earlier:

I think it would be possible to reduce the wages [of spinners] because there is always a sufficiency of hands, but it has not been the policy of the masters to do so. They will not do it knowing that the lower the workpeople are reduced in circumstances, the less dependence can be placed on their attention.[28]

The secondary sector: coarse spinners and rural mills

Leaving aside for the moment skill premia and union effects, earnings of medium-count and coarse spinners were consistently less than fine spinners and they were more variable (table 6.2). A comparison of earnings and piece rates of spinners and handloom weavers lends confirmation that the secondary labor market was more responsive. It is well known that without protection from trade unions or government regulation, the labor market for handloom weavers was exceptionally loose and flexible, and it probably came as close to an auction market as any market in the period did.[29] The number of handloom weavers working in their homes or small shops grew rapidly after 1780 as improvements in factory-spinning technology created an abundant supply of yarn to be woven. The conjunction of the slump in textile prices after the French Wars and the rapid advancement and investment in power-loom technology propelled handloom wages on a downward course. During the period 1822 to 1832 alone, piece rates for calico, a medium cloth, fell by nearly 50 percent (table 6.3).[30]

A series of piece rates in coarse spinning, albeit fragmentary, is available for a comparable period. As in handloom weaving, the fall was significant: the price paid for no. 40 fell by 30 percent. To be sure, there are differences between the handloom and spinners' series. Most of the change in spinning occurred after 1828, that is, two years after the recession of 1825–26, but in weaving, piece rates adjusted quickly to the trade decline. Nonetheless, the evidence for coarse spinning cannot reject the hypothesis that urban firms in the secondary sector cut rates in response to market forces.

In the rural sector, earnings were lower in the first instance because of their relationship with agricultural rather than urban industrial wages; but

Table 6.3 *Weaving and spinning piece rates, 1822–1832*

Year	Weaving[a]	Spinning[b]
1822[c]	100.00	100.00
1823	92.84	102.40
1824	82.90	110.00
1825	86.21	100.00
1826	57.76	93.60
1827	64.40	80.00
1828	64.92	100.00
1829	46.33	80.00
1830	60.73	76.80
1832	52.70	70.40

Notes:
[a] Calico.
[b] No. 40.
[c] 1822 = 100.
Sources: Weaving: John S. Lyons, "The Lancashire Cotton Industry and the Introduction of the Powerloom, 1815–50," Ph.D. dissertation, University of California, Berkeley, 1977, 243. Spinning: Michael Huberman, "Invisible Handshakes in Lancashire: Cotton Spinning in the First Half of the Nineteenth Century," *Journal of Economic History* 46 (December 1986), 993.

because the effort problem was less acute in this sector, the differential stuck. Recall that rural mills had more margins to work at than their urban rivals, but as the proportion of labor in total costs bulked large, given the opportunity, they would have cut piece rates. Moreover, because of the dependent position of their workers, if employers cut rates there would have been little pressure to raise them when business recovered. The evidence is consistent with this notion. The Gregs' factory in Styal employed 435 workers in 1841, but despite its size male mule spinners in the 1840s earned about 11s 6d, 7s 6d less than their Manchester counterparts.[31] To get a true measure of the real wage disparity the nominal wage gap must be corrected for rental and cost-of-living differences, and urban disamenities. But even using the most favorable estimates against finding disparity, a real wage gap of about 11 percent remains.[32]

This finding corroborates Williamson's recent estimates that there existed a corrected wage gap of about 13 to 30 percent between urban and rural sectors.[33] Williamson described this phenomenon as market disequilibrium, an outcome of the slow movement out of the countryside. On the other hand, the model in chapter 5 implies that wage gaps between primary and secondary sectors could persist, and in the context of rural mills I interpret the evidence to mean that paternalism succeeded in eliciting effort at low cost. The gap can be seen as the wage premium needed to elicit effort in large urban firms. In support, the wage gap between the Gregs' and Manchester mills persisted, if not widened, throughout the second half of the century.

There are accounts of rural mills facing a labor shortage in the mid-1830s, but instead of raising wages they began looking further afield for families. The compensation package had not changed; instead the geographic scope of the market expanded or contracted, depending on the availability of local labor. As late as 1875 labor turnover at Quarry Bank was low; only in the early 1900s did families begin to leave, and until then, according to the historian of the firm, labor relations were uniformly good.[34] It was not in the interest of an employer, W. R. Greg wrote, to maintain "artificially . . . a rate avowedly above the market price of labor, for he shall turn a deaf ear to destitute multitudes who come to him begging for employment."[35]

The Ashworth factories outside Bolton spun fine yarn and they were large, the New Eagley mill employing 709 workers in 1867. But like other rural mills, its wages, after making the necessary adjustments, were lower than those found in urban centers. In the 1840s there was a heated exchange in the Bolton newspapers and in parliament about Henry Ashworth's treatment of his workers. The controversy centered on the millowner's outspoken position on trade unions, hour legislation, and free trade, and, as a result, the statistical evidence reported was exaggerated in one direction or another. Nevertheless, Boyson, Ashworth's biographer, acknowledged that piece rates paid by the firm were at least 10 percent lower than those in Bolton in the 1840s.[36] Earnings averaged about 33s at the Ashworth's mills and ranged between 25s and 43s in Bolton in the 1830s and 1840s.[37] The reported difference is small but it is an underestimate, because Ashworth fined his operatives more often than his Bolton competitors.[38] For the 1860s and later the evidence is unambiguous; by all accounts, the firm's earnings and piece rates were persistently about 15 to 20 percent lower than those found in Bolton.[39]

Unlike owners of urban fine-spinning mills, it was Henry Ashworth's philosophy and practice to raise or lower rates of pay according to the state of trade and the supply of labor.[40] Estimates of piece-rate changes in table 6.4 are based on data collected from the New Eagley mill output

Table 6.4 *Piece-rate changes: Ashworth's New Eagley mill, 1832–1852 (percentages)*

Variable [a]	1832–52	1832–36, 1843–45, 1851–52	1837–42, 1847–48
Earnings	134.32	14.41	325.67
Piece rate	88.86	4.25	220.43
Output	46.16	10.16	105.24

Notes:
[a] Quarterly statistics.
Method: See table 6.1.
Source: Ashworth Quarterly Stock Account.

ledger for 1832–52. The data are only available by quarters and are less precise than figures for M&K; yet a clear trend does emerge. For the entire period and noticeably in the bad years of 1837–42, the mean rate of change of output was less than the rate of change of piece rates. As expected, piece-rate changes are smaller than output changes in good years, 1832–36, 1843–45, and 1851–52.

In summary, rural mills had developed a cost-effective strategy of eliciting effort. Despite their older technology, the Gregs' and the Ashworth's mills survived in the fiercely competitive textile industry and it was only late in the century before labor unrest and turnover posed a threat to the patron–client relation at both firms. Nevertheless, the proportion of output produced by the rural sector declined steadily, and even rural employers themselves recognized that their employment practices were unrepresentative. It was the general tendency in the trade not to alter rates of pay, W. R. Greg conceded, because an employer was "so often expected to give his men their usual wages."

Primary and secondary wages: controlling for skill levels

The wage comparisons made in previous sections are imprecise because they do not correct for skill or union effects. But even after correcting for these effects, wage differences between large and small firms persist. The correspondence between size of establishment and employment conditions in the first factory industry has been the subject of much debate among social and labor historians. In an important contribution, Patrick Joyce in *Work, Society, and Politics* argued that sometime around the middle of the century employers exercised their authority in the factory and put an end to the social unrest that had threatened the fabric of Lancashire in the

Table 6.5 *Weekly earnings and firm sizes in 1833*

Average weekly earnings (in d)	Number of firms employing labor force			
	< 150	151–350	> 350	Total
0–100	16	3	2	21
101–125	30	19	20	69
> 126	18	25	26	69
Total number of firms	64	47	48	159

Source: Stanway's 1833 survey as reprinted in Andrew Ure, *The Philosophy of Manufacturers* (London: Charles Knight, 1835), 390–91.

1830s and 1840s.[41] He suggested that with population movements stabilizing in urban centers, work began to dominate the lives and define the existence of factory operatives, and they came to identify their interests with those of their masters. To establish his argument, Joyce distinguished between large or feudal firms, which were a sign of population and market stability, and small firms, an indicator of early and rapid economic and demographic expansion. The former had a sense of duty and obligation to their workers and paid high wages; workers would respond deferentially and, as a result, industrial relations were tranquil. In small mills, however, the opposite held. Joyce cited contemporary accounts of wage and employment conditions to support his argument. Even in the 1840s, he found that for Oldham, the "shared life-style of master and man [in a small firm] was a source of unpopularity," and relative to large concerns, they paid low wages.[42] Joyce's arguments are not inconsistent with the fair wage model, although my approach emphasizes to a greater extent the bargaining power of spinners as opposed to their deferential attitude.

Joyce's argument has proved controversial. There is a long-standing belief in the literature that small employers were better able to identify with their workers. Referring to Oldham, D. A. Farnie and D. S. Gadian argued that, in small firms, tensions between the parties were diminished because it was common to find bosses who were former spinners.[43] But small firms were also well known for their long hours of operation and for maltreating and grinding their workers, and in theory workers at these firms should have been compensated for these disamenities. Taking a different perspective, but arriving at a similar result, Craig Calhoun claimed that at small firms workers were in a better position to demand higher wages. "Small factories can be seen as important resources for collective action, since small size [is] conducive to the formation of community and

Table 6.6 *Weekly earnings and firm sizes in 1833 by region*

	Bolton	Manchester	Stockport	Oldham	Glossop
Number of firms	12	43	19	22	12
Average number					
of workers	453.08	402.21	330.84	171.59	79.75
Average count	72	71	31	34	41
Weekly earnings (in d.):					
Spinners	347.71	325.64	291.46	312.68	274.80
Overlookers	303.43	392.55	316.69	277.30	364.90
Piecers	50.16	70.37	70.41	74.03	58.96
Drawing tenters	70.82	101.73	92.38	95.31	87.78

Source: Table 6.5.

hence to collective action."[44] Similarly, John Foster found that labor militancy was greater in Oldham than in regions like Bolton where firms were larger.[45]

The most exhaustive cross-sectional study of firms available, factory inspector John Stanway's survey of 1833 (table 6.5), confirms the correspondence between size and earnings postulated by Joyce.[46] The survey has its limitations. It was restricted mainly to south Lancashire (thus excluding Preston) and contained a relatively high proportion of large firms. Despite these drawbacks, those who have used the survey have found that it provides a reasonable view of the industry and imparts no statistical biases. For the 159 firms surveyed, the null hypothesis that there was no positive relation between size and average earnings is rejected.[47] This result holds when the survey is broken down by region (and therefore size of firm) in table 6.6. With the exception of Stockport, the average earnings of spinners increases with the size of firms in the region. I also estimated equations with earnings as the dependent variable, and size of firms (measured by the number of workers) and count as the independent regressors.[48] In a double-log form the size coefficient is the only significant variable.

These results do not sit well with standard theories of compensation. If workers at small firms were maltreated, assuming that markets worked well, their earnings would have been greater than those at larger concerns, because they would have included a compensating differential. Nor can earning gaps be explained by skill differentials. Scattered evidence reveals that all workers in large firms, irrespective of occupation, age, and gender, received higher earnings. In 1833 overlookers earned more at large concerns, and over the period 1833 to 1841 the earnings of male and female piecers at Bolton mills increased and exceeded rates at smaller Oldham mills.[49] The timing of the change meshes with the introduction of the new wage policy, but these were not strictly efficiency wages.[50] The basic shirking model can attribute the high wages of spinners in large firms to monitoring problems; it cannot explain why piecers in these establishments also received high earnings. There is no reason to assume that piecers' tasks were any more difficult on longer mules, in the same way that a secretary at a large firm also earns high wages, even though his skills are no different from a secretary at a smaller concern. A fair wage model can explain this phenomenon. The fixing of the male mule spinners' wage generated spillover effects. Within large firms, workers used the pay of their upper- and lower-paid co-workers as reference groups in negotiating their fair wage. Thus, even though they were a minority in the factory, spinners' pay premia impacted on the remuneration of the entire workforce. As in modern labor markets, in Lancashire cotton spinning, regardless of skill level, the average worker in a primary sector firm tended to receive positive wage premia.

The labor market at the middle of the century: another snapshot

The growth in the average size of firms and the increasing concentration of the industry in urban regions around 1850 erased gradually the divisions between large and small, and fine and coarse mills. The demise of the rural sector was relative and by 1850 probably less than 10 percent of yarn was spun in this region.[51] Labor-market integration, however, did not imply a return to thoroughgoing competition.

There is strong evidence of learning. Although there remained firms like those in Preston which continued to cut piece rates and engage in bitter negotiations with their workers, by 1850 the fair-wage strategy was being adopted by an increasing number of firms in the industry. Recall that at the middle of the century the average firm employed about 200 workers and there was little investment in new methods of supervision. To remain competitive even medium-sized firms were compelled to bargain over effort levels. The spread of fair wages is visible in G. H. Wood's widely used earnings and employment series.[52] Table 6.7 reports the flexibility of piece-rate changes between 1838 and 1852, a period which covered two cycles. If piece rates were sensitive to changes in prices, then the ratio of earnings to the value of output should not exhibit cyclical movements. For the data underlying the table, the standard deviations about trend for the logarithms of value and volume of output per worker, and average earnings, are 0.424, 0.304, and 0.116. Indeed, earnings exhibit countercyclical movement. Both the volume and value of output are below trend, while average

Table 6.7 *Earnings and output expressed relative to trend, 1838–1852*

Period	Average real earnings[a]	Value of output per employee[b]	Volume of output per employee
1838–42[c]	1.008	0.940	0.989
1843–45[d]	0.978	1.091	1.094
1846–48[c]	1.032	0.968	0.941
1849–52[d]	0.979	0.993	0.987

Notes:
[a] All cotton operatives.
[b] Price – no. 40.
[c] Trough years of business cycle.
[d] Peak years of business cycle.
Method: Calculated by regressing the logarithm of the variable in question on a constant, time, time squared, averaging the deviations within the given periods, and then exponentiating their averages.
Sources: Earnings: George H. Wood, *The History of Wages in the Cotton Trade During the Past Hundred Years* (Manchester: Hughes, 1910), 127–28.
Employment: G. N. von Tunzelmann, *Steam Power and British Industrialization to 1860* (Oxford: Oxford University Press, 1978), 239. Price deflator: A. D. Gayer, W. R. Rostow, and A. J. Schwartz. *The Growth and Fluctuations of the British Economy, 1790–1850* (Oxford: Oxford University Press, 1952), 468–70; Paul Rousseaux, *Les mouvements de fond de l'économie anglaise: 1800–1903* (London, 1930), 262–63. Output: Thomas Ellison, *The Cotton Trade of Great Britain* (London, 1886), table 5. Price: J. A. Mann, *The Cotton Trade of Great Britain* (Manchester: Thomson, 1860), 96.

earnings are above trend, in the bad years of 1838–42 and 1846–48. During the relatively good years of 1843–45 earnings are below trend. By the middle of the century the labor market operated as one entity in which the dominant response to a decline in demand was output adjustment, not piece-rate cuts.

An alternative approach: prices and quantities

The data reported in the previous sections have their limitations. The firms studied may be in some way unique, and the 1833 survey gives only a snapshot of a fast-changing industry. As for the average earnings and employment series, Wood himself recognized their weaknesses. He collected earnings and not piece rates, and wages were uncorrected for unemployment or changes in hours worked during trade declines – and such changes

Table 6.8 *Disaggregated yarn output, 1822–1852 (millions of lbs.)*

| Year | Type of yarn[a] | | | | |
	F2	F1	FC	C2	C1
1822	8.13	12.44	22.48	41.37	31.71
1823	26.40	14.64	27.82	50.1	35.21
1824	14.27	16.49	28.12	49.4	33.92
1825	9.32	16.01	29.53	53.88	35.47
1826	9.52	10.29	23.33	46.32	28.62
1827	11.26	10.79	32.72	50.51	30.67
1828	11.04	12.70	38.14	67.6	39.67
1829	9.22	14.36	37.22	64.71	39.85
1830	8.68	16.08	47.22	79.4	46.16
1831	10.11	15.35	55.12	90.8	44.49
1832	11.42	15.10	50.04	93.12	54.49
1833	11.37	11.80	59.34	100.00	51.07
1834	8.40	11.99	70.05	113.85	55.23
1835	7.52	11.27	73.59	121.97	57.80
1836	9.22	18.81	85.51	126.52	51.24
1837	8.39	13.26	90.72	120.88	39.43
1838	8.19	12.63	100.99	149.70	57.65
1839	6.47	11.23	90.64	144.40	62.64
1840	8.63	7.87	117.85	174.23	61.28
1841	7.82	8.44	114.26	172.76	83.58
1842	8.50	7.60	110.56	168.12	62.14
1843	9.32	9.24	130.64	198.78	73.83
1844	9.95	13.25	141.64	207.81	75.21
1845	10.68	12.75	160.57	233.27	80.80
1846	13.14	14.65	178.94	241.77	69.68
1847	10.04	10.23	108.61	178.68	74.97
1848	11.72	10.13	157.00	238.89	87.48
1849	15.47	14.43	182.07	248.70	75.06
1850	17.28	20.59	154.60	212.54	69.77
1851	18.13	17.08	181.09	253.69	61.07
1852	17.83	19.48	219.22	281.91	79.96

Notes:
[a] In decreasing order of fineness from left to right.
Method: The method of construction is found in an appendix to chapter 6.

were not insignificant. Moreover, the series contain missing observations and it is difficult to assess trends for the period before 1835. Finally, Wood's series is not sufficiently detailed to compare the earning differentials of large and small firms in fine and coarse spinning, and the response of firms to a demand shock.

In this section I propose an alternative approach to evaluate labor-market adjustment based on the relation between earnings and layoffs, and prices and output. Although the relation between earnings and prices is inappropriate in explaining wage levels of large and small firms, it does shed light on the response of firms to demand shocks. As demand contracted, if earnings and piece rates were flexible, price changes would have been greater than output changes; but if firms paid fair wages the opposite would have held. What makes the approach attractive is the availability of detailed data on the prices and output of a wide variety of yarn types in fine and coarse spinning that can be used to infer wage and employment adjustment in large and small firms.

I have constructed output series of different yarn types following the industry's practice to use longer stapled cottons for the spinning of finer counts of yarn.[53] Disaggregated annual imports of cotton, corrected for wastage and inventories held at mills, can then be used as estimates of output broken down into different counts.[54] The appendix to this chapter describes the details of construction; table 6.8 gives the final series. Output series C1 is based on the import of Uplands and East Indian cottons and represents the output of counts less than no. 20; C2 represents the production of nos. 20–40; FC, nos. 40–60; F1, nos. 60–80. Together the output of these counts represent about 96 percent of the industry's production. The remainder, F2, represents counts greater than no. 80, and its proportion of total output is in line with contemporary estimates.[55] Although the series are inappropriate for evaluating rural and urban differences, as constructed the series provide an approximate mapping of changes in earnings at fine or large firms, and coarse or small concerns.

The sum of the disaggregated series does not equal the total of Thomas Ellison's series, the widely used aggregate series (table 6.9).[56] Ellison took the average weight of imported bags of cotton to calculate total consumption and an average wastage rate to estimate losses in converting cotton into yarn. On the other hand, the disaggregated series are constructed using the actual weights of the bags and a scale of wastage rates. But the differences between the two series are minor. Both series show steady expansion in output; the correlation between the series is 0.97; and their coefficients of variation, and mean and median rates of change are similar. Both series indicate declines in output in 1826, 1839, 1847, and 1850. The anomaly between the increase in the disaggregated series between 1840

Table 6.9 *Total output and inventories, 1822–1852 (millions of lbs.)*

	Output		Inventories	
	Disaggregate	Ellison	Raw cotton	Yarn
1822	116.1	128.2	14.3	28.0
1823	154.2	138.1	7.7	27.4
1824	142.2	149.0	16.3	33.6
1825	144.2	150.6	9.5	32.6
1826	118.1	134.9	21.9	42.2
1827	136.0	177.2	21.9	44.9
1828	169.2	195.9	34.3	50.5
1829	165.4	198.5	34.7	57.3
1830	197.6	222.0	27.4	62.7
1831	215.9	233.7	33.1	58.8
1832	224.1	249.6	27.2	71.7
1833	233.6	263.5	27.5	67.8
1834	259.5	274.3	19.1	78.7
1835	272.2	286.2	16.3	82.5
1836	286.3	313.6	24.3	85.2
1837	272.7	328.6	33.5	105.1
1838	329.2	378.3	50.8	113.7
1839	315.4	342.7	27.3	99.0
1840	370.9	412.7	44.1	107.5
1841	387.9	393.8	30.1	115.7
1842	356.9	407.3	42.4	136.5
1843	421.8	469.7	51.7	49.2
1844	447.4	488.6	51.5	130.1
1845	498.1	543.0	52.7	131.9
1846	518.2	554.2	53.1	157.1
1847	382.5	401.6	22.7	116.5
1848	505.2	513.0	37.5	127.1
1849	535.8	565.3	37.4	144.1
1850	474.8	526.7	37.5	120.2
1851	531.7	585.9	39.5	127.1
1852	618.4	657.5	58.7	124.5

Sources: Disaggregated output: sum of series of table 6.8. Ellison output: John S. Lyons, "The Lancashire Cotton Industry and the Introduction of the Powerloom, 1815–50," Ph.D. dissertation, University of California, Berkeley, 1977, 143. Raw cotton inventories: Thomas Ellison, *The Cotton Trade of Great Britain* (London, 1886), Appendix. Yarn inventories *George Holt Trade Circular*, 1852.

and 1841, and the decline in Ellison's aggregate figures, can be attributed to an increase in the import of East Indian cottons and the corresponding growth in C1 output. All other sectors decline between 1840 and 1841, except for F1 which increased marginally.

The distinctive feature of disaggregated output is the uneven growth of the individual series. At one extreme, F1 had absolute declines in sixteen years; at the other, FC had eight years of decline. Such was the extent of the unevenness that aggregate growth masked a decline in the output of individual types of yarn. Thus, Ellison's series hides minor or sectoral fluctuations such as occurred in 1825–26 in fine spinning, and in 1835–36 in C1 production. Even during major depressions, when Ellison reported stable, even increased, growth, the individual series indicate output cutbacks. Between 1836 and 1837 total output increased, but all series except FC declined. Similarly, total output increased between 1841 and 1842, but all series except F2 decreased. The magnitude of the sectoral declines was also greater than the aggregate declines. The standard deviation of FC for years of absolute declines is 12.47; for Ellison's series, it is 9.11.

Before assessing the relative size of output and price adjustments, the origins of the output cutbacks must be considered. As constructed, the disaggregated series may reflect both demand and supply shocks, but there is reasonable evidence to suggest that demand factors dominated. Contemporary literature reported that on occasion firms responded to a rise in supply prices by reducing cotton consumption and cutting output.[57] The response could only be successful if firms colluded to restrict output, but in competitive Lancashire – at least before the introduction of wage lists and the concomitant organization of employers into permanent Masters' Associations – attempts at collusion were short-lived.[58] In any event, supply shocks could not have had a significant impact because there was a variety of cottons of similar staple length that were substitutes. The Liverpool cotton market was stocked with cottons from around the world and it was serviced by a large number of importers and speculators.[59] The cotton market was efficient. Spinners placed orders on short notice and generally held limited stocks of cotton, equivalent on average to three to four weeks of production.[60] During normal business years it was the "custom" of the industry, *The Economist* observed, that spinners "bought little more than will cover the orders they have taken, and they very seldom exceed the necessary quantity."[61]

Authorities on the state of trade emphasized that output changes were associated with sudden and unexpected shifts in demand. Although means of communication existed in the yarn market, firms had difficulty anticipating demand changes. Ashworth wrote that the producer of cotton goods "works in complete ignorance of the number and purchasing power of his customers"; and in the early stages of the 1847 crisis, the *Manchester Guardian* reported that the "market will be to a great extent regulated by the demand and upon this important branch of the subject it is impossible at the present moment to offer any satisfactory opinions."[62] In the home market, among other factors, unanticipated changes in the Bank of England's credit and monetary policies and unpredictable harvests caused major and unforeseen shifts in demand. The foreign market, which accounted for more than 30 percent of yarn sales, was susceptible to even greater and swifter changes. Unlike the Liverpool market, the yarn market had no associated trade circular. The information that passed between agent and producer was often slow and unreliable, and the poor communication only exacerbated demand shocks.[63]

The volatility of cotton and yarn stocks provides evidence of the relative impact of supply and demand shocks on output. If supply was unpredictable, it would be expected that cotton stocks held by firms would be unstable. But the purchase of cotton at the Liverpool market was a smooth and reliable process and stocks held by firms declined steadily over the period.[64] On the other hand, yarn stocks show greater volatility and the trend coefficient is not significant. Still, the instability of yarn stocks may not be associated with the unpredictability of demand, if firms used stocks as buffers in response to a shock in demand. The implication is that fluctuations in output may exaggerate the actual amount of quantity adjustment. The evidence does not support this view. If yarn was produced to stock and to smooth output, the variance of the *level* of inventories would exceed the variance of the *rate of change* of output.[65] But the standard deviation of the level of yarn stocks (4.55) is smaller than that of the rate of change of Ellison's output series (11.23). Finally, the negative correlation coefficient between output and yarn stocks (−0.33) supports the view that demand changes were unpredictable. Any change in inventories was unintended and was quickly met by a reduction in output.

Whether or not large firms paid fair wages and adjusted employment instead hinges on the relative size of price and output changes. Output fluctuations are compared with two indicators of wage changes: the final product prices and the "margins," a measure of (gross) value added calculated by deducting costs from the final prices. From the available cotton and yarn prices reproduced in table 6.10, I have constructed margins to correspond to the disaggregated output series.

Standard deviations of rates of change are used to measure variability in table 6.11.[66] As expected, in the fine-spinning sector, because of the large size of its firms, output fluctuations were larger than price and margin changes for the entire period; but among small firms, which were mainly found in coarse spinning, output, price and margin changes were roughly

Table 6.10 *Yarn and cotton prices, 1822–1852 (d/lb.)*

Year	Yarn prices				Cotton prices			
	No. 30	No. 40	No. 100	No. 140	East Indian	Upland	Egyptian	Sea Island
1822	17.50	16.75	48.00	83.25	7.04	7.93	—	17.63
1823	18.75	16.75	45.00	80.00	6.85	8.25	—	17.25
1824	19.25	15.50	50.25	71.00	6.45	8.78	10.85	15.29
1825	19.25	17.50	66.63	85.34	9.03	10.64	14.25	25.81
1826	13.00	13.00	45.25	78.00	5.50	6.67	7.88	15.63
1827	12.50	12.50	42.63	78.67	6.32	6.36	7.75	13.43
1828	12.13	11.75	42.50	77.58	4.56	6.29	8.06	15.38
1829	12.50	11.75	42.50	77.25	3.69	5.77	7.25	12.85
1830	12.25	12.25	38.50	72.17	4.98	6.81	8.50	13.68
1831	10.50	11.25	32.84	57.17	4.48	5.71	8.41	13.41
1832	11.75	11.25	37.00	57.00	5.21	7.00	8.31	12.13
1833	13.13	12.88	36.50	59.50	6.15	8.53	11.08	15.63
1834	13.75	13.62	40.00	60.00	6.86	8.86	14.78	19.44
1835	15.88	15.25	47.00	62.00	7.36	10.09	15.60	25.25
1836	15.50	16.25	59.75	80.75	6.99	10.06	14.76	24.13
1837	12.75	17.00	50.00	70.00	4.69	6.85	11.36	21.88
1838	12.00	16.00	45.67	66.67	5.10	6.91	11.44	22.07
1839	11.00	13.75	52.75	76.50	5.68	7.41	12.37	24.39
1840	10.25	13.00	44.00	66.50	4.53	5.86	10.25	17.57
1841	9.50	12.00	39.00	60.17	4.38	6.14	10.03	16.25
1842	9.25	10.88	32.00	52.50	3.86	4.99	7.87	11.47
1843	9.00	10.75	32.00	50.00	3.41	4.55	6.62	13.97

Table 6.10 (cont.)

Year	Yarn prices				Cotton prices			
	No. 30	No. 40	No. 100	No. 140	East Indian	Upland	Egyptian	Sea Island
1844	9.00	10.63	36.67	57.67	3.67	4.69	7.54	15.35
1845	8.88	10.19	38.67	60.50	3.16	4.33	7.57	15.31
1846	10.63	11.07	36.33	56.00	3.63	5.07	7.74	15.25
1847	8.00	10.38	40.00	59.25	4.25	6.14	8.62	15.31
1848	7.25	8.25	30.50	47.00	3.17	4.41	6.81	10.56
1849	8.13	8.13	35.00	48.50	3.96	4.97	6.25	12.60
1850	11.00	10.88	40.50	58.00	5.12	7.27	8.75	15.72
1851	9.75	9.25	36.00	54.00	4.03	5.75	7.74	15.81
1852	9.75	9.13	48.00	60.00	4.36	5.64	8.19	19.56

Sources: No. 30 (water twist) and no. 40 (mule weft) from John S. Lyons, "The Lancashire Cotton Industry and the Introduction of the Powerloom, 1815–50," Ph.D. dissertation, University of California, Berkeley, 1977. Nos. 100 and 140, best-quality mule yarn, from M&K Yarn Sales Book. Cotton prices are averages of the last week in March, June, September, and December. Quotations taken from Liverpool Mercury.

Table 6.11 *Prices and quantities: standard deviations of annual rates of change, 1822–1852*

Variable	1822–52	1822–37	1838–52
F2	45.03	62.60	16.60
No. 140	12.10	12.60	12.03
M140	14.69	11.69	12.60
F1	20.27	15.65	24.48
No. 100	16.40	17.17	16.20
M100	19.70	22.20	18.07
Ellison	11.23	8.56	13.68
Dis. sum	13.54	12.93	14.58
FC	17.59	15.29	20.08
No. 40	11.57	10.23	12.93
M40	17.63	20.63	15.48
C2	13.69	12.16	15.54
C1	17.50	14.40	20.43
No. 30	13.50	14.20	12.50
M30	17.67	16.30	19.94

Notes and sources: The margins are calculated from the prices in table 6.10: M140 = no. 140 – Sea Island; M100 = no. 100 – Egyptian; M40 = no. 40 – Upland; M30 = no. 30 – East Indian. Output series are from tables 6.8 and 6.9.

the same size; and for the entire industry, Ellison's output series exhibited less variability than the corresponding average price. Over the period, however, as the average size of firms increased in coarse spinning, output changes grew larger in the sector. After 1838, changes in FC output were greater than changes in M40, and the price of no. 40 and changes in C1 were greater than changes in M30 and no. 30.

The data in table 6.11 are uncorrected but a similar picture between output and price changes emerges after adjusting in table 6.12 for the rapid growth in output and technical change in the period.[67] For each grade of output, good years were identified as years when output was above trend and bad when output was below trend. For these good and bad years average deviations of output and prices from trend were calculated. If firms paid fair wages, in periods of demand contractions, the average values of the deviations of prices and margins should be less than the deviations of output, whereas the opposite should hold in good years. The evidence conforms to this pattern in all sectors.[68] When C2 and F2 output were below trend, the corresponding prices were above trend. For the FC series and Ellison's series, the fall in prices was generally less than that of

Table 6.12 *Prices and quantities expressed relative to trend, 1822–1852*

| | Values expressed relative to trend | | | |
| | Good years | | Bad years | |
Variable	Mean	Median	Mean	Median
C2	1.043	1.046	0.951	0.954
No. 30	0.999	0.975	1.005	1.031
FC	1.053	1.051	0.948	0.958
No. 40	1.031	1.029	0.971	0.979
M40	1.056	1.072	0.951	0.955
F2	1.143	1.103	0.924	0.928
No. 140	0.987	1.004	1.023	1.044
M140	1.000	1.011	1.010	1.020
Ellison	1.031	1.025	0.964	0.973
No. 40	1.014	0.981	0.971	0.979
M40	1.017	1.005	0.969	0.961

Note:
The logarithm of each variable was regressed on a constant and time. For each category of output (e.g., C2), years were classified as good years if output was above trend, and bad years if output was below. Using the exponentiated deviations from trend from the regressions, average and median values were calculated from output, prices, and margins for good and bad years.

output. In good years for all sectors, when output was above trend, price changes were relatively smaller or even below trend.

It would be premature to conclude, however, that output fluctuations were the product of the fair wage policy. It is possible that the output fluctuations reported in the tables reflected a combination of employment adjustment and the exit of firms. However, firm histories document that only in coarse spinning did entry and exit contribute to output fluctuations, and that after 1835 their importance declined.

In fine spinning between 1833 and 1842 markets stagnated, but the number of firms in the sector in Manchester remained stable.[69] In the depression of 1841–42, only one fine-spinning mill ceased production in Manchester, and it was well below the average size of mills in the sector. On the other hand, the entry and exit of firms dominated output fluctuations in coarse spinning for the first half of the period. In the upturn of 1822–25, there was a large increase in the number of mills and firms; in

Manchester alone twenty new mills were constructed in the expansion of 1823 to 1825, which amounts to an increase in firms of more than 20 percent. In the ensuing contraction and recovery, there was a noticeable stability in the industry. In 1826, there were 92 mills, rising to 95 in 1829, and 96 in 1832.[70] However, these figures are net of entry and underestimate the turnover of firms. Lloyd-Jones and LeRoux, using the Township of Manchester rate books, maintained that for the same period no fewer than sixty-five firms or concerns entered the industry in the town, whereas sixty-three left.[71] Most of these firms were very small, usually sharing space in a mill; only eighteen had a ratable value of £150 or more.

The entry and exit of firms contributed to the output fluctuations in coarse spinning. This is evident for the 1825–27 period of depression and recovery. Over this period FC output first declined by 20 percent and then had a recovery of 40 percent. Lyons estimated that thirty-three new integrated firms entered the industry between 1827 and 1835 and it is reasonable to assume that half this number entered in 1827 and that integrated firms produced FC yarn.[72] Based on the composition of output there were probably about 163 firms in this sector at the time, each producing about 270,000 pounds of yarn annually.[73] At this rate seventeen new firms would have produced 4.59 million pounds of yarn, and this increase could explain about 49 percent (4.59/(FC 1827 – FC 1826) × 100%) of the additional output in 1827.

The contribution of entry and exit to output fluctuations diminished over the period. In the downturn of 1841, Horner reported that twenty-six spinning and integrated (spinning and weaving) firms shut down, about 3.2 percent of firms operating.[74] The firms were generally smaller than average and could have produced at most 270,000 pounds of yarn annually. The total contribution of exiting firms to the reduction in output between 1841–42 would have been about 23 percent (26 × 270,000/(dis. sum 1842 – dis. sum 1841) × 100%). During the ensuing recovery of 1843–45, about the same proportion of output can be attributed to the entry of firms. In the Lancashire and Cheshire cotton-textile district, according to Horner, there were fifty-one investments in new mills in the recovery period.[75] It is reasonable to assume that about three-quarters of the new mills were in the spinning or integrated sectors and that each mill could have produced about 430,000 pounds of cotton annually.[76] Since many of the mills were constructed in 1844 and 1845, the new mills could have contributed at most 33.5 million pounds (2 years × 430,000 pounds per mill × 39 mills) of additional output between 1842 and 1845.[77] But this would represent only 25 percent of the increased output (33.5/(Ellison 1845 – Ellison 1842) × 100%) in the recovery. Thus, in contrast to the 1820s, the relative contribution of firms entering the industry to the increase in output was cut in half. The vast proportion of output fluctuations in the 1840s can be attributed to fair wage inflexibility.

Summary: modern and Golden Age labor markets

In a recent study Charles Brown and James Medoff presented extensive evidence that modern large firms and large establishments tend to pay higher wages than smaller ones for equivalent jobs.[78] Even after allowing for the possibility that large employers are able to attract higher-quality workers, they find that most of the size effect remains. These results do not sit well with straightforward demand and supply analysis. Instead, they support the notion that wages are an outcome of bargaining over a surplus between workers and firms similar to the process described in chapter 5.

For Lancashire the evidence is consistent with this model as well. The labor market, at least in the 1830s and 1840s, was broadly divided along the lines of firm size: in the secondary sector small firms paid contingent wages; workers of the same quality in the primary sector received higher earnings. Workers everywhere wanted to protect customary standards in order to manage risk, but only in large firms were they able to bargain for them and receive pay premia.

Thus the wage fails to act as the key market clearing instrument in both modern and Golden Age labor markets despite their differences and governmental regulation. The point is that wage stickiness is not necessarily a product of union intransigence and employer ignorance; it may arise in an environment in which risk is not completely diversifiable and where there is insufficient or asymmetric information. In this regard, the origins of "sticky wages" can be found as far back as the first factory industry.

Appendix

Following Blaug's method, the disaggregated yarn output series was constructed using annual evidence from the *Trade Circular Reports* on imports, weights of bales, and consumption of cotton. Weights of bales were found from total imports in pounds and total bales imported (table 6A.1).[79] The constructed series is consistent with that available for the 1850s in Mann.[80] Consumption (imports less bags reexported or left in the hands of dealers) was calculated as the product of the number of bags consumed and their weight (table 6A.2). Different grades of cotton based on their staple length or fineness were then grouped using the following weights:

$$F2 = .5(Egyptian) + Sea\ Island$$
$$F1 = .5(Brazilian) + .5(Egyptian)$$
$$FC = .5(Alabama) + West\ Indian + .5(Brazilian)$$
$$C2 = .5(East\ Indian) + .5(Uplands) + .5(Alabama)$$
$$C1 = .5(East\ Indian) + .5(Upland).$$

The procedure allowed for the exhaustion of all net imports. The composition of the groups and the weights attached are based on spinning manuals and other accounts of the quality, mixing, and supply of cotton imports.[81] The division of cottons within groups is thus somewhat arbitrary, but different combinations of weights and components were tried and the results were not altered significantly.

To arrive at output (table 6.8), inventories of cotton at mills and wastage were deducted. Since disaggregated series of inventories are unavailable, it was assumed the composition of cottons held as inventories was identical to the composition of cotton imports. Following contemporary accounts, wastage rates were assumed to begin at 9 percent for the production of coarse yarn, C1, and to rise 1 percent with each output grade.[82] No doubt some waste was recycled by both spinners and weavers of waste, but I assume that contemporary wastage rates are net of the recycled proportion.

Ellison's procedure is identical except for his use of the average weight of bales imported and a constant wastage rate of 11 percent.

Table 6A.1 *Weights of bales of raw cotton, 1822–1852 (lbs.)*

	Type			
Year	US	Brazil	East Indian	Egyptian
1822	306	172	329	—
1823	315	163	386	265
1824	326	173	322	229
1825	330	171	331	204
1826	331	176	324	216
1827	335	172	284	239
1828	341	174	379	214
1829	339	181	309	245
1830	341	173	356	232
1831	360	186	336	222
1832	350	178	322	223
1833	363	174	346	262
1834	367	186	369	231
1835	373	174	346	262
1836	379	185	346	235
1837	380	179	355	226
1838	384	178	375	216
1839	383	171	355	192
1840	388	173	356	219
1841	397	177	356	224
1842	409	175	364	229
1843	411	189	361	198
1844	415	187	373	186
1845	418	183	377	178
1846	431	176	377	240
1847	417	181	377	233
1848	436	199	370	249
1849	429	188	389	239
1850	416	176	386	245
1851	428	178	373	238
1852	428	184	383	251

Method: Imports in lbs. divided by number of bales.
Sources: George Holt Trade Circular and *Marriott and Rogers Trade Circular.*

Table 6A.2 *Cotton consumption by source, 1822–1852 (millions of lbs.)*

Year	Sea Island[a]	Egyptian	Brazilian	West Indian	Alabama or Orleans	Upland	East Indian
1822	10.37	0.00	23.67	7.72	24.70	61.09	16.30
1823	29.20	4.99	24.50	5.28	35.53	63.72	17.10
1824	12.78	10.61	26.00	4.71	38.96	71.40	10.78
1825	6.18	10.34	22.25	6.15	41.90	63.71	18.88
1826	6.35	12.83	10.87	3.56	46.70	65.11	8.24
1827	11.72	8.34	16.23	5.37	68.63	73.88	8.92
1828	11.26	7.47	22.22	4.42	74.65	88.48	14.54
1829	9.50	6.18	29.12	3.48	66.77	93.50	10.57
1830	8.16	6.13	32.40	2.57	84.33	96.67	17.40
1831	9.68	7.15	30.63	1.80	108.58	98.67	13.37
1832	9.45	10.22	26.31	1.53	96.84	113.19	19.44
1833	12.55	3.80	24.29	1.56	121.56	102.33	21.77
1834	9.50	1.57	25.78	1.72	140.31	109.58	19.82
1835	8.87	4.48	21.16	1.36	151.74	114.36	19.51
1836	7.47	7.87	24.13	1.29	181.40	94.34	25.85
1837	6.13	9.15	23.11	1.20	202.01	87.70	8.51
1838	6.33	8.77	22.76	1.15	234.46	109.92	34.32
1839	5.28	5.47	21.10	0.94	197.47	108.82	39.54
1840	7.91	6.15	13.00	0.65	279.52	107.86	41.23
1841	6.11	7.08	12.37	1.15	262.14	94.57	55.46
1842	7.57	6.48	12.19	0.45	262.30	95.47	55.65
1843	8.06	7.66	14.70	0.95	310.21	138.13	41.99
1844	7.19	10.20	20.87	1.23	372.52	132.59	45.00
1845	6.52	9.83	20.86	1.05	373.19	157.43	57.01
1846	6.14	16.70	18.74	0.90	419.42	124.30	42.91
1847	6.14	12.04	11.64	0.60	244.64	111.00	62.60
1848	9.08	9.39	14.08	0.48	361.14	147.80	57.28
1849	12.87	19.04	22.10	0.71	411.90	125.91	49.40
1850	11.44	19.65	30.30	0.17	341.53	96.26	87.94
1851	12.89	18.57	22.41	0.33	410.36	118.14	41.50
1852	10.02	24.51	23.07	0.53	489.59	127.97	82.99

Notes:
[a] In decreasing order of fineness from left to right.
Source: George Holt Trade Circular.

7   Short hours and seniority in the "hungry 'forties"

The wage policy of entrepreneurs in a period of depression is very largely a question of circulating capital . . . if wages are maintained, there is an obvious incentive to reduce the number of men employed. But if a man is dismissed, it may not be possible to recover him again when he is wanted in the future; and thus, if the employer looks to the future, he may well think it worth while to retain some of his men even if their present employment involves him in losses. Further, if he can afford to keep on those men whom he does retain without cutting their wages, he has a stronger claim on them in the future; and the same reason which prompts him to keep them employed prompts him to refrain from cutting their wages.[1]

Commitment vs. the market

Wage stickiness is not in itself a sign of labor-market failure. Firms may have kept piece rates and earnings fixed if the costs of negotiating small changes were large, or simply if cutting wages proved to be pound-foolish and penny-wise. Andrew Ure made exactly this point.[2] There were other margins at which firms could have cut back more easily, such as reducing stocks of cotton and yarn, the impact of these cuts varying with the count of yarn spun. This line of reasoning has its limits. While it might be appropriate in explaining small nominal wage deviations over the normal business cycle, it is less convincing in explaining why firms persisted in paying above market clearing wages during long periods of decline in demand, like those that hit the Lancashire economy in the 1840s.

The spot model maintains that firms forced to lay off workers when faced by a considerable demand shock would have used the occasion to improve the quality of their labor forces, keeping productive workers on and dismissing the rest. They would have had little reason to shorten the workday; if need be, firms would have adapted to fixed rates of pay by operating at longer hours and implementing shift or night work, as was the case in the American South.[3] Nor would firms have had an incentive to keep older, and at times less productive, workers. Firms would have been indifferent to the effect these policies had on worker morale, because in a spot market, firms are not concerned about their reputations as good or "honorable" employers.

In contrast, the fair wage maintains that firms are keen on keeping workers and abstaining from wage cuts. If firms renege on their promises and cut piece rates arbitrarily, they could lose their investments in building reputations as fair employers and workers would react strategically. Employers can signal their commitment to their fair wage, and to their workforces, if they cut output rather than workers and piece rates, and this could be achieved by short-hour working. When forced to lay off, firms protect seniority in order to preserve long-term attachments. Only if commitments are kept repeatedly on both sides of the market can cooperation evolve.

The economic climate of the 1840s tested the fair wage policy initiated in Manchester after the dispute of 1829. The depression of 1841–42, which Hobsbawm has called "almost certainly the worst of the century," was followed by a brief upturn in the middle of the decade, but by late 1846 there were early signs of a renewed trade decline that lasted until 1849.[4] During these years firms were compelled to adjust employment levels in order to maintain their commitments about piece rates. At M&K the general policy was to work short time. As early as the downturn of 1830, the firm's strategy was to "accommodate [itself] to the market, rather than throw [its] workpeople out of their employment."[5] M&K's approach was representative of a general commitment among middle-sized and large firms in Manchester and Bolton to protect long-term attachments. During minor downturns and the early and late stages of a recession, firms worked short hours, and if business did not recover they began laying off younger workers first.

This chapter seeks to explain the pattern of employment adjustment in Lancashire. Workers' defense of short time can be attributed to their life-cycle concerns, and their determination to preserve the standard relation between effort and pay. They saw short time as a means to spread the available work fairly, and they also maintained that short time was an alternative to piece-rate cuts. Firms, especially larger ones, accommodated these demands, because by working short time they showed their commitment to fair wage and employment standards. But if inventories built up with no signs of recovery, firms began laying off workers. Firms let younger workers go first to preserve attachments with older workers. Seniority provisions were popular not solely because the median or average worker was protected from layoffs, as is commonly argued today, but also because workers of all ages saw the system as just and fair.[6]

Short hours: the received wisdom

Consider a world without unemployment insurance, with relatively risk-averse workers, and in which firms are able to adjust hours costlessly. In these conditions an efficient contract would dictate that all labor input adjustments would be made by changing hours per worker rather than employment.[7] But contemporary millowners and commentators, appealing to the capital intensity of their operations and limited (ex post) substitution between capital and labor, were almost unanimous in the view that hour adjustment was costly. Employers had definite interests in the working hours of their employees.[8] The fixed costs of running a textile factory, which included rent, interest on machinery, local rates, salaries, and insurance were substantial, and there was a preference for multishift work. According to one estimate reported by Horner, for a firm employing 230 workers, unit costs would have increased by 1.3 percent for each hour cut from the normal workweek of sixty-nine hours. After reviewing similar evidence for other mills he believed to be representative of the industry, Horner observed that during a trade decline a "mill-owner working full time may be a loser, [but] a mill-owner working short time must be a loser."[9]

The fixed-cost argument dominates studies of the cotton-textile industry found in the secondary literature. To support his explanation of steady growth in the Victorian period, Lee surveyed the arguments of millowners reported by the factory inspectors and concluded that the growth of output was unchecked because short-hour practices were uncommon. Production maximization helped to spread the large fixed costs in cotton spinning over as large a volume of output as possible. "The maximization of production and also of productive capacity represented the appropriate business strategy for most firms."[10] Extending this line of reasoning, larger firms should have had a greater incentive than their smaller rivals to work short time, because of fixed capital and labor requirements; moreover, because of the forces of competition and the mobility of labor and capital, there should be little observed differences in short time between regions.

There are problems with the fixed-costs view. Until the second quarter of the nineteenth century, the capital costs of entry in coarse spinning remained relatively modest and the overriding concern of most millowners was the availability of working capital. A further problem is that evidence on the proportion of fixed costs contained in parliamentary reports was often inflated by millowners to support their claim that legislation to reduce hours of work would result in higher unit costs and lower profits and wages.[11] Still, for large concerns like M&K and Horrockses, these claims might have had some validity. From another perspective, however, the arguments echoed Senior's infamous position that the whole of the manufacturers' profit was derived from the last two hours of work in the day and that legislative interference would wipe out the margin of profits. The limitations of this line of reasoning are well known.[12] Among other problems, Senior made the standard assumption that there was a fixed relation between hours and effort, asserting that the workload was light and the mechanization of the industry had developed to the extent that operatives had little control over output. Anticipating the findings of chapters 2 and 3, Marion Bowley, Senior's biographer, questioned this assertion: "No one [contemporary] thought of suggesting that the assumption of unchanged productivity per man-hour, whether the length of the working day was ten hours or more, used in the calculation was valid."[13]

R. C. O. Matthews put forward a different explanation why firms did not work short time on a regular basis.[14] To Matthews the marginal cost curve of the representative firm of the period was ⌐-shaped. The horizontal portion of the curve represented the entry of firms and the gradual filling up of empty factory space. Matthews identified two such periods, between 1824 and 1833, and between 1834 and 1840. With a completed factory, a firm in normal times operated on the vertical stretch of its cost curve. Demand would have to fall considerably onto the horizontal stretch of the cost curve or below it before there would be any contraction in output or short time, but Matthews argued that these occasions were rare. Like others Matthews assumed a constant relation between hours and effort, but there remain other problems with his analysis. For Manchester, A. A. Le Roux and Roger Lloyd-Jones found that "far from being exhausted by the end of the first subperiod [1833], semi-reserve capacity was near its highest level for the period under consideration."[15] The result is that, putting aside theoretical shortcomings, Matthews' model, like the fixed-costs view, does not mesh with the history and the technology of the industry.

Short hours in 1841

Despite the flaws with the fixed-costs view and Matthews' model, the evidence on capacity utilization would appear at first pass to confirm that short-hour working was uncommon.[16] Horner's 1841 survey of 1,164 spinning and weaving mills in all regions of Lancashire, the most detailed undertaken in the period, has been frequently cited to support the conclusion that short time was rare.[17] Between 1836 and 1841, Ellison reported

Table 7.1 *1841 survey results by operation*

Operation	All firms	By size			By type[a]			
		<150	150–300	>300	C	F	SW	W
Full-time	526	342	111	73	257	56	157	56
Machinery	51	26	9	16	21	2	27	1
Closed	62	45	12	5	37	1	17	7
Short-time								
At visit	115	67	21	27	39	18	41	17
Other	163	84	41	38	74	8	70	11
Total	917	564	194	159	428	85	312	92

Notes:
[a] C = Firms spinning yarn less than no. 60.
F = Firms spinning yarn greater than no. 60 and firms spinning both fine and coarse yarn.
SW = Firms spinning and weaving all counts.
W = Firms weaving only.
Source: PP 1842 (31) XXII.

that an "immense amount of over trading had been done, and the markets all over the world were glutted with English goods."[18] But despite the decline in demand Horner found that 76.20 percent of firms worked full time (sixty-nine hours per week), 11.85 percent had stopped, and only 11.94 percent worked short time.

There are flaws with the survey results that, once corrected, reveal a different picture. The category of full time includes firms operating at full capacity or sixty-nine hours throughout 1841 and firms that on the date of the inspectors' visit, sometime between September and December 1841, operated at sixty-nine hours but had worked short time in some earlier period. Including these firms, represented by "Other" in the short-time category in table 7.1, reveals that about 30 percent of firms were on short hours sometime in 1841.[19] By this accounting, short time of some type was five times as great as complete closures (permanent layoffs). Many of these firms reported working 48-hour weeks, some working four- or five-day weeks and others nine- to ten-hour days; the average duration of short time was about five and a half weeks.[20] The addition of the unreported firms also affects the sectoral impact of short time. Whereas 19 and 13 percent of weaving and integrated establishments respectively reported short time at the time of visit only, including other firms alters these figures to 30 and 35 percent.

Although the vast majority of firms would appear to have worked full time, the problems with the timing of the survey are compounded because economic activity varied between sectors and between the months of the survey. Horner himself noted this problem in his introduction to the survey:

There is probably an alteration in the circumstances facing mills that in that time [i.e., the period between the date of the survey and the survey's compilation], some that were working full time at that period of the visit may now be working short time, and in other mills the reverse may be the case.[21]

According to Burn's statistics on the state of trade, the weekly average of cotton bought by the industry fell dramatically during the second quarter of 1841 compared to previous years, but recovered to normal levels during the last quarter.[22] It was customary for cotton stocks to be spun quickly into yarn and the drop in cotton consumption from March to May would have translated into a slowdown in production throughout the summer months and probably into October as well. Newspaper reports and trade circulars confirm this pattern of activity.[23] Horner observed for the period ending in September "that the trade is in a state of extreme depression and without distinct prospect of improvement."[24] The trade news also reported that the coarse-spinning and the integrated sector (which wove coarse yarn) were hardest hit by the downturn.[25] Still, there were signs of improvement in the latter part of the year, signaled by an increase in demand for coarse yarn in Germany. To meet the demand in November and December, firms purchased about 135,000 bales of raw cotton, the largest amount for any two-month period in 1841.[26]

To check whether or not there was wide variation in capacity utilization rates between sectors and over the period of the survey, the returns were broken down by month in table 7.2. About 55 percent of all firms and 60 percent of coarse-spinning concerns were surveyed in November and December when trade was showing a slight improvement. As expected, table 7.3 reveals that the majority of the coarse-spinning firms reported full-time work in the last two months of 1841, but there were also fifty-six firms that reported working *short time in the past*, probably in the third quarter. If these firms are counted in the short-time category for September and October, then about 42 percent ($(18 + 22 + 56/171 + 56) \times 100\%$) of coarse-spinning firms and 45 percent of integrated concerns worked short time in this period. The respective figure in fine spinning was 34 percent.

In conjunction with the date of visit, the survey when broken down by size of firm reveals a pattern inconsistent with the view that large concerns generally operated at full time. Only 26 percent of small firms (employing

Table 7.2 1841 survey results by month

Month	All firms	By operation					By type[a]				By size		
		Full time	Machinery[b]	Closed	Short-time		C	F	SW	W	<150	150–300	>300
					At visit	Other[c]							
September	155	95	7	18	25	10	77	13	48	17	108	29	18
October	252	151	16	15	29	41	94	40	91	27	149	48	55
November	297	163	19	16	43	56	140	15	108	34	186	63	48
December	213	117	9	13	18	56	117	17	65	14	121	54	38
Total	917	526	51	62	115	163	428	85	312	92	564	194	159

Notes:
[a] C = Firms spinning yarn less than no. 60.
F = Firms spinning yarn greater than no. 60 and firms spinning both fine and coarse yarn.
SW = Firms spinning and weaving all counts.
W = Firms weaving only.
[b] Firms not working at full capacity because of machine repairs.
[c] Firms that worked short time in 1841, but not on date of visit.
Source: PP 1842 (31) XXII.

Table 7.3 1841 survey results by operation, type, size, and month

| | | By type[a] | | | | | | | | By size | | | | | |
| | | C | | F | | SW | | W | | <150 | | 150–300 | | >300 | |
Operation	All firms	SO[b]	ND[c]	SO	ND	SO	ND	SO	ND	SO	ND	SO	ND	SO	ND
Full time	526	109	148	34	22	72	85	31	25	167	175	49	62	30	43
Machinery	51	5	16	1	1	17	10	0	1	9	17	2	7	12	4
Closed	62	17	20	1	0	11	6	4	3	26	19	5	7	2	3
Short time															
At visit	115	22	17	11	7	14	27	7	10	34	33	9	12	11	16
Other	163	18	56	6	2	25	45	2	9	21	63	12	29	18	20
Total	917	171	257	53	32	139	173	44	48	257	307	77	117	73	86

Notes:
[a] C = Firms spinning yarn less than no. 60.
F = Firms spinning yarn greater than no. 60 and firms spinning both fine and coarse yarn.
SW = Firms spinning and weaving all counts.
W = Firms weaving only.
[b] September and October.
[c] November and December.
Sources: PP 1842 (31) XXI.

Table 7.4 1841 survey results: coarse-spinning and integrated firms

| | Coarse spinning | | | | | | Integrated | | | | | |
| | | September and October | | November and December | | | September and October | | | November and December | | |
Operation	Total	0–150	>150	0–150	>150	Total	<150	150–300	>300	<150	150–300	>300
Full time	257	90	19	115	33	157	29	23	20	24	29	32
Machinery	21	4	1	12	4	27	5	2	10	4	3	3
Closed	37	15	2	15	5	17	6	3	2	2	3	1
Short time												
At visit	39	20	2	14	3	41	5	3	6	3	9	15
Other	74	14	4	42	14	70	5	3	17	12	16	17
Total	428	143	28	198	59	312	50	34	55	45	60	68

Source: PP 1842 (31) XXII.

fewer than 150 workers) worked short hours when visited or at some time in the past, but the corresponding figures for middle-sized (150 to 300 workers) and large firms (over 300 workers) were 32 and 40 percent. These figures underestimate the proportion of short-time firms because of the interaction between size and the date of the survey. The vast majority of middle-sized and large firms were visited in the last two months of 1841. Again, as expected, few firms worked short time during these months. But when large firms which reported short time in the past when visited in the last two months of 1841 are included in the September and October totals, about 53 percent ((18 + 11 + 20)/(73 + 20) × 100%) of these concerns worked short time in the two-month period (table 7.3). The corresponding figure for middle-sized firms is 47 percent.

Table 7.4 reports the interaction among the type of production, the date of survey, and the size of firm for selected sectors.[27] Only 35 percent of integrated concerns reported some short-time working. However, if large (over 300 workers) integrated concerns that reported short time in the past when surveyed in the last two months of 1841 are included in the September and October totals, about 55 percent of large concerns worked some short time in the period. The corresponding figure for middle-sized and coarse-spinning firms is 48 percent.

Horner's survey did not capture the depth of the depression. The recovery expected in November and December 1841 never materialized. Firms were stuck with accumulating stocks of yarn and many resorted to short time again in the early months of 1842. At this juncture the Manchester Chamber of Commerce advocated that firms work 20 to 30 percent less than full capacity.[28] By March many mills had stopped completely and the ensuing downturn has become an historic benchmark.[29] Recovery was not underway until early 1843.

The unemployment rate during the crisis has been the subject of much controversy, but from Horner's survey the proportion of workers laid off fully or partially in the early stages of the depression can be calculated. Horner's uncorrected result was that about 24 percent of the textile workforce was either not at work or only partially employed in the last four months of 1841.[30] However, using a much broader definition, the unemployed comprised 42 percent of the workforce if those who were recorded as fully employed on the survey date but had worked short time in the past as recorded in the tables are included in the unemployed category. Moreover, following procedures set out above and including workers who in November and December were recorded as being on short time in the past in the September and October unemployment figures, about 53 percent of workers were laid off partially or completely during the worst two months of 1841.

The corrected results reveal the sensitivity of the 1841 survey to the date of the inspectors' visit and to the size of firms. If more firms had been visited in the first two months, then the survey would have shown a higher proportion of short-time firms, in some cases exceeding 50 percent of the total number of firms studied. Because of the greater number of large firms working short time, this resulted in an even higher proportion of workers being laid off. In sum, the evidence for 1841 reveals that short-time unemployment was neither trivial nor random. Rather, it had a discernible pattern that needs to be integrated into the larger question of how labor markets in the period worked.

Short hours as fair hours: a work- and life-cycle perspective

M. A. Bienefeld in his study of hours of work in the nineteenth century gave little attention to short-time practices, although he did make reference to differences between actual and normal hours of operation. For social and labor historians it has been the convention to subsume analyses of short time in the history of the struggle for a shorter workweek.[31] Two recent studies have given short-hour working the attention it merits. For 1847, Boot found a large proportion of firms working short time in the early stages of the recession.[32] His claim that short time reduced labor turnover, however, begs the question of whether firms should have kept their best workers only and laid off the rest. Another drawback is that Boot's findings are restricted to Manchester. The view that short time reduced turnover costs is also defended by George Boyer in his work on the Poor Law.[33] He argued that, since firms paid only a proportion of the rate payments, they did not incur the total relief bill, and since part-time workers were eligible for relief benefits, firms lowered training and hiring costs by keeping workers on short time. It remains unclear why firms did not keep their best workers only. Boyer's model is also incomplete, because it does not explain the variation of short time by region, type, and size of establishment.[34]

There is a more substantive difference between my approach and Boyer's. For Boyer, the availability of assistance implies that the cost of job loss was lowered for unemployed and part-time workers, thereby raising the wage premium preventing them from withholding effort. The fair wage model of chapter 5 predicts otherwise. Short time had mutual gains for both workers and firms. Workers were concerned about their life-cycle needs, whereas firms were concerned about the quantity and quality of output. In addition, both parties saw short time as a means to preserve lengthy attachments, and worksharing reduced the premium required to prevent spinners from withholding effort.

Life-cycle concerns best explain workers' demand for short hours. Although kinship networks did provide support during trade declines, the incidence of a general trade decline was spread across all family members, and short time was a fair way to spread the burden of unemployment. Earnings were often supplemented by poor relief, but many workers, as I described earlier, loathed going to the authorities; for them short time was their only source of income.

There was also the popular belief that short time would curtail overproduction and dampen the severity of the recession. Although these arguments may ring hollow to modern economists, the rhetoric can be understood in a life-cycle model. "The old fad of English overproduction," as Samuel Andrew of Oldham put it in 1875, had its origins in the commonly held view that business downturns were the result of competitive pressures on firms to increase output steadily.[35] Overproduction led to price wars between firms and downward pressure on wages, and to check these forces workers petitioned employers to work short time. They were well aware that it was always in the interest of firms to restore full-time hours and the petitions clearly state that short time was an *alternative* to piece-rate cuts.[36] "If the markets are flat," workers argued in 1848, "the legitimate course to be pursued is to limit the supply to the demand and thus maintain both prices and wages."[37] Workers claimed as well that if rates and earnings were maintained at fair levels, domestic demand could be sustained, protecting future levels of production and employment. It has also been advanced that male textile operatives saw short time as a means to reinforce the patriarchy of the domestic economy inside the factory.[38] Male workers, especially those in coarse spinning, had to keep guard against replacement in the factories, and short time kept them attached to their employers; at the same time, it enhanced their role as breadwinners during a slump.

Why would individual firms respond to workers' demands for work-sharing? Consider the classic cartel problem with perfect labor markets. An individual firm welcomes output cutbacks by its rivals. Since it is difficult to monitor and enforce quotas, the individual firm has an incentive to undercut rivals. If all firms do this, the cartel would be broken, prices would fall, and so would wage rates. Rational firms would therefore not spend resources forming and enforcing output cuts. As a prisoners' dilemma, cartels should not work, but consider that in Lancashire the labor market was not perfect and firms paid their workers a wage premium, the fair wage. Under these circumstances, the cartel was not ostensibly a means to reap monopoly profits, but a means of preventing firms from producing at full capacity and putting downward pressure on piece rates. Short-time working collectively agreed upon was an arrangement compelling individual firms to abide by the fair wages they themselves had agreed to pay. If successful, short-time agreements would then be a powerful force in regulating the industry, especially in decreasing inventories.

Short time also reduced firms' labor costs. Keeping workers attached to groups of firms, short time helped generate and maintain the general skills of factory work, or what William Mass and William Lazonick referred to as "the general capability to work" and the "habituation to factory work."[39] Short time had the advantage of promoting the exchange of knowledge and skills between older and younger workers. There was a geographic dimension to this development as well. The regional basis of the industry was at once a result and a cause of "locally concentrated supplies of experienced factory labour."[40] Because they held general skills, workers could in principle move between firms, but short time in economic crises like 1841 had the benefit of keeping them attached to specific regions.

There were other ways in which short time reduced firms' unit costs. By preserving the fair wage, short time contributed to the industry's productivity performance. Firms may not have wanted productivity to increase when short time was in place, for the same reason as they did not want inventories to accumulate; but by accommodating workers' demand for short time, it could be expected that firms would benefit from better morale and hence higher productivity when full hours of work returned. This was of special concern to large firms, regardless of specialty, that had made substantial investments in fixed capital.

Evidence in support of the productivity relation is indirect; in fact, the best studies of increased effort are those reports examining the link between productivity increase and changes to the legal workweek. Like their attitude to short time, workers persistently supported changes to the normal workday and responded positively when hour changes were introduced. A number of employers in Bolton made public the results of experiments in 1844 and 1845 they had conducted on the effects of one- and two-hour reductions.[41] They attributed their finding of steady output levels to both the diligence and the health of workers. One manager observed later in the decade that workers were "more attentive [and] they turn out better work"; still another reported in his mill that "they work with more vigor and pleasure while they do it."[42] Wage evidence confirms these appraisals. Wood found that, though hours worked fell in 1847, by 1849 wages had recovered to their initial level. He wrote:

In a large mill in the North and North-East Lancashire district, time workers were reduced *pro rata* with the reduced hours, but piece workers generally made up their former earnings without any advance in piece rates, as soon as trade, which was very depressed in 1847 and 1848, revived.[43]

The preservation of long-term attachments reduced labor costs in another way. In the earlier variants of the shirking model, like Bulow and Summers', firms eschew short time because it lowers the present value of the job, giving workers a greater incentive to shirk; this would entail a higher equilibrium (or no-shirking) wage. The underlying assumptions in this class of models, it can be speculated, helped to explain why worksharing declined in popularity during post-1945 cyclical downturns.[44] As constructed, these models exclude the likelihood that in an environment of uncertain demand where there is limited unemployment insurance, workers might give value to long-term attachments. Under these conditions, firms will try to avoid temporary layoffs to maximize the value of the job. More formally, it can be shown that the longer the credible promise of future employment, the lower will be the wage premium a firm must offer to elicit full effort from workers.[45]

Not all firms benefited from a short-hour working strategy. Like other large mills, Horrockses mill in Preston offered workers guaranteed employment through boom and slump, but offsetting this provision was their penchant to pay rates consistently below the prevailing average. It is not surprising, then, the mill's experiment with cutting hours resulted in no significant increase in output.[46] As I described in previous chapters, the firm had a poor reputation in the labor market and most likely workers perceived that the reduction in hours was a gesture and not a credible commitment to institute a policy of a shorter workday. Expectations were confirmed in 1852 and 1853 when the firm, like others in Preston, reneged on a promised repayment of wages.

Collective decision making: the marginal vs. average worker

We know that short time gained currency with the spread of fair wages and that it became the conventional response to decline in demand.[47] Still, the failure of some of the largest firms to work short time in 1841 needs to be considered.

There were gains for some individual firms and workers to break the standard of short time and this may explain the mixed results for 1841. Older workers who had higher earnings and had accumulated some savings may have been willing to trade off hours for leisure; younger workers may have preferred a longer workday and higher earnings. The result may have been a separating equilibrium. Those who had a greater preference for labor found employment at firms which operated twelve hours per day or full time and those who desired leisure went to work at firms operating on short time. There is some evidence of this pattern for the pre-1850 period. Horner reported that firms in urban centers were reluctant to work short time in fear of losing their best, meaning youngest and most productive, workers.[48]

Yet a salient feature of labor markets in periods of rapid industrialization, across time and space, was the difficulty firms had in catering to marginal workers. The sorting and allocating problem was complex, and the costs of setting up a homogeneous workforce were not insignificant. Alternatively, firms could have offered employment to workers with heterogeneous preferences, but firms' experience with the relay system, in which different sets of children worked shifts, proved to be difficult to organize and administer. The failure to offer contracts with variable hours meant negotiating standard hours of work with a mixed group of employees. A collective choice problem therefore existed. Like any public good, hours of work would have changed when the preferences of the *average* (or median) rather than the *marginal* worker changed. And it is clear from the accounts I have previously referred to that, at least for the average worker, short time was the preferred response to a decline in trade.

The ever-present tension between private and social gains meant that the average firm and worker needed some mechanism to punish defectors and enforce compliance.[49] The press gave a public platform for the revelation of abuses and the exchange of information. Throughout the 1830s and 1840s, both the radical and the mainstream press highlighted employers who abided by the short-time convention and blacklisted those working longer hours; this type of sanctioning was later practiced by the *Cotton Factory Times* which was founded in 1885.[50] During the 1847–48 recession, a report for Bolton identified the Knowles firm, which had been known as a ratebuster for thirty-five years, as having begun to work short time.[51] The language and action of workers during the Stalybridge dispute of 1892–93 was typical of the strength of community standards of behavior. The union acknowledged the right of an individual worker to sell his labor to the highest bidder – and, one can infer, to find employment at firms operating at full time during recessions – "but this was a right that was subordinate to what they also called 'the interests of the trade,' interests that were the concern of employers and workers together."[52]

Despite lacking the authoritative properties of written rules, short-hour working became regularized, prescribing the actions of individual firms and workers and how the parties behaved to each other. Here is another illustration of custom reconciled to the market, protecting what was perceived to be fair and just. Although the functional form relating enforcement costs to rule adherence is not obvious on a priori grounds, as short

Table 7.5 *Size of firms, population growth, and short-time working in Lancashire towns in 1841*

Towns	Average size of firms	Firms on short-time (percentages)[a]	Population growth 1821–41[b]
Rochdale	105.1	32.5	1.610
Oldham	115.8	26.7	1.966
Whalley	118.1	35.5	1.740
Bury	162.2	26.3	1.909
Bolton	217.5	35.7	1.582
Ashton-under-Lyne	243.9	36.6	1.782
Manchester	263.6	27.0	1.868
Blackburn	281.4	42.5	1.605
Preston	286.8	17.8	2.105

Notes:
[a] Measured as firms working short time or recording some short time in 1841.
[b] Ratio of 1841 to 1821 population.
Sources: Size of firms: R. A. Sykes, "Some Aspects of Working-Class Consciousness in Oldham, 1830–1842," *Historical Journal* 23 (March 1980), 168. Short time: PP 1842 (31) XXII. Population growth: Patrick Joyce, *Work, Society, and Politics: The Culture of the Factory in Later Victorian England* (Brighton: University of Sussex Press, 1980), 104; Craig Calhoun, *The Question of Class Struggle: Social Foundations of Popular Radicalism During the Industrial Revolution* (Chicago: University of Chicago Press, 1982), 188; PP 1843 (342) XXII, 145.

time grew in popularity after the middle of the century, enforcement costs fell. "In the limit when enforcement costs fall to zero," Alexander Field observed, "the weight of tradition, through a process understood only imperfectly, may make it simply *unthinkable* for any agent to violate the current practice, in spite of individual incentives to do so."[53] Like the fair wage, short-hour working had evolved into a rule of thumb that was a guide to future course of action.

Short time: regional differences in enforcement

Short time in 1841 confirms the role of baragaining over wages and hours at the local level, despite small distances between towns. Table 7.5 breaks down Horner's survey of capacity utilization during the downturn of 1841 by town. In areas dominated by large firms like Bolton, Ashton-under-Lyne, and Blackburn, the percentage of firms on short time exceeded the average for Lancashire. In areas more heavily represented by small firms, as in Oldham and Rochdale, the opposite generally held. However, the relation between size and short hours was not found everywhere. In Whalley, which in the 1840s specialized in coarse yarn the average size of firms was about that found in Oldham, but the percentage of firms on short time was almost identical to the figure for Bolton. On the other hand, in Bury, which had a significant proportion of middle-sized firms, the proportion of firms on short time was equal to Oldham's. Most dramatically, Preston stands out as a town where short time was unpopular.

The ability of Preston employers to organize themselves and cut wages must be part of an explanation why its mills continued to work at full time. But there were other forces at work. The costs of monitoring and enforcing agreements would be lower where there was repeated bargaining over effort levels and hours, and where there was continuity in relations. Population movements, as Joyce suggested, offer a crude index of the stability of towns and their communities of workers and firms. In Preston, Oldham, Manchester, and Bury, population change was rapid and short-time arrangements less prevalent than in the more stable communities of Bolton, Blackburn, Rochdale, and Whalley. In sum, although the 1841 evidence suggests a relation between firm size and short time in some towns, it also lends support to Pat Hudson's claim that "struggles around the control and character of work were undertaken largely at the regional level."[54]

An exception to the rule: rural mills

Rural firms could enforce high levels of effort at low wages, and, as a result, they had little incentive to practice short-hour working.[55] Rural enterprises did reduce output, but the timing of short-time work did not coincide with cyclical downturns. Much of this downtime was due to water shortages and broken water wheels; besides, fluctuations in output at rural mills were smaller than at their urban rivals. Rural employers' statements confirm that they found short time an extravagant strategy to elicit effort. In light of the previous discussion, rural employers catered to the average preferences of their workforces, but because paternalism had shaped their values, it was less likely that these workers would signal a preference for short time. Even those workers who preferred leisure would have had difficulty in exercising their choices, because at rural sites firms controlled access to and hours of operation of clubs, reading rooms, and the like.

After the middle of the century rural employers altered their practices. The Gregs, like many other employers, worked short time at Styal during the Cotton Famine of the 1860s.[56] The patron–client relationship was breaking down, albeit slowly, and, like other firms, rural mills had to recruit workers and reduce turnover. It may be speculated that short time was adopted by rural millowners because of learning effects, and because of the need to conform to standard practice for fear of being ostracized and sanctioned.

First-in–last-out: layoffs and seniority

Short-hour working was limited to brief downturns and the early and last stages of recessions.[57] At other times firms were forced to lay off workers. If firms' hiring and firing decisions were based solely on skill attributes, then it would be expected that older workers would be let go first. Spinning on either a mule or a self-actor required a combination of physical strength, keen eyesight, and manual dexterity, and all observers agree that such skills declined as workers got older.[58] Mitchell's survey of earnings in 1833, which plots weekly wages against age, exhibits a pronounced bump at ages thirty-one to thirty-five – 275d per week compared to 250d at thirty-six to forty, 240d at forty-one to forty-five, and a steeper gradient at younger ages.[59] Even though payment was by the piece, age did matter. As the strength, vision, and dexterity of spinners over thirty-five deteriorated, they produced more broken yarns. Since workers neither paid for their raw materials nor owned and invested in their equipment, firms could presumably reduce wastage and replacement costs by employing younger, more dexterous workers.

Age would also figure in the employer's calculation in another way. Firms worked to order in highly competitive and specialized yarn markets and it was essential that they maintained quality and filled orders quickly, which meant that they needed guaranteed output. Younger, more productive workers would seem to guarantee this.[60]

The problem with this view of productivity is that it ignores the possibility that firms could achieve higher levels of effort from the *entire* workforce – and over time – by offering employees the commitment of lengthy attachments. Seniority was seen as just and fair; it was accepted as the customary and right thing to do. The line of reasoning extends from my earlier explanation of why spinners preferred stable piece rates over their work and life cycles. Older workers whose productivity at the firm declined and whose alternative opportunities contracted wanted the possibility of lengthy tenure because it provided some take-home pay; it also smoothed their consumption stream. As for younger cohorts, the layoff of senior workers would have signaled to them that they should not expect lengthy attachments; using the framework of the basic incentive model, the present value of their job would have fallen and they would shirk. Younger workers wanted to be assured that they too would have a job when they aged. If firms honored their commitment about piece rates and layoffs, workers of all ages would reciprocate and give more effort in all states of nature.

For the 1840s, one would be hard-pressed to find younger spinners and piecers voicing disapproval of a layoff strategy that hit them hardest. This is all the more surprising because children/piecers were not assured of taking over their fathers' mules. Filling vacant mule positions was left to the discretion of employers and after 1850, in some regions, with the agreement of the spinners' trade unions.[61] Indeed, it was common practice that unstaffed mules would be filled by unemployed spinners rather than piecers. Younger workers' acceptance of the layoff rule may have reflected an optimism that the industry would rebound, as it had from previous trade declines, and that there would be a resumption of new investment.[62] Their actions were also tied to the preservation of the fair wage itself.[63] It was widely perceived that older spinners were the guardians of customary standards and the leaders of work-to-rule campaigns. Thus, in Bolton, trade union officials warned inexperienced spinners "not even [to] hint that we intend to do as much work in eleven hours as we do in twelve."[64] If firms fired senior members of the work group, this would have been construed by the younger cohort as an attack on the fair wage, and since it was in their own interest that the standard be preserved, they were willing, to use Solow's phrase, to "sit tight" and wait out the recession.[65]

Ages of spinners taken from the unpublished census manuscripts of 1841, 1851, and 1861 can be used to assess the layoff strategies of firms. The years of enumeration trace a business cycle. The period 1841–51 saw crises and layoffs in 1842 and 1847–48; the period 1851–61 saw growth, especially in coarse spinning.[66] If seniority did matter, the ratio of older to younger workers should increase between 1841 and 1851 and fall thereafter.

Samples were taken for Manchester, Oldham, and Bolton. Local histories and directories helped locate in the enumeration books districts where spinners resided. The point of entry was then randomly selected and every second spinner's age, family position, and birthplace were noted.[67] On average, the samples contain 200 spinners, which samples more than 10 percent of the total number of spinners in Manchester and 15 to 20 percent of the number of spinners in Oldham and Bolton.[68]

The validity of the sample needs elaboration. Demographic changes and urbanization had little effect on average ages. The age structure did not change greatly over the period.[69] Despite the rapid growth of Oldham, the proportion of the male population over twenty years of age remained roughly the same and equal in all three towns. As for reliability, studies of other industrial regions have confirmed the accuracy of the ages reported.[70] The occupations given to enumerators are more troublesome. Residents who were over sixty years old and who reported themselves as spinners would have had difficulty in performing some spinning tasks, so they were left out of the sample. Others included in the sample may have falsely reported their occupation as spinner because they had been forced into early retirement or into occupations that did not carry the social distinction of spinning. While false reports add spurious older members to the sample, there is an offsetting error. The sample includes young boys and women who reported themselves as spinners, even though in all likelihood the young boys were piecers, and the women throstle spinners. On average this group comprised' about 2 percent of the sample, or probably enough to cancel the inclusion of retired or former spinners. As a final check on the accuracy of the samples, the reported ages for 1841 are close to Shuttleworth's findings for 1832.[71]

Table 7.6 records the ages of spinners. Of special interest is the percentage of spinners over thirty-five, since contemporaries thought this marked the end of peak productivity years. Still other observers believed the boundary between productive and unproductive years came at thirty, so the choice of thirty-five favors the finding that firms retained a larger proportion of younger and productive workers during the depression years. Nevertheless, in all towns the percentage of employed spinners over thirty-five increased between 1841 and 1851. In the 1851–61 period, when business recovered, firms recruited younger workers, and the percentage of workers over thirty-five fell in Oldham and Manchester. In Bolton the percentage of older workers rose slightly, perhaps indicating the relatively slower expansion of fine-spinning markets.[72]

Layoffs in the secondary sector

Although it is impossible to distinguish between the ages of spinners at large and small mills in the urban census samples, firm-level evidence for the rural sector, albeit fragmented, is available. In the secondary sector there was little reason to provide long-term commitments to individual workers in order to raise effort levels. It would be expected that, during trade declines, firms in the sector could lower labor costs by retaining their most productive workers. Census ages for Turton, where many of Ashworth's workers resided, reveal that older spinners were relieved of their duties during the 1840s.[73] The employment records of the Gregs illustrate a similar pattern. The percentage of female workers of all ages employed at Styal in their card, spinning, and mule rooms was 52 percent in the good business year of 1844, rising to 61 percent in 1847, but falling

Table 7.6 *Age distribution of spinners, 1841–1861*

Town	Age	Distribution of spinners from samples (percent)		
		1841	1851	1861
Manchester	Under 20	8.3%	7.2%	4.2%
	20–24	16.4	15.2	26.2
	25–34	33.3	30.2	24.0
	35–44	24.7	27.3	25.4
	Over 45	17.3	20.1	20.2
	Average age	35.4	36.4	34.4
	N	203	204	215
Bolton	Under 20	7.9%	3.1%	3.8%
	20–24	15.6	14.2	22.6
	25–34	37.1	40.4	30.1
	35–44	26.1	27.8	29.3
	Over 45	13.3	14.5	14.1
	Average age	34.7	35.6	35.6
	N	208	209	197
Oldham	Under 20	2.8%	2.0%	7.2%
	20–24	13.4	14.3	20.2
	25–34	36.3	33.9	26.5
	35–44	33.4	30.8	23.1
	Over 45	14.0	19.1	23.0
	Average age	36.7	37.3	36.0
	N	188	189	199

Sources: 1841 – PRO/HO 107/576–80, 546, 534–36;
1851 – PRO/HO 107/2225–30, 2241, 2209–12;
1861 – PRO/RG9 2927–30, 3016–20, 2820–26.

to 56 percent in 1849 when trade recovered. At the same time, the average wage moved in the opposite direction.[74] Older workers were not lost to the firms, however. It was in the interest of rural mills to keep the family units intact, and many older spinners were found new work packing, sweeping, or cleaning in the mill or repairing roads and walls on the estate.[75]

The outcome at rural mills was similar to that found in large urban mills. At both types of mills workers maintained long-term attachments. At M&K's and Lee's Manchester mills, the average tenure was about seven years; Ashworth boasted that the average tenure at his mills was eight years; at the Gregs' mills family names reappear in the wage books generation after generation.[76] These identical outcomes should not obscure the processes by which they were achieved. Lengthy attachment at rural mills was the result of occupational shifting and the stability of the family unit, whereas in urban mills tenure was extended to ensure directly high levels of individual effort.

Conclusion: preserving the fair wage

In their comprehensive account of modern British economic growth, Matthews and his collaborators found that in the second half of the nineteenth century the reduction in hours worked, through its effect on the quality of labor input, contributed significantly to the growth in productivity.[77] The standard explanation of the link between labor quality and productivity is that the workweek in the heyday of industrialization was excessively long and that legislation of the ten-hour workday in 1850 and 1853 reduced the fatigue of workers and raised their general health. There was a greater intensity of work, implying fewer mistakes, better quality, and higher output per person-hour. In emphasizing the role of statutory changes to the workweek at the expense of firm-level studies, the standard view has underestimated changes in hours of work that were mutually arranged by individual employers and workers. Little attention has been paid to the role of short-hour working by extending attachments on negotiated effort. Indeed, the secondary literature has asserted that short-hour working was insignificant and that there was no bargaining over effort levels.[78]

The evidence on hours and the age profile of spinners in Lancashire in the 1840s suggests that effort levels were variable. Both parties were left better off by negotiating hours and seniority provisions. Thus the fair wage survived the "hungry 'forties" because firms and workers designed a layoff package that would preserve it. Layoff schedules and short hours were enforced by both parties and, as a result, wage and employment arrangements moved further away from their market ideal.

8 Rules and standards: wage lists in Lancashire

The standard rate was not an original conception of trade
unionism: it was essentially the means whereby principles which
custom stamped as right and proper were solidified into a system,
which it was the function of trade unionism to maintain as rigidly
as possible. At the end of the nineteenth century, as throughout its
course, the mediaeval conception of the just wage still lingered in
the minds of the wage-earners in the guise of a reverence and trust
in custom as affording a criterion which was desirable in itself,
and which also afforded practical guidance in steering amidst the
reefs and shoals of their negotiations with the capitalist.[1]

The labor market after 1850

A feature of well-developed labor markets in which repeated communications exist between the parties is that multiple wage and employment practices become regularized. This arises because labor markets function more
efficiently if terms and categories are standardized into a few recognizable
packages, and because the evolution of contractual forms exhibits strongly
self-reinforcing learning processes on both sides of the market. The questions that must be considered are why some set of rules is chosen as
opposed to another, and how these rules are enforced. Some rules, such as
seniority provisions in Lancashire, often remain rules of thumb; other
rules become codified. In a strict economic sense both informal and formal
rules carry the same weight in restricting the parameters and choices of
decision makers, but written rules may require additional resources to
make any changes to them. Written rules, like those found in the Talmud,
get passed down from generation to generation without any changes. They
have a future and a past, whereas oral traditions or rules of thumb may be
simply regularities that only have a past.[2]

As prescribed by either written or unwritten rules, conformity has an added feature. It reduces enforcement expenditure and signifies that public sanctions and boycotts could be placed on individuals breaking standards of behavior, even if it is in the personal interest of the penalizers – workers and firms – not to conform. Because of the taboo attached to undercutting or ratebusting, and because penalizers fear that they too may be punished, firms and workers do what is right. The close-knit towns of southern Lancashire, in which factory and community intersected, and in which both workers and employers had well-organized and frequently shared social, religious, and political institutions, reinforced and preserved such behavior.[3]

To many social and labor historians, the 36-week Preston strike in 1853–54 was a watershed in labor-market development in Lancashire. The historians of the dispute found that, during one important march, workers carried banners proclaiming "A Fair Day's Wage For A Fair Day's Work."[4] Their demand for the restoration of a 10 percent wage cut was not honored and their union was crushed. The dispute in some histories marked an end to the period of confrontation that had begun with the introduction of machinery in the first factories; workers had learned the "rules of the game," and the market had triumphed. But, whereas some employers, like Henry Ashworth, saw the gains made in Preston as a victory of "property against communism," others expressed concern about the loss of market share. Following employers elsewhere, the lords of Preston began searching for an alternative relationship with their work-forces. An outcome of the dispute, as in Manchester in the 1830s, was a regional piece rate – a compendium of wage rules – that regulated earnings and put an end to work stoppages.

The received wisdom is that the early lists, like the type used in Manchester, were not permanent and that this method of pay became widespread only with trade union consolidation, sometime after 1850.[5] In this later period the Bolton and Oldham lists were the most widely used; the former regulated wages in fine-spinning, the latter in coarse-spinning areas. By the end of the century the lists were well-established institutions, determining the earnings of 75 percent of spinners in Lancashire and Cheshire and governing industrial relations as the "force of laws."[6]

Despite their significance, the origins of the lists, their makeup, and their effect on labor-market development remain uncertain. Even the Webbs, the leading authorities on industrial relations in the period, were reluctant to address these issues. "It is difficult to convey to the general reader," they wrote, "any adequate idea of the important effect which the elaborate [spinning lists] have had in Lancashire . . . [Yet] the principles upon which the lists are framed are so complicated that we confess, after prolonged study, to be still perplexed on certain points."[7]

It is not my intention to describe the intricacies of the lists and how they were negotiated and altered after 1850.[8] Rather, using the basic model of chapter 5 as a framework, my aim is to show why this set of rules developed as opposed to another, and to evaluate the effect of the two dominant lists on labor-market development. I will argue that the post-1850 lists codified standard rates of pay set in the earlier period – that is, before union consolidation – incorporating elements of the fair wage and employment package negotiated by workers and firms.

There were important changes in labor-market operations after the middle of the century. In 1850 workers' demands, like those in Preston, centered upon their uncertainty over the restoration of a piece-rate cut, but by the middle of the 1870s they were better assured that firms would honor their commitments. Reputations were secured and both parties meted out sanctions against those breaking the rules of the labor market embedded in the lists. The labor market had evolved into an institution, but a paradox remained: because the standard rate was safeguarded, piece rates could be adjusted below and above it, making the aggregate labor market more responsive to changes in demand or supply than at any time in the nineteenth century.

The Bolton list: worker-sponsored technical change

An early study of the method of compensation stated that the "first list known in the spinning trade was that adopted at Preston in 1859," and that the remaining major lists were put in place in the next twenty-five years.[9] This statement has left the impression, repeated in the literature, that the origins of the major lists are found in the mid-Victorian boom and that they were an outgrowth of trade union consolidation. S. J. Chapman, however, speculated that the lists were not introduced at the same time. He wrote that the Bolton list was "said to date back to 1813, but corroborative evidence is lacking."[10]

The list to which Chapman referred is clearly dated 1813 and appears to have been a regional and not a private or mill one.[11] Contemporary accounts confirm the practice of paying by lists in the town. The *Manchester Guardian* reported that workers and firms in Bolton were renegotiating a list of prices in 1823; in his survey of methods of pay in the textile industry in 1833, factory inspector Cowell noted the existence of the list; later in the decade, Preston spinners went out on strike for the Bolton list of prices.[12] The list stipulated prices paid per pound of yarn, and to account for the longer time necessary to spin finer yarns, prices increased with count spun. In operation it was a pure piece-rate list, with no adjustments for either the length or speed of the mule.

The early introduction of the Bolton list and its structure can be attributed to the pace of technical change and the size of firms in the town. Crompton was an erstwhile resident of the town, and after the introduction of his mule, Bolton quickly became the center of the medium- and fine-spinning trade in Lancashire. The town benefited from the sector's growth and technical dynamism; by 1811 it had thirty-three mills, employing on average 150 workers. As was the case in Manchester, Bolton mills needed a way to elicit effort from spinners, but because of their size and the early introduction of long mules, they confronted an effort problem. We know that male spinners took advantage of their bargaining position. Bolton, according to E. P. Thompson, was "the most insurrectionary center in England from the late 1790s until 1820s" and, among other issues, workers persisted in their demand for a regional list that would establish a standard rate of pay across firms and different vintages of machinery.[13] Large firms in the town were willing to go along with these demands, because the list would eliminate work stoppages and protect their investments in fixed capital. Moreover, the list moderated competition, particularly the wage cutting that had ensued when smaller firms with older technology cut rates at the first signs of a trade decline. Smaller firms could not compete at standard rates; in addition, they were a minority in Bolton and large firms were able to enforce the list by supporting striking workers at these firms.[14]

For firms, the list had obvious drawbacks. Since wages were paid per pound of yarn spun, unit labor costs on new and old machinery were identical. The Bolton list, therefore, made for equal labor costs between mills of varying efficiency and for unequal earnings. Of course, firms would get some of the benefits of technical change because, by raising effort levels and reducing stoppages, the lists reduced unit fixed costs. As long as prices rose this was a satisfactory arrangement, but with profits eroding after the French Wars and with the intent of breaking the spinners' organization, firms in the town joined together in 1822 to introduce the principle of discounting, whereby rates paid as set by the list would decline with the length of the spinning mule. A protracted and bitter strike ensued.[15] Anticipating the outcome of the Manchester conflict of 1829, employers prevailed, but, during the course of the dispute and its aftermath, they complained of the difficulty of finding qualified male spinners to replace recalcitrant workers.[16] They had come to realize the benefits of stable industrial relations in getting good work out.

Workers were naturally reluctant to share the surplus that they had had to themselves since 1813, but the new list retained some benefits. Even after the introduction of discounting, the new list protected them from the unremunerated intensification of their labor, and in this respect their standard was protected. For a mule of a given size rates of pay per pound of output were fixed and spinners would capture the gains if employers attempted to speed up work or extract more effort. The standard of paying higher rates for finer counts of yarn was maintained, and, finally, employers could not change unilaterally any of the rates without revising the entire list.

The lists negotiated in Bolton after the middle of the century did not tamper with the standard of 1823, which gave workers the benefit of their increased effort. The established list was not undercut, because the proportion of smaller firms in the town remained stable. Additionally, the list was unresponsive to changes in technology. The introduction of the self-actor in fine spinning, which began in the 1860s and which was nearly complete by the late 1880s, increased speeds of operation, yet there was no substantive change in the list's makeup. To observers writing in the early twentieth century, this was a *chance manquée*. Under the Oldham list, as we will see, workers and firms shared the benefits of increased speed, but in Bolton these gains were captured entirely by spinners as they had been in the first half of the century. This is a clear example of worker-sponsored technical change. Moreover, as mule sizes increased in fine spinning, the list was not altered accordingly. Employers gained no advantage from extending mules beyond 806 twist spindles or 1,100 weft spindles.[17] Changes to the list were incremental; its original makeup endured because it was a proven method of ensuring labor peace and a productive labor force.

The standardization of wages is a common occurrence in a well-developed labor market like Bolton's. The number of firms had stabilized and, relative to other regions in Lancashire, population inflows had moderated by the 1840s, if not earlier. The necessary conditions were in place for regularized and repeated communications and contracts between the parties. In this environment, rules or standards took hold and could be enforced. "By their very nature," Gavin Wright observed, "labor markets are subject to 'increasing returns,' which is to say that they function more efficiently when terms and categories are standardized into a few recognizable packages."[18] The extent of these returns was such that they could offset the costs associated with the list's makeup, and particularly the disincentive to invest in longer or newer spinning machinery.

The Oldham list: splitting the gains

Until 1850 or so, the average size of firms and the available labor supply in Oldham made it unnecessary for employers to pay by a list. It was customary in Oldham "for each master to make separate bargains with his workpeople"; still others did not give the "particulars" of their rates of pay.[19] The expansion of factory industry occurred later in Oldham than in Bolton, and in the early period a large number of firms rented or shared space and power in a larger mill. The "room and turning system" maintained the small firm as the typical unit of production. Farnie wrote that the system "accentuated the degree of competition, increased the mortality rate among factory masters," and again, in contrast with Bolton, prevented "the family firm from establishing an hereditary monopoly of local industry under a separate caste of employers."[20] Given their chances of survival, small Oldham firms had little reason to develop long-term attachments that were essential in preserving mill and regional lists. In this environment, firms would have had great difficulty enforcing rules and standards.

As long as mills remained small, the effort problem was held in check. Overlookers were not necessary and spinners worked directly under their employers. Technical progress was slow until the 1840s and firms incurred small costs in setting rates of pay. The relatively higher proportion of women and young male spinners in the coarse-spinning sector made it difficult for male spinners in the sector to organize, at least initially, a strong and continuous union presence that challenged rate cuts or threats of replacement.

The growth of large and permanent firms in Oldham commenced with the wide-scale diffusion of the self-actor after 1867, ushering in a decade of unprecedented expansion that undermined the position of the small employer, insofar as it entailed an enlargement in mill size.[21] The emergence of joint-stock companies made it possible for smaller firms to take advantage of the new technology and respond to the shortage of room and turning space. The expansion was rapid. The boom of 1873–75 – the greatest in Oldham's history – saw the creation of seventy limited partnerships. By the middle of the 1880s the average sizes of Oldham and Bolton firms were almost identical.

Without any commensurate investment in managerial structures, the increase in scale unleashed the effort problem. As was the case in fine spinning a generation earlier, after 1860 coarse-spinning firms could not replace workers easily and had to find an alternate way to elicit effort. Firms became increasingly dependent on their minders to recruit and supervise junior workers and, as before, it was widely believed that these tasks were best performed by men. Trade union activity intensified, culminating in the establishment in 1870 of the Oldham-based Amalgamated Association of Operative Cotton Spinners. Among the union's most pressing demands was the enforcement of a regional list; the two sides tested each other's strength through a series of confrontations which broke out in the early 1870s. In May 1872, 200 mills shut their doors, locking out some

20,000 operatives.[22] A resolution was eventually reached, but the protracted dispute had posed a threat to the viability of the new limited-liability companies, since many employers lost minders to firms that continued working and to neighboring towns. Oldham firms had come to the realization that they needed to rely on a core group of male spinners to ensure a steady flow of output.

The Oldham list of 1872 was a contract by which workers gained a standard wage and firms elicited high levels of effort. The list paid spinners the highest wages in Lancashire for spinning coarse counts, and although there were later revisions, its makeup remained the same. It calculated how much yarn could be produced normally on mules of different speeds and lengths after deducting time for cleaning, doffing, and accidental stoppages. To find the piece rate per 1,000 hanks of yarn, normal production was divided into the standard weekly wage, a time component to which each spinner was entitled. The actual gross earnings of the minder were calculated as this piece rate multiplied by the number of 1,000 hanks actually spun, adjusted upward or downward by a percentage determined by collective bargaining over the business cycle. The Oldham list, therefore, made for equal earnings, but unequal labor costs per pound of yarn spun. Later variants of the Oldham list also included a speed clause which split the gains in output between firms and workers.

Differences between the two major lists can be attributed partly to the technologies used in the regions. Minders of self-actors had less control over effort than fine spinners on common mules. Most of the self-actors in Oldham were produced by the local firm of Platt Bros., and the standardization across firms made it easier for managers to acquire information on how much output could be produced in a given time.[23] The time component in the list would have been practical only if firms had some notion of what could be produced in a given period. This is consistent with Eugene Fama's observation that, without information about the flow of hourly effort or output, payoffs for time gave the worker an incentive to supply hours without effort, and that firms would therefore opt for a pure piece-rate system.[24]

The makeup of the list had implications for average wages (table 8.1). Throughout the century the ratio of Oldham to Bolton average earnings remained stable at about 92 percent. This stability is all the more remarkable because of the greater productivity increases and investment in coarse spinning, and because whatever skill differential that existed between the two sectors diminished with the introduction of self-actors in fine spinning. If the labor market operated as a spot market, then Oldham earnings should have increased relatively.[25] Yet, it would also be inaccurate to conclude that earning stability was the result of worker organization, because

Table 8.1 *Weekly earnings of spinners in Bolton, Oldham, and Preston: 1833–1890*

Year	Weekly wage (in s)		
	Oldham	Bolton	Preston
1833	26.08	28.50	22.50
1841	24.00	27.50	20.50
1860	28.00	31.43	20.00
1870	31.50	33.70	24.00
1880	29.75	32.50	27.25
1890	35.33	41.58	34.00

Source: George H. Wood, *The History of Wages in the Cotton Trade During the Past Hundred Years* (Manchester: Hughes, 1910).

by the third quarter of the century unions were as well organized in Oldham as in Bolton.

I believe the "wage contour" had its origins before 1850.[26] In the early period, union development was more volatile in Oldham and women could be found spinning in the town; as a result, the fair wage negotiated was lower down on the contract curve. A geographic dimension in wage determination was well established before the middle of the century and, as in modern labor markets, it became a component of the fair wage itself. The Bolton list, one employer stated, ensured "that our prices might be generally known as being higher than in other towns."[27] Not only did workers want to ensure uniform piece rates and earnings within regions, but they wanted to protect their position in the regional hierarchy. Wages, therefore, had both industry and geographic dimensions, and the lists established after 1850 standardized these differentials.

The Preston list: the end of confrontation

By the middle of the century, as we have seen, Preston employers had built a powerful association and cut piece rates at the first sign of a decline in demand. Firms in the town also worked considerably less short time than anywhere else in Lancashire. Yet, after the dispute of 1853–54, Preston firms, like those elsewhere, were prepared to negotiate a piece-rate list. Their motivation appears to have been the loss of market share incurred during the lengthy dispute. Prior to 1850 Preston competed with Bolton in the spinning of medium to fine counts, but after the confrontation it began to manufacture more medium to coarse yarns.[28]

The Preston list, which some authorities date to 1853, was revised in 1859 and again in 1866.[29] The date of its introduction falls between those of the first Bolton and Oldham lists. It was costly to engage in repeated conflict, and like large firms elsewhere Preston employers needed to find a way to elicit effort. As for its makeup, the list was based on the Bolton list; it was a pure piece-rate system and there was no speed clause. Rates decreased with the length of the mule, up to 1,000 spindles on twist mules and 1,100 on weft mules; thereafter a uniform price was paid. Discounting gave spinners the major portion of the gains from mule size. Despite these advantages earnings in Preston remained below those found in Oldham throughout the century, although the latter spun coarser yarn. The weight of regional and historical dimensions in bargaining maintained differentials, even after the introduction of regional lists.

Adapting and enforcing rules

The Bolton and Oldham wage lists evolved into the two dominant district lists. Beginning in the 1830s, spinners in Bolton organized financial assistance to strikers in neighboring regions to "ensure the payment of customary rates"; a similar pattern was observed in Oldham.[30] However, at least in principle, the regional coverage of the lists was inconsistent with their structure. As written, the lists implied that it was cheaper to use the Bolton list to spin coarse yarn, and that it was less expensive to use the Oldham list to spin fine yarn. Figure 8.1 illustrates the relation between labor costs and counts set by the lists. Given the proximity of the towns in Lancashire, the high mobility of capital, and the obvious benefits for firms and workers to break the district lists, it is remarkable that they became dominant in the first place. Evidently, some mills attempted to take advantage of price differentials, the existence of which John Jewkes and E. M. Gray acknowledged: "The observable differences have no real relation to technical conditions, but are the outcome of chance, or the unforeseen offspring of some muddled historical struggle." Why did such differentials persist in the face of competition? Jewkes and Gray grounded them in "sanction and prestige," but this explanation begs the question as to the mechanisms used by firms and workers to enforce regional standards.[31]

An episode in Darwen – a coarse-spinning town – illustrates the delicate balance between private and social gains. In the mid-1890s, with the market for fine yarn expanding, a mill began spinning fine counts of yarn using the Oldham list.[32] Workers demanded the higher wages set by the Bolton list and a dispute ensued. With the intention of preserving the

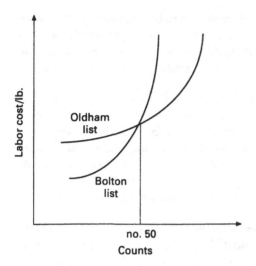

8.1 Labor costs and counts of yarn: the Bolton and Oldham lists

Oldham list, the vast majority of firms supported the workers' demand, and, in the end, the maverick firm was forced to resume spinning coarse yarn.

Thus, the lists, like short hours, were protected by community norms. Enforcement was rooted in the community networks of Lancashire. Joyce has described in detail the bonds between firms and workers both inside and outside the factories after 1850 when population movements stabilized. "At the center of this sense [of community] was the neighbourhood, and very near the heart of the neighbourhood feeling the factory."[33] Workers and firms developed their own rules of what was just and fair, and both parties could monitor each other closely. Those who did not fit in moved elsewhere.[34]

The lists promoted unionization, since formal organizations could more easily administer them. But acting like monopolists seeking to maximize revenue by discriminating among buyers of labor time, unions did not go so far as to demand a uniform rate throughout Lancashire. For employers, the lists reduced negotiation costs. Employer associations, organized ostensibly to administer negotiations, also took the initiative to use the lists as a means to regulate competition and reduce uncertainties in labor and product markets.[35] In Oldham, as elsewhere, the local association of employers sponsored trade union attempts to organize outlying areas and impose the standard rate of pay on smaller concerns that, in the past, had initiated rounds of wage and price cuts, and protracted and costly labor disputes. Moreover, the list forced employers to become managers of labor and to master the intricacies of the method of pay. Spinning manuals of the period provided detailed instruction on how to calculate wages, and there is some evidence that after 1875 firms hired more overlookers in the spinning rooms.[36]

Combined, the development of trade unions and employers' associations at the district level contributed toward and preserved the regional specialization of the industry. Alfred Marshall observed that regional specialization in textiles depended on well-developed marketing and distribution networks, but he underestimated the role of the lists in encouraging an available and inelastic supply of labor. Workers in each region were ensured the highest wages in Lancashire for spinning the type of yarn for which they had training.

Inside the mill both workers and firms adapted themselves to the method of pay. The lists consolidated the organization of production in which the spinner or minder recruited, supervised, and paid his piecers. In Bolton, where the available supply of piecers was greatest, the list stipulated the gross wages of spinners, who were left to strike a bargain with their piecers. Although the Oldham list in principle gave piecers a proportion of the minders' standard earnings, they were in effect paid by time.[37] Thus, the two major district lists motivated spinners to drive their assistants hard, because they did not share the gains with the team. In line with our previous discussion of wage contours, the piecer–spinner earnings ratio remained relatively stable in the second half of the nineteenth century.[38] This cannot be explained by ordinary laws of demand and supply. Because of the excess supply of piecers, their wages should have fallen relatively; at the same time, there is little compelling evidence to suggest that the excess supply of younger workers exercised any downward pressure on spinners' wages.[39] Instead, the pay ratios are consistent with the notion that all textile workers who were governed by the lists received fair wages.

To a limited extent, firms adjusted to the lists by changing material inputs. Coarse-spinning firms would use inferior and cheaper cotton, but inferior cotton produced more end breakages and generated more work for the spinning team. The strategy would lower net costs as long as the minder could force his assistants to work harder to mend the additional broken threads. This approach had its drawbacks, giving rise to frequent and bitter bad-spinning disputes that were finally resolved, albeit unsatisfactorily, in the Brooklands Agreement of 1893. Disputes over inferior cotton were less frequent in fine spinning because firms had little leeway in the type of cotton used; however, firms in the sector tried to pay for lower counts of yarn than were actually spun in attempt to reduce costs.[40]

Extending the length and improving the timing and speed of spinning mules were the principal means by which employers adjusted to the lists. Steady improvements in the self-actor increased the ratio of spindles to spinners and offset the productivity losses associated with inferior cotton. The increase in manning ratios was an adaptive response to the high wages paid to spinners. In coarse spinning, the nature of the list meant that workers and firms shared the benefits of the new investments. Between 1876 and 1907, spindleage in this sector grew by 105 percent and unit costs as specified by the Oldham list fell by 15 percent.[41] Recall, in contrast, that the Bolton list *in principle* deterred technical change. Because this list had no speed clause, piece rates remained constant on long mules with more than 806 twist spindles; as result, unit costs as determined by the list fell slightly, by only 2 percent between 1876 and 1907. Nonetheless, investment in fine spinning increased in the late nineteenth century, although not at the rate witnessed in coarse spinning. The number of spindles in Bolton rose by 75 percent between 1882 and 1913. By the first decade of the twentieth century, the average mule carried 1,100 spindles. The continued investment of firms was based on their expectation that increased labor effort on these new longer mules would cover the rise in fixed expenses.

Because the lists were well enforced, both parties could adjust to them: workers raised their efforts, while firms made continuing investments in machinery. The average real earnings of spinners from 1870 to 1913 increased by 1.5 percent per annum, slightly exceeding the increase in productivity of 1.27 percent.[42] Wood made some preliminary calculations of the relative contributions of effort and technical change to the rise in earnings after 1850.[43] Between 1860 and 1906, average earnings of operatives rose by 69 percent. Wood attributed 7 percent of this gain to increased rates of pay and 13 percent due to the employment of relatively more adults. The remaining 49 percent, he concluded, was the result of "increased efficiency of operatives and machine." Estimates of the productivity change in coarse spinning permit the residual to be broken down further. Jewkes and Gray found that during the same period the number of spindles and the speed of mules increased by 44 percent, but since workers captured only half of the gain, this means that 27 percent (= 49 percent − (44/2) percent) of the rise in average earnings in Lancashire is attributable to the greater efficiency of operatives.[44] Wood's procedure shows that increased effort accounts for between 12 and 15 percent of the rise in spinners' earnings in Oldham and Bolton.[45] The magnitude in the increase of effort appears large, but it is consistent with the annual improvement in labor quality for the entire British economy which Matthews and his collaborators found as a result of changes in hour legislation after the middle of the century.[46] Samuel Andrew, the secretary of the Employers'

Association of Oldham, best summarized the interplay between machinery and labor efficiency:

We have at this moment the most capable labor in the world. It is born and brought up well suited and disciplined in to its work; under its wage-lists, with the present improved machinery we can depend upon it fulfilling its duty with the accuracy of clockwork.[47]

Flexible institutions

After 1875 the lists became the centerpiece of industrial relations. "Look after the lists, and wages will look after themselves" was the spinners' maxim.[48] Although disputes persisted over issues like the use of inferior cotton and how to adjust earnings to compensate for faster speeds and time required for doffing and cleaning, most accounts acknowledge the lists' conciliating and coordinating functions in reducing stoppages in production.[49] The aim of this section is not to review these negotiations, which have been addressed elsewhere, but to evaluate how the rule of paying by lists affected wage and employment adjustment.

As in many earlier disputes, from the workers' perspective at issue in the Preston strike of 1853–54 was firms' taking advantage of market conditions and reneging on a commitment to restore a wage cut. Citing poor trade prospects, Preston employers claimed they could not raise piece rates as they had earlier promised. Clearly, if firms had private information about prices and markets unavailable to workers, they always had an incentive to announce that the state of trade was bad.[50] However, this policy was incompatible with eliciting high and steady levels of effort, because firms that tried to force a wage cut found it difficult to recruit other workers in the future, and because it incited work stoppages. Even for Preston there is evidence of firms having difficulty in recruiting workers throughout the 1850s.[51] An alternative arrangement was for capital and labor to agree on a mutually beneficial division of the surplus; however, cooperation could only have emerged after a learning process in which each party recognized the motives of and trusted the other. Thus, if Lancashire firms kept to their commitments about the fair wage, their statements about the state of trade would be credible. Union organizations, which the lists promoted, played an integral part in checking this process, since it was costly for individuals to acquire information about the state of trade. Rule XVI of the spinners' trade union's constitution of 1860 instructed the general secretary to purchase "such publications, periodicals, or newspapers, as shall be found to convey the soundest and most reliable information on that subject [the state of trade]."[52]

After 1850, commitments were kept. Neither the Bolton nor Oldham standard was tampered with and, as a result, workers had a built-in guarantee that any piece-rate cut would be restored. Thomas Ashton, head of the Oldham spinners, observed that, to avoid stoppages and strikes, "the best plan is for employers and employed to agree upon a rule of wages as a standard, and let the general state of trade afterwards govern such rate of wages up or down, always allowing reasonable profits for capital."[53] By the third quarter of the century, it was less common for workers to demand fixed rates of pay, irrespective of the state of trade, and there was a general acceptance that the list could be adjusted upward or downward over the business cycle.[54] The Brooklands Agreement, which was called by a leading employer "the most complete treaty between capital and labor that has ever been framed," routinized these adjustments to just one change in any year of no more than 5 percent.[55] In terms of figure 5.2, this meant that the fair wage position on the contract curve was maintained if the curve shifted to accommodate changes in profits and workers' utility. The standard, according to the author of the first history of the lists, was left intact:

The lists have not succeeded in removing all probability of dispute between employer and employed. They have, it is true, introduced uniformity into the payment of wages in the cotton trade, *caused wages to be payable on definite and known principles*, adjusted the wages of different classes of spinners, and defined strictly the duties of the operative; but they do not make wages vary either with the varying cost of the raw material or the varying prices realized for the finished product. The standard, in other words, implies a given condition of trade. A changed condition, e.g., a rise or fall in the price of yarn, when fully established results in a percentage being added to or taken from the wages payable. The method of determining the occasion and the amount of alteration is determined by negotiation between the association of employers and the association of spinners.[56]

Within a generation after the introduction of the fair wage policy, the lists regularized the adjustment of labor markets to a trade decline. The results were akin to a profit-sharing scheme in which employment is stabilized and the wage is tied to some cyclical indicator.[57] In the first and last stages of a downturn the golden rule was to work short hours. At M&K, for example, workers were placed on short time throughout the Cotton Famine of the early and mid-1860s, and no one was permanently laid off; during the 1906–07 recession, S. J. Chapman and H. M. Hallsworth found a similar response and concluded that short time was the "commonest form of unemployment in the Lancashire cotton industry."[58] But if short time failed to draw down stocks and the downturn worsened, unlike the earlier period, a mechanism, mutually agreed to by the parties, was in place that lowered piece rates.

Table 8.2 shows the positive relation between annual changes in coarse

Table 8.2 *Annual changes of lists and margins, 1853–1914 (percentages)*

| | Bolton (1853–82) | | Oldham (1875–1914) | |
Statistic	List	no. 100 margin	List	no. 30 margin
Mean	–0.04	–0.14	0.06	–0.02
S.d.	2.95	5.34	3.64	3.96
S.e.	0.51	0.93	0.58	0.64
Min.	–10.53	–11.02	–11.76	–6.76
Max.	5.26	14.22	8.00	11.39
Range	15.79	25.32	18.76	18.15
Correlation coefficient	0.26		0.65	

Source: Lists: Alan Fowler and Terry Wyke, eds., *The Barefoot Aristocrats: A History of the Amalgamated Association of Operative Cotton Spinners* (Littleborough: George Kelsall, 1987), 246. Margins: John Jewkes and E. M. Gray, *Wages and Labour in the Lancashire Cotton-Spinning Industry* (Manchester: Manchester University Press, 1935), 211; M&K Sales Book.

yarn margins, the widely accepted state-of-trade indicator, and changes in the Oldham list between 1875 and 1914. The fit between annual changes in the Bolton list and margins for fine spinning is less precise, but still the minimum values of rates of change are nearly the same. Using prices and quantities as proxies for wages and employment (the same procedure employed in chapter 6), table 8.3 compares labor-market adjustment before and after the middle of the century. In contrast with the early period, when output changes dominated price movements, for 1853 to 1887 the standard deviations of output and price changes were almost identical in fine spinning.[59] In coarse spinning for a later period, 1875–87, price changes were nearly twice as great as output fluctuations, whereas for 1838–52 the reverse held. Thus, despite the institutional rigidity imposed by the lists, or perhaps it is more accurate to say because of it, the late nineteenth-century labor market exhibited greater wage flexibility – and employment security – than it did in 1850.

This is not a surprising result. In a comparative study of labor markets in history, George Grantham observed this tendency. He argued that in the early stages of labor-market development it was not uncommon for firms to accommodate the average preferences of workers. Firms did not normally vary employment packages continuously at all possible margins, but instead offered fixed packages to workers in order to minimize negotiation

Table 8.3 *Output and prices: annual rates of change, 1838–1890*

Variable	Years	Standard deviation (annual rates of change)
C1	1838–52	20.43
No. 30	1838–52	12.50
F1	1822–52	20.27
No. 100	1822–52	16.40
Output	1853–87	6.81
No. 40	1853–87	14.20
No. 100	1853–87	6.11
Output	1875–87	6.16
No. 32	1875–87	14.20
Output	1866–90	6.30
No. 100	1866–90	8.18

Sources: Output and prices for 1838–52: tables 6.8–6.10; output, 1853–90: Mark Blaug, "The Productivity of Capital in the Lancashire Cotton Industry During the Nineteenth Century," *Economic History Review* 13, no. 3 (1961), 376; no. 32: John Jewkes, and E. M. Gray, *Wages and Labour in the Lancashire Cotton-Spinning Industry* (Manchester: Manchester University Press, 1935), 211; no. 40: Thomas Ellison, *The Cotton Trade of Great Britain* (London, 1886), Appendix; no. 100: M&K Sales Book.

and transaction costs. This tendency for employers to target groups rather than individuals, Grantham continues, "gives special importance to the social structures from which the supply of laborers is drawn."[60] But as labor forces matured, wage and employment packages changed accordingly. In the case of Lancashire, this meant preserving the institution of the fair wage, but also adapting it to secure steady employment, even if this meant changes above and below the standard.

Conclusion: wage determination and local effects

In a frequently cited article, Gregory Clark attempted to show that across different countries real wages in the textile industry varied with the level of efficiency and intensity of individual workers. He attributed the wage–effort relation to "local effects," by which he meant market forces outside the control of workers and firms themselves. The contingent wage in the industrial sector is set by its opportunity cost, or, in the familiar two-sector case, agricultural wages. Clark concluded that international trends in development can be inferred from the wage–effort relation in textiles. He wrote:

It would not be correct, however, to interpret the above [noted findings] as indicating that the key difference in worker efficiency in textiles lay in the strength of unions in textiles, the nature of bargaining between labor and management in the factories, or the labor recruitment strategies of different textile industries . . . Whatever constrained the choices of workers in cotton textiles, or whatever determined their preferences, must have applied to all of the local labor force. Unfortunately the sources on the textile industry do not allow me to go with any confidence beyond this limited ascription of responsibility to local influences. But this in itself is not a modest or an uncontroversial claim.[61]

The problem with Clark's claim is that it does not fit the sources for the British cotton-textile industry itself, the terrain and industry which is at the center of his argument. The evidence for Oldham and Bolton reveals that earnings did not always move with changes in productivity or efficiency, using Clark's yardsticks of manning ratios and capital per worker. By all accounts, productivity and investment growth were far greater in coarse than in fine spinning, and wage movements in the two areas should have reflected these changes in "local effects." However, earnings in both regions before the middle of the century appear to have been set by local standards of fair wages that were negotiated and enforced by workers and firms, and that were later codified in regional piece-rate lists. These local effects were clearly not the type to which Clark referred.

Part IV

Conclusion

9   More lessons from the cotton mills

All in all it is easy to understand how the convention that wages are only cut *in extremis* became entrenched in labor markets before unions were significant and before Keynes attached so much weight to their downward rigidity.[1]

The myth of the textbook labor market

The strong belief in economics is that over time and in a unilinear path wages have become less flexible.[2] Labor markets today, it is believed, look very different from markets in the nineteenth century – the Golden Age of wage flexibility – because of changes in occupational and industrial mix, collective-bargaining coverage, methods of payment, average job duration, workforce demographics, and government regulation. In earlier periods, spot relationships held, with the wage rate acting as the key market clearing instrument; in modern labor markets, worker–firm attachments are more likely to be long term, and lifetime compensation agreements dominate short-run concerns.

Based on the belief that wages have become more rigid, and that rigidity reduces welfare, economists have proposed various schemes that impose costs on the use of particular types of compensation schemes that are believed to make wages less sensitive to cyclical changes. These proposals include bans on multiyear collective-bargaining agreements, and tax incentives for profit-sharing or bonus systems linked to some measure of profits.

Current policy proposals need to be reconsidered, however. The evidence does not sit well with the basic or standard labor market model, even in the Golden Age. In the heyday and heartland of industrialization, firms and workers had good reason to form long-term attachments and to negotiate rigid piece rates and earnings. By 1850, if not earlier, a framework was in place that provided workers and firms with a basis to engage in repeated negotiations; after 1850, when and where commitments were upheld, piece rates and earnings moved in response to changes in the cycle. Hence in Lancashire wages became less and not more rigid over time. There is no a priori reason to believe, therefore, that in the absence of government regulation, wide-scale social insurance, and formal collective bargaining, wages will clear the market.

With the intention of provoking new directions for research, this chapter addresses the implications of these findings for recent debates in British economic history and the economic history of labor markets. I begin with a reevaluation of recent research in labor history.

The moral economy of the mill floor

Buttressed by the new gradualist interpretation of economic growth during the crucial years of the industrial revolution, recent work in British social and labor history has sought to reveal the continuity of eighteenth-century work habits, work organizations, and technologies.[3] These accounts, with varying degrees of emphasis, have challenged the older view that the market triumphed over custom. In place of rapid growth, development is widely believed to have been uneven; putting-out and small workshops existed alongside and complemented the factory sector, and in the process old skills were retained and new skills developed. Neither workers nor firms are identified as monolithic. The assertion that workers lost skills has been replaced by the view that workers exercised control of the labor process. It is no longer held that workers learned the rules of the game; indeed it appears they actively played a role in making them as well. In these accounts conflict *and* compromise were equally probable outcomes.

This research agenda is in part a reaction to an overemphasis on cotton textiles in the earlier literature, and the claims of radical changes in work organization and technology in the industry. To Hobsbawm, who wrote, "whoever says industrial revolution, says cotton," the new research has responded: whoever says industrialization, says also woolens, pottery, and buttons.[4] But despite claims to the contrary, cotton is representative. Like these other industries, its path of development was uneven: large and small firms and rural and urban mills coexisted; old technologies competed against newer vintages; and methods of compensations and wage and employment adjustment varied between sectors and regions. In this environment it is difficult to conclude that capital and labor were monolithic.

But there is a more important reason why Hobsbawm's emphasis on cotton remains warranted. Whether the classical labor market deviated from the auction market standard is an important question, because it focuses attention on the nature of labor-market development in the first factory industry. Herein lies the contribution of economic history to labor history. Using the insights of modern labor economics, I have shown that a modern-looking wage and employment package was negotiated by workers and firms. Institutions like the fair wage were created to reduce uncertainty and the costs of production and exchange; the kind of institutions that were appropriate for the putting-out stage were very different from those necessary for the factory age. This finding has broader implications for the social and economic history of Britain. Although aggregate or sectoral economic growth might not have been as rapid as had been claimed by economic historians of the 1950s and 1960s, the new wage and employment packages that evolved in Lancashire in the first quarter of the nineteenth century were manifestations of changes in the risk and information environment that were very much part of the industrial revolution.

This approach and its findings extend Randall's interpretation of the role of custom and the market.[5] Randall argued that in the late eighteenth century, in both the West Riding of Yorkshire and the West of England, social systems developed, including labor-market arrangements, in "which habituation and practice became ossified and reified as custom." In Randall's account, regulatory legislation, such as apprenticeship provisions and wage-fixing clauses, provided woolen workers with their most significant source of strength to temper changes in technology and work organization; when parliament repealed this body of legislation beginning in 1809, workers found themselves unprotected from market forces and many turned to Luddism.

For the cotton industry, there was an alternative path in which labor-market arrangements evolved. Structure in the late eighteenth century, as Randall correctly pointed out, was created to reduce uncertainty, but it does not necessarily follow that these arrangements were inviolate. A new social and economic context created new points of reference for judging what was right and fair.[6] In response to a changing environment of risk and uncertainty, a new structure was put into place in the factory period in which the fair wage established itself as the moral economy of the mill floor. Custom was not constructed in opposition to the market economy; rather, as Randall has written, the "origins of the moral economy have to be found within a capitalist economy." Although there is nothing in the process of institutional change to insure that efficient institutions will evolve, what is remarkable is that in certain sectors and regions of the cotton industry it only took one generation – and further comparative research is necessary to evaluate whether this was slow or rapid – for a relatively new structure to take hold.

I have avoided referring to the outcome as an "internal labor market" for the same reason that I have criticized the invention of the stylized model of the Lancashire labor market. Certainly, the cotton-spinning labor market shared many of the features of modern labor markets, including idiosyncratic tasks, ports of entry, internal promotion ladders, and a division between large and small, primary and secondary firms. But identical outcomes should not obscure different processes. Modern internal labor markets respond to the demands of large multidivisional firms and the supply of well-disciplined and mature labor forces. But in Lancashire structure was a response to workers' uncertainty about the market, and employers' incomplete and imperfect information about effort levels. The contribution of economic history to labor economics lies, therefore, in demonstrating that despite common features and outcomes, every labor market, even the textbook model, has its own history.

The dual labor market and workers' welfare

How British workers fared during industrialization has been a subject of intense debate in economic history for almost a century. It will remain an important research area because it informs our perceptions about the relative roles of government and the market in improving and protecting living standards. Did wage and income gaps widen and did unemployment increase during the critical years of industrialization? Or did the market work efficiently providing workers with the opportunities to share the benefits of economic growth?

As it stands, the evidence is mixed.[7] Jeffrey G. Williamson, putting forward an optimistic view, claimed unambiguously that "real wages rose rapidly during the industrial revolution," and that "no conceivable level of unemployment could have canceled the near doubling of full time wages up to 1850." He found that industrialization saw impressive gains in the standard of life of over 60 percent for farm laborers, over 80 percent for "blue-collar workers," and over 140 percent for all workers. However, these gains were not evenly distributed. After the French Wars, the ratio of the *average* skilled worker's (including spinners) pay to that of an unskilled worker increased markedly. Williamson's underlying series have been the source of considerable debate, but perhaps the chief difficulty with his findings is that they do not mesh with alternative estimates of welfare. Joel Mokyr has found that consumption per capita showed no discernible increase at least until 1850; studies reveal that the heights of British workers signaled little or no improvement during the early years of industrialization.

A basic assumption in much of this literature, most often implicit, is that labor markets before 1850 worked smoothly and efficiently.[8] This might reflect the fragmentary evidence on wages and employment, but it also underscores the lasting impact of the myth of the Lancashire labor market. For the early decades of the century this vision is accurate, but by 1830 there were clear signs that the labor market deviated from its textbook model. Labor markets are not static; they develop rules, regularities, and institutions, and the direction in which the market evolves holds implications for wage and employment adjustment. Thus, the preliminary task in standard-of-living analyses must be to consider the nature of the labor market itself. Indeed, if the competitive assumption is relaxed, aspects of the conflicting evidence on the well-being of workers can be reconciled.

Assume the economy has a labor market, such as that for cotton spinners in the 1830s, composed of two sectors: a primary sector that offers a fair wage package comprising stable or fixed earnings, long-term attachments, seniority provisions, and short-time working; and a secondary sector in which firms provide a package consisting of short-term attachments and contingent wages.[9] Workers are assumed to be homogeneous and randomly sort themselves between sectors.

Cotton spinners' experience varied according to the size of establishment (and to the region) where they initially found, by happenstance, work. Coarse spinners moved easily into fine spinning and vice versa, but spinners in small firms could not replace workers in large firms, even if they offered themselves at lowered wages. In larger establishments employers had less than full information about effort levels and, as a result, earnings were fixed above market levels. The wage gap between primary and secondary sectors persisted, because if large firms offered market wages, workers would have given less than full effort.

If the dual labor market model fits, as I have tried to argue it does for cotton spinning, there existed a range of experiences for any particular class of workers during industrialization, some whose incomes rose steadily, others who were less fortunate – but not of their own preference or levels of investment in human capital. In the 1830s and early 1840s, when the division between the primary and secondary sector is most transparent, assessments of the average worker's earnings or pay ratios of unskilled and skilled workers obfuscate the divergence of experiences within occupations and industries. As the relative size of the primary sector grew, owing to the increase in establishment size, it becomes possible to write about the experience of the average worker. It is not a coincidence that by 1850, about the time the median cotton-spinning firm faced a managerial constraint, both pessimists and optimists agree that average incomes improved steadily.

Short-time working in the 1840s illustrates how the dual labor market model reconciles opposing views on the standard-of-living question. Jeffrey Williamson argued that the annual unemployment rate in the 1840s was at most 15 percent, but because he assumed no variation in hours worked, he failed to account for changes in part-time or underemployed workers, like those on short time. In contrast, Hobsbawm estimated that between 30 and 75 percent might have been destitute in the course of the slump, and like other pessimists he gave attention to the debilitating effects of short time on earnings and consumption.[10] Revised estimates of short time and a reinterpretation of the new evidence in chapter 7 give little support to either view. Contrary to Williamson, short time was significant especially in the primary sector; contrary to Hobsbawm and others, short time was not always a sign of destitution. Undoubtedly, earnings of short-timers fell, but as evidenced by short time's popularity it also insured workers against arbitrary piece-rate cuts and provided them with long-term attachments. Thus, at large firms short time smoothed income and consumption flows over the life cycle, and it was the *absence* of short time that reduced lifetime earnings at smaller concerns.

The behavior of immigrant and rural migrant workers is closely related to the standard-of-living controversy and provides another research area in which the dual labor market hypothesis might prove to be instructive. Urban centers during the peak of the industrial revolution were well known for their bad housing, poor sanitation, and general squalor. The possibility of infrequent employment and low wages also dampened the experience of immigrants. Pollard attributed the flow of immigrants to their preference for employment possibilities. "People move, not so much for better-paid jobs, but for jobs," and that "many migrants did not even come for jobs, but for the expected opportunity of finding jobs."[11] Pollard's reasoning can be formalized in the popular Todaro model which assumes that favored jobs are allocated by lottery, and that the potential immigrant calculates the expected value of the job, and compares it with the certain employment in the rural sector. In Todaro's words, "as long as the urban–rural [wage gap] continues to rise sufficiently to offset any sustained increase in the rate of job creation, then the lure of relatively high permanent incomes will continue to attract a steady stream of rural migrants into the ever more congested urban slums."[12] The Pollard–Todaro model makes straightforward predictions, among others, that immigrants will earn lower incomes than non-immigrants, the latter having first claim on the better jobs; and that immigrants should cluster in the low-wage–high-unemployment sector.

To many analysts, this model of migration is an incomplete explanation. Do immigrants really desire low-wage jobs? For Britain, Williamson tested a Todaro-like model and found that its cities absorbed immigrants with considerable ease, and with the exception of the Irish, male immigrants into Britain's cities did not exhibit lower earnings than non-immigrants, and nor did they exhibit higher unemployment rates.[13] By his own admission, Williamson's results are speculative. His evidence is restricted to the census of 1851, and for this census year the enumerators had not asked how long an immigrant had been resident in the city; it is also difficult to estimate the earnings immediately following immigration. Despite these drawbacks, Williamson concluded that British cities could have absorbed more immigrants if it were not for imperfect factor markets. In particular, he isolated the failure of capital markets to invest in urban infrastructure. This view may be accurate in explaining why economic growth during the French Wars was delayed or slowed down by crowding-out of private investment in favor of government debt, but by 1850 this constraint was certainly less binding.

Bridging the Todaro model and Williamson's results, the findings in this book suggest an alternative approach to the migration puzzle. Williamson might be correct in that there was no a priori reason why immigrants could not take on spinning positions, as they surely did in the early years. But analyses of migration behavior need to consider that labor markets and structures evolve. As labor markets became integrated within the textile sector, it did not follow that they became more competitive. With the development in the 1830s of the fair wage policy, and the promotion of workers internally, favorable jobs were rationed, and as in the Todaro model it became less likely that immigrants held them. If immigrants could bid down wages, as Williamson implicitly assumes, their earning profiles would have matched non-immigrants. But like other workers, immigrants could not engage in this type of undercutting, and as a result they congregated in the secondary sector. In other words, immigrants did not hold false perceptions and their behavior was in no sense irrational; rather, it was the structure of the labor market and the fair wage that impeded them. If there had been greater opportunities or if expansion was quicker, more workers could have taken jobs at primary-sector wages. Thus, contrary to Williamson, insufficient demand might have been the culprit in the failure of urban Britain to absorb more immigrants.

In response to these claims, a skeptic might argue that the institutional features explicit in the dual labor market model simply mask the true or real labor market. Wages could reflect movements in shadow prices not easily identifiable, and there may be some margin left out of the analysis. In this view, for example, earnings of primary workers, after taking account of their extra effort, represented a compensating differential. This approach, of which Clark's statement of the role of unions and employers in wage determination described in chapter 8 is a classic example, is based on the conception that institutions are more or less unimportant to economic activity.

This line of reasoning is unsatisfactory. By narrowing choice, institutions shape economic decisions, and there are strong feedback mechanisms in the process. The institutional framework also helps explain why a certain set of rules gets adapted as opposed to another. "Labor markets," Gavin Wright observed, "can evolve in many different directions, but they cannot move in all directions at once."[14] Past decisions impact on future choices and decisions have different degrees of reversibility. The hiring of male workers on longer mules in the 1820s prevented a return to the high turnover and market reliance policies of the early decades; it also meant that technical change would move in the direction of adding more spindles, instead of throstle and ring spinning which were often performed by women. This does not imply, however, that labor-market development was unilinear. Another feature of institutions is that they provide a framework for learning processes on both sides of the market. In Lancashire, institutions that initially fixed piece rates and reduced the likelihood of broken commitments about pay and effort norms later gave rise to flexibility with favorable macroeconomic effects.

Persistent institutions and economic decline

If the standard-of-living controversy envelops historical research on the period before 1850, then the debate on the causes of British economic decline informs research on the last quarter of the nineteenth century. The debate remains prominent because of its implications for policy: was the slowdown in growth inevitable or could appropriate measures have been taken to stimulate economic performance? Owing to its place as the first factory industry, the cotton-textile industry has held center stage in the controversy.[15]

One view, which was popular with commentators in the 1920s and 1930s, was that institutions choked flexible responses by firms and workers, and as result, the industry could not compete internationally. Keynes, for example, condemned the widespread practice of short time.[16] For others, the regional piece-rate lists represented the institutional failure of the British textile industry.[17] They made the British textile industry uncompetitive because rates of pay were fixed like the elements in the periodic table; as a result, new technology could not be introduced without changing their basic makeup. These observers went on to argue that union intransigence and employer ignorance led to the adoption of and adherence to the lists.[18]

Why, then, did these institutions persist? Conventional economic theory does not offer much guidance on this problem. To some analysts, institutions are scrapped according to the principles of benefit–cost analysis.[19]

The conservative principle prevails so long as the overhead costs associated with a new institution are expected to be above those associated with an existing institution. Although this approach provides a reasonable analysis of origins, it leaves unexplained why so-called inefficient or suboptimal institutions survive.

The history of Lancashire institutions sheds some light on the issue of persistence, or what has been referred to as inertia. Without making any claims about optimality, far from impeding growth, structure in the labor market abetted productivity by raising levels of effort and putting an end to work stoppages. It might have been possible to alter the institutional framework if it had been legislated by a third party, as Polanyi and others have asserted, but structure in the industry was self-imposed, pre-dating factory legislation and the consolidation of trade union organizations. Once in place institutions could have been changed, but their legacy was a powerful one, since present and future choices were necessarily shaped by past decisions. To draw up a new set of arrangements would have entailed high costs in developing new reputations; it is also difficult to estimate the enforcement costs of the new arrangements.[20] Both parties had an incentive to keep arrangements intact and this meant adapting to structure or making incremental changes, rather than scrapping it entirely. To illustrate, whereas Bolton-style lists discouraged investment in new equipment, firms were not deterred from investing in older mules, because their work organization and method of pay were proven methods of raising productivity. The success of the wage lists lay in the ability of firms and workers to keep at bay the forces of competition and to enforce their codes of behavior through community associations that had a strong regional bases. The claim of many commentators that high labor costs embedded in the lists impeded the diffusion of the new ring-spinning technology has merit only insofar as it recognizes that the older technology had benefits that were difficult to relinquish.

To be sure, there were inherent flaws with the system as it developed. First, although the fine-spinning sector continued to expand, according to Jewkes and Gray, structure as embedded in the lists biased investment toward coarse spinning. This meant that British industry had to compete head on with low-wage producers like India and Japan. Second, structure reinforced the predisposition toward regional, and thereby vertical, specialization in spinning and weaving. Third, there were limits to institutional adaptation. Structure originated in a specific technological and workplace environment. Using the mule, spinners and minders exercised control over the effort and output of the team for which they received the benefits, but these institutions were not transferable across technologies. As long as spinners could expend more effort and get more work out of their assistants, the system worked well, but there were both physical and technical limits to this type of adaptation.[21] In sum, the system had its paradoxes: it promoted coarse spinning on self-acting mules, exactly the specialty and choice of technique that was steadily losing ground.

Having said this, there is a larger point to be made about institutional inertia. At some point, perhaps as late as the interwar years when Keynes admonished the industry about the persistence of short-time work, the effort-inducing capacity of Lancashire's institutions had clearly worn off. Even for the earlier period, there is little doubt that individual workers and firms could have done better by working full time or paying by a different list. The point is that institutions persisted well after firms and workers had exhausted all margins of exploitation, including physical capacities of expending more effort. Nevertheless, there was a lack of massive undercutting and the fair wage prevailed. "Tradition," the social historian John Walton has written, "should never be underestimated in Victorian Lancashire."[22] In time, norms of economic behavior became institutionalized or regularized, not only because the costs of enforcing these norms declined, but because both workers and firms acted according to tradition rather than analysis.[23] Each principal feared change. It was "when in Manchester do as the Mancunians do" – and this meant paying fair wages.

Notes

1 Introduction: the myth of the Lancashire labor market

1 Manufacturer Alexander Richmond's responses to the Parliamentary Select Committee on Artisans and Machinery: PP 1824 (51) V, 70.

2 The model is easily extended to the case of heterogeneous jobs and labor. See Kevin Lang, Jonathan S. Leonard, and David Lilien, "Labor Market Structure, Wages, and Unemployment," in Kevin Lang and Jonathan S. Leonard, eds., *Unemployment and the Structure of Labor Markets* (New York: Basil Blackwell, 1987), 2.

3 For a recent review of this literature, see N. Gregory Mankiw, "A Quick Refresher Course in Macroeconomics," *JEL* 28 (December 1990), 1645–60.

4 Jeffrey G. Williamson, *Did British Capitalism Breed Inequality?* (Boston: Allen and Unwin, 1985), 205.

5 Robert M. Solow, "On Theories of Unemployment," *AER* 70 (March 1980), 10.

6 A. W. Phillips, "The Relation Between Unemployment and the Rate of Change of Money Wage Rates in the United Kingdom, 1861–1957," *Economica* 25 (May 1958), 283–300.

7 Paul Samuelson and Robert M. Solow, "Analytic Aspects of Anti-Inflation Policy," *AER* 50 (May 1960), 177–94; also, Jeffrey Sachs, "The Changing Cyclical Behavior of Wages and Prices: 1890–1976," *AER* 70 (March 1980), 78–90. These and similar findings on increasing wage rigidity are still widely held. Commenting on the origins and demise of Keynesianism, Leonard Silk (*New York Times*, March 27, 1992, C2) wrote that before 1945 fiscal policy could work because "labor played a passive role in capitalism, gratefully taking whatever wages they could get. Governments could apply fiscal stimulus without worrying that it would kick off inflation while there were still workers looking for jobs."

8 Robert J. Gordon, "Why US Wage and Employment Behaviour Differs from that in Britain and Japan," *Economic Journal* 92 (March 1982), 37.

9 Karl Polanyi, *The Great Transformation* (Boston: Beacon Press, 1944), 102.

10 T. S. Ashton, *The Industrial Revolution, 1760–1830* (London: Oxford University Press, 1948), 87.

11 Eric J. Hobsbawm, *Labouring Men* (London: Weidenfeld and Nicolson, 1968), 347–50.

12 Edward P. Thompson, "The Moral Economy of the English Crowd in the Eighteenth Century," *P&P* 50 (February 1971), 76–136.

13 Patrick Joyce, *Work, Society, and Politics: The Culture of the Factory in Later Victorian England* (Brighton: University of Sussex Press, 1980). The quote at the end of the paragraph is from page 55.

14 Spinners were paid exclusively by the piece. Throughout I will refer to piece rates or rates of pay wherever appropriate to distinguish the method of pay from the ambiguous term "wages." Earnings refers to the piece rate multiplied by output. By fair wages I mean the combination of rates of pay and output that secured a fair day's pay for a fair day's work. Unless otherwise noted, earnings are reported on a weekly basis.

15 Of course it can be argued that the market is an institution in itself, but this is a subject well beyond the scope of this book. Instead my focus is on how one particular labor market evolved from the model found in a standard textbook.

16 The pathbreaking work was George Akerlof's: "The Market for 'Lemons': Quality Uncertainty and the Market Mechanism," *Quarterly Journal of Economics* 84 (August 1970), 488–500. Information problems are basic to the transactions-costs approach of Oliver E. Williamson, *The Economic Institutions of Capitalism: Firms, Markets, Relational Contracting* (New York: Free Press, 1985), and credit rationing models. On the latter, see Joseph E. Stiglitz and Andrew Weiss, "Credit Rationing in Markets with Imperfect Information," *AER* 71 (June 1981), 393–411.

17 This line of reasoning is elaborated in Samuel Bowles and Herbert Gintis, "The Revenge of Homo Economicus: Contested Exchange and the Revival of Political Economy," *Journal of Economic Perspectives* 7 (Winter 1993), 83–102.

18 Anthony O'Brien, "The Cyclical Sensitivity of Wages," *AER* 75 (December 1985), 1124–32; Steve G. Allen, "Changes in the Cyclical Sensitivity of Wages in the United States, 1891–1987," *AER* 82 (March 1992), 122–40; Christopher Hanes, "The Development of Nominal Wage Rigidity in the Late Nineteenth Century," *AER* 83 (September 1993), 732–56. For related studies, see Susan B. Carter and Richard Sutch, "Sticky Wages, Short Weeks, and Fairness: The Response of Connecticut Manufacturing Firms to the Depression of 1893–94," University of California Historical Labor Statistics Project, Working Paper no. 2, 1992; William A. Sundstrom, "Real Wages or Small Equilibrium Adjustments? Evidence from the Contraction of 1893," *EEH* 29 (October 1992), 430–56.

19 Richard Price, "The Labor Process and Labor History," *SH* 8 (January 1983), 57–73; Patrick Joyce, "Labour, Capital, and Compromise: A Response to Richard Price," *SH* 9 (January 1984), 67–76.

20 James A. Jaffe, *The Struggle for Market Power: Industrial Relations in the British Coal Industry, 1800–1840* (Cambridge: Cambridge University Press, 1991), 4.

21 William Lazonick, *Competitive Advantage on the Shop Floor* (Cambridge, Mass.: Harvard University Press, 1990).

22 Patrick Joyce, *Visions of the People: Industrial England and the Question of Class, 1848–1914* (Cambridge: Cambridge University Press, 1991).

23 Fustian was a mixture of linen warp (the hard yarn running lengthwise in a piece of woven cloth) and cotton weft (the soft yarn interlaced at right angles to the warp). Using cotton, the spinning wheel was incapable of making a strong warp. This description of the early history of cotton manufacture and technical and organizational change relies on A. P. Wadsworth and J. de L. Mann, *The Cotton Trade and Industrial Lancashire* (Manchester: Manchester University Press, 1931); and Maxine Berg, *The Age of Manufactures: Industry, Innovation, and Work in Britain, 1700–1820* (Oxford: Basil Blackwell, 1985).

24 Proto-industrialization in Lancashire is evaluated in John K. Walton, "Proto-industrialization and the First Industrial Revolution," in Pat Hudson, ed., *Regions and Industries: A Perspective on the Industrial Revolution in Britain* (Cambridge: Cambridge University Press, 1989), 41–68.

25 This paragraph is based on John S. Lyons, "Family Response to Economic Decline: Handloom Weavers in Early Nineteenth-Century Lancashire," *Research in Economic History* 12 (1989), 45–91; Richard Sutch, "All Things Reconsidered: The Life-Cycle Perspective and the Third Task of Economic History," *JEH* 51 (June 1991), 271–89.

26 Berg, *Age of Manufactures*, 158.

27 The classic statement on pre-industrial work habits is Edward P. Thompson, "Time, Work-Discipline, and Industrial Capitalism," *P&P* 38 (December 1967), 56–97. The quote is taken from page 73.

28 Robert J. Morris, *Class and Class Consciousness in the Industrial Revolution, 1780–1850* (London: MacMillan, 1979), 52; Mark Harrison, "The Ordering of the Urban Environment: Time, Work, and the Occurrence of Crowds, 1790–1835," *P&P* 110 (February 1986), 135; Gary Cross, ed., *Worktime and Industrialization: An International History* (Philadelphia: Temple University Press, 1988), especially his introduction and pages 5–7. See also the exchange between David S. Landes, "The Ordering of the Urban Environment: Time, Work, and the Occurrence of Crowds, 1790–1835," *P&P* 116 (August 1987), 192–99, and Mark Harrison, "A Rejoinder to David Landes," *P&P* 116 (August 1987), 199–206.

29 Adrian Randall, *Before the Luddites: Custom, Community, and Machinery in the English Woollen Industry, 1776–1809* (Cambridge: Cambridge University Press, 1991), 32. See also John Rule, *The Experience of Labour in Eighteenth-Century English Industry* (New York: St. Martin's Press, 1981), 194; Bob Bushaway, *By Rite: Custom, Ceremony, and Community in England* (London: Junction Books, 1982).

30 David Landes, *The Unbound Prometheus: Technological Change and Industrial Development in Western Europe from 1750 to the Present* (Cambridge: Cambridge University Press, 1969), 59–60; John Styles, "Embezzlement, Industry, and the Law in England, 1500–1800," in Maxine Berg, Pat Hudson,

and Michael Sonenscher, eds., *Manufacture in Town and Country Before the Factory, 1750–1900* (Cambridge: Cambridge University Press, 1983), 173–210; Lars Magnusson, "From Verlag to Factory: The Contest for Efficient Property Rights," in Bo Gustafsson, ed., *Power and Economic Institutions: Reinterpretations in Economic History* (London: Edward Elgar, 1991), 206–09.

31 With the addition of spindles, jennies were moved to factories and men began to operate them. It was claimed that their increased size required greater physical exertion, although women continued to operate them as well. Jenny mills survived into the nineteenth century, but they were surplanted by water-frame, and then mule-spinning, factories: Wadsworth and Mann, *Cotton Trade*, 481; Ivy Pinchbeck, *Women Workers and the Industrial Revolution* (London: Virago Press, 1980), 148; Neil J. Smelser, *Social Change in the Industrial Revolution: An Application of Theory to the Lancashire Cotton Industry, 1770–1840* (London: Routledge and Kegan Paul, 1959), 89–90.

32 S. D. Chapman, *The Cotton Industry in the Industrial Revolution*, 2nd edn. (London: MacMillan, 1987), 29.

33 Andrew Ure, *The Philosophy of Manufacturers* (London: Charles Knight, 1835), 15–16; R. S. Fitton, *The Arkwrights: Spinners of Fortune* (Manchester: Manchester University Press, 1989).

34 S. D. Chapman, "Introduction," in Gilbert French, *The Life and Times of Samuel Crompton* (Bath: Redwood Press, 1970), viii–ix.

35 S. D. Chapman, *Cotton Industry in the Industrial Revolution*, 29.

36 This description of mule spinning relies on Isaac Cohen, *American Management and British Labor: A Comparative Study of the Cotton-Spinning Industry* (New York: Greenwood Press, 1990), 31–32.

37 The automation of common-mule spinning is elaborated further in chapter 4.

38 Cohen, *American Management*, 14–15; Berg, *Age of Manufactures*, 235–46.

39 Frances Collier, *The Family Economy of the Working Classes in the Cotton Industry, 1784–1833* (Manchester: Manchester University Press, 1964), 17.

40 John Kennedy, "A Brief Memoir of Samuel Crompton, with a Description of His Machine Called the Mule and the Subsequent Improvement of the Machine by Others," *Memoirs of the Literary and Philosophical Society of Manchester* 5 (1831), 335–36; PP 1834 (167) XIX, D1, 167.

41 Michael Anderson, *Family Structure in Nineteenth-Century Lancashire* (Cambridge: Cambridge University Press, 1971), 37–38. For a study of Oldham, see Bryan Roberts, "Agrarian Organization and Urban Development," in J. O. Wirth and R. L. Jones, eds., *Manchester and Sao Paulo: Problems of Rapid Urban Growth* (Stanford: Stanford University Press, 1978), 85, 102. Census samples for Manchester, Bolton, and Oldham in 1851 reveal that most spinners were born in the towns in which they were working. Their average age was about thirty-five years.

42 Phyllis Deane, *The First Industrial Revolution* (Cambridge: Cambridge University Press, 1962), 97; Sidney Pollard, *The Genesis of Modern Management* (London: Edwin Arnold, 1965), 204; H. J. Habakkuk, *American and British Technology in the Nineteenth Century: The Search for Labor-Saving Inventions* (Cambridge: Cambridge University Press, 1962), 134.

43 Arthur M. Okun, *Prices and Quantities: A Macroeconomic Analysis* (Washington, D.C.: Brookings Institution, 1981), 62.

2 Custom against the market: the early labor market

1 "Journeyman Cotton Spinner," quoted in Robert G. Hall, "Tyranny, Work, and Politics: The 1818 Strike Wave in the English Cotton District," *International Review of Social History* 34, no. 3 (1989), 451.

2 C. H. Lee, *A Cotton Enterprise, 1795–1840: A History of M'Connel and Kennedy, Fine Cotton Spinners* (Manchester: Manchester University Press, 1972), 101–06, 162.

3 John L. Hammond and Barbara Hammond, *The Town Labourer, 1760–1830* (London: Longmans Green, 1917), 11; Lee, *Cotton Enterprise*, 114; see also R. S. Fitton and A. P. Wadsworth, *The Strutts and the Arkwrights, 1758–1830: A Study in the Early Factory System* (Manchester: Manchester University Press, 1958), 230.

4 Gavin Wright, "Cheap Labor and Southern Textiles Before 1880," *JEH* 39 (September 1979), 657.

5 "Different packages will attract different workers, and will have different implications for costs and productivity . . . The important point is that different packages will have different degrees of reversibility; hence the choice made at one point in time will continue to affect choices made in the future. It follows that to really understand labor arrangements of today, you have to know their history": Gavin Wright, "Labor History and Labor Economics," in Alexander J. Field, ed., *The Future of Economic History* (Boston: Kluwer, 1987), 323.

6 This paragraph relies on Michael Huberman, "Invisible Handshakes in Lancashire: Cotton Spinning in the First Half of the Nineteenth Century," *JEH* 46 (December 1986), 990–91. For Saint Monday, see sources cited in Hall, "Tyranny, Work, and Politics," 449; D. A. Reid, "The Decline of Saint Monday 1766–1876," *P&P* 71 (January 1976), 78.

7 Butterworth Diaries, 3 March 1834, Oldham Local Interest Centre; *MG*, 9 October 1824.

8 Some mill owners attributed irregular attendance and work habits to drinking on and off the job: Rowbottom Diaries, 21 October 1829, Oldham Local Interest Centre; PP 1816 (397) III, 472; PP 1833 (450) XX, D2, 126; PP 1833 (519) XXI, D2, 164; *MG*, 27 November 1824.

9 Michael Anderson, "Sociological History and the Working-Class Family: Smelser Revisited," *SH* 1 (October 1976), 325.

10 Angus B. Reach, *Manchester and the Textile Districts in 1849*, ed. C. Aspin (Rossendale: Helmshore Local History Society, 1972), 29–33, 110.

11 Anderson, *Family Structure*, 136–69.

12 During severe economic contractions poor relief restricted diets to the extent that some forms of physical relief work – like road work – could not be undertaken: David J. Oddy, "Urban Famine in Nineteenth-Century Britain: The Effect of the Lancashire Cotton Famine on Working-Class Diet and Health," *EHR* 36 (February 1983), 68–86. On the stigma effect, see L. Lynne Kiesling,

"Institutional Choice Matters: The Poor Law and Implicit Labor Contracts in Victorian Lancashire," *EEH* 33 (January 1996), 65–85. The introduction of the New Poor Law in 1834 made little difference to the pattern of behavior: John K. Walton, *Lancashire: A Social History, 1558–1939* (Manchester: Manchester University Press, 1987), 195. George Boyer (*An Economic History of the English Poor Law, 1750–1850* [Cambridge: Cambridge University Press, 1990], 233–65) has recently challenged the view that assistance was meager. Nevertheless, the overall impact of the poor law on labor-market decisions is ambiguous. The stigma effect raised the cost in going to the authorities; on the other hand, beginning in the 1830s or so, removal may not have been a threat, since an increasing number of spinners was born in Manchester. Because of these offsetting influences, I assume throughout this book that poor relief had a neutral effect on both suppliers and demanders of labor time. This might bias the case against my argument that spinners received pay premia, because if relief was substantial it would have lowered the cost of job loss, thereby raising the fair wage required to prevent workers from withholding effort. I discuss this further in chapter 6.

13 Boot found a lag of six weeks between becoming unemployed and receiving relief: H. M. Boot, "Unemployment and Poor Law Relief in Manchester, 1845–50," *SH* 15 (May 1990), 217–29.

14 Anderson, *Family Structure*, 163.

15 Rowbottom Diaries, 8 February 1827, 19 October 1829; *MG*, 26 November 1836.

16 On the role of reference groups, see William Brown and Keith Sisson, "The Use of Comparisons in Workplace Wage Determination," *British Journal of Industrial Relations* 13, no. 1 (1975), 23–51.

17 H. A. Turner, *Trade Union Growth, Structure, and Policy: A Comparative Study of the Cotton Unions in England* (Toronto: University of Toronto Press, 1962), 53–78; John Mason, "Mule Spinner Societies and the Early Federations," in Alan Fowler and Terry Wyke, eds., *The Barefoot Aristocrats: A History of the Amalgamated Association of Operative Cotton Spinners* (Littleborough: George Kelsall, 1987), 14–35.

18 Pollard, *Genesis of Management*, 38–47.

19 This is Fitton's assessment in *Arkwrights*, 151. Unless otherwise specified, quotes in this paragraph are from this source.

20 HL 1818 (90) XCVI, 192.

21 See Henry M'Connel's statement in PP 1833 (450) XX, E9. Also, Per Bolin-Hort, *Work, Family, and the State: Child Labour and the Organization of Production in the British Cotton Industry* (Lund, Sweden: Lund University Press, 1989), 37.

22 Wage data in this section are from George H. Wood, *The History of Wages in the Cotton Trade During the Past Hundred Years* (Manchester: Hughes, 1910), 14, 15, 28. These are nominal earnings. Prices fluctuated during this period and any real earnings estimates are sensitive to dates selected. Using Lindert and Williamson's northern urban cost-of-living series, prices fell by 18 percent from

1810 to 1820, but only by a little more than 8 percent between 1809 and 1819: Jeffrey G. Williamson, *Did British Capitalism Breed Inequality?*, 212.
23 Herman Freudenberger, Frances J. Mather, and Clark Nardinelli, "A New Look at the Early Factory Labor Force," *JEH* 44 (December 1984), 1089.
24 PP 1816 (397) III, 240–41, 261, 274–75.
25 In 1819 legislation prevented children between nine and sixteen years old from working more than twelve hours a day in cotton mills. The law was poorly enforced. Employers spread out the labor of children in shifts and parents underreported the ages of their children. For a recent assessment, see Gary Cross, *A Quest for Time: The Reduction of Work in Britain and France, 1840–1940* (Berkeley: University of California Press, 1989), 25–28. Further hour modifications were made in 1825 and 1831, and in the late 1830s and 1840s. I refer to this legislation in chapter 7.
26 Stephen A. Marglin, "What Do Bosses Do? The Origins and Functions of Hierarchy in Capitalist Production," *Review of Radical Political Economics* 6 (Summer 1974), 33–60.
27 David S. Landes, "What Do Bosses Really Do?," *JEH* 46 (September 1986), 585–624. For a reassessment of the Landes–Marglin debate, see Maxine Berg, "On the Origins of Capitalist Hierarchy," in Gustafsson, ed., *Power and Institutions*, 173–94.
28 As late as 1841, the average medium- and coarse-spinning firm (defined in this book as spinning counts below no. 60) employed 109 workers (N = 470); the average fine-spinning firm, 191 workers (N = 80); integrated, 349 (N = 32; there were few integrated mills in 1815); the average for the entire industry was 205 workers: Roger Lloyd-Jones and A. A. LeRoux, "The Size of Firms in the Cotton Industry: Manchester, 1815–41," *EHR* 33 (February 1980), 76; V. A. C. Gatrell, "Labour, Power, and the Size of Firms in Lancashire Cotton in the Second Quarter of the Nineteenth Century," *EHR* 30 (February 1977), 98.
29 Cohen, *American Management*, 31.
30 This section relies on Michael Huberman, "Industrial Relations and the Industrial Revolution: Evidence from M'Connel and Kennedy," *Business History Review* 65 (Summer 1991), 345–78. The archives of the firm have been widely consulted. See, among others, G. W. Daniels, *The Early English Cotton Industry* (Manchester: Manchester University Press, 1920); Roland Smith, "Manchester as a Centre for the Manufacture and Merchandising of Cotton Goods, 1820–30," *University of Birmingham Historical Journal* 4 (1953–54), 47–65; Collier, *Family Economy*. The most thorough account of the firm's activities is Lee's *Cotton Enterprise*. Despite the breadth of the secondary literature, the sources on production and industrial relations at the firm remain untapped.
31 In an early study of M&K, Daniels argued that it was a "typical cotton-spinning firm from that stage of the Industrial Revolution when the cotton industry was beginning its rise to prominence." In his recent study of capital formation, Richardson offered a more cautious view, but concluded that despite its size and specialty M&K was not unique: G. W. Daniels, "The Early Records of a Great Manchester Cotton-Spinning Firm," *Economic Journal* 25 (1915), 175;

Philip Richardson, "The Structure of Capital During the Industrial Revolution Revisited: Two Case Studies from the Cotton-Textile Industry," *EHR* 42 (November 1989), 502. The role of M&K is complicated since it combines elements of a representative and leading firm. After the strike of 1829, which I discuss in the next chapter, the firm, with a handful of other large Manchester fine-spinning firms, began to develop new strategies in the labor market that were eventually pursued by many other firms around 1850.

32 The evidence is from a comparison of the employment records of nine Manchester factories for 1818: HL 1818 (90) XCVI, Appendix.

33 This account is based on Lee, *Cotton Enterprise*, 10–90.

34 Fixed capital includes capital and stocks; total capital figures are net of credit outstanding: Richardson, "Structure of Capital," 499.

35 M&K Inventory Book, John Rylands Library, University of Manchester, Manchester; Lee, *Cotton Enterprise*, 162.

36 A comprehensive treatment of the early strikes and union formation can be found in Mason, "Mule Spinner Societies."

37 M&K Letter Books, 4 November 1811, 23 October 1813, 17 September 1818.

38 HL 1819 (24) CX, 237. If the exclusionary policies established by male spinning unions were indicative, then the threat of hiring women on small common mules, like those being used at M&K, was widespread. The strikes waged against the hiring of women in Scotland in 1811 and in Manchester in 1818 are further evidence that the threats of replacing men were often carried out.

39 John Sutcliffe, *A Treatise on Canals and Reservoirs* (Rochdale, 1816), 36.

40 "Certain large mills in 1818, like M'Connel and Kennedy, employed women and young boys on small mules": Hall, "Tyranny, Work, and Politics," 450. Hall cites statements of employers, overseers, and workers before the commissions on factory conditions.

41 R. G. Kirby and A. E. Musson, *The Voice of the People. John Doherty, 1798–1854: Trade Unionist, Radical, and Factory Reformer* (Manchester: Manchester University Press, 1975), 370; J. W. M'Connel, *A Century of Fine Spinning* (Manchester, 1906); see also Collier, *Family Economy*, 17.

42 Lee, *Cotton Enterprise*, 114; HL 1818 (90) XCVI, Appendix 6. The increase in the proportion of female workers was not the result of a decline in the number of male mechanics or engineers. Although after the turn of the century the firm stopped selling spinning mules, it retained mechanics and engineers to build and maintain its own increasing complement of machinery. In 1818 the firm employed about fourteen mechanics, and by the 1830s, about twenty. Source: M&K Deeds and Documents.

43 HL 1819 (24) CX, 342.

44 M&K Inventory Book.

45 Lazonick, *Competitive Advantage*, 83.

46 Based on a comparison of 1811 and 1817, for which data are available on wages and unit costs. With output increasing by about 25 percent, and with fixed costs about 20 percent of unit costs in 1811, unit costs would have fallen by 5 percent. The total wage bill fell by 10 percent, and with unit labor costs about 50 percent

of total costs in 1811, unit costs would have fallen by another 5 percent. Calculations were based on 1811 prices. Sources: cost estimates for 1811 from Kennedy's statement reproduced in Edward Baines, *History of the Cotton Manufacture of Great Britain* (London: Cass, 1835, reprinted in 1966), 353; wages: M&K Cash Ledger.

47 The equation *waste* = *a* + *b(count)* was estimated by ordinary least squares, using rates of change of monthly observations between 1810 and 1818 (N = 108). The regression was significant ($F = 7.05$) with an $R^2 = 0.108$. Regressions were also run for levels and logs of waste and count; the results did not alter significantly. Source: M&K Yarn Output Book.

48 If multiple end breakages were not pieced up, then the mule would have come to a complete stop. This "downtime" would have lowered productivity. The output growth in table 2.1 is thus net of downtime.

49 Statement before the factory commissioners cited in Cohen, *American Management*, 64.

50 The overlooker problem is examined in greater detail in chapter 4.

51 Lazonick, *Competitive Advantage*, 84–85. Lazonick's evidence is from the testimony of workers and overlookers in the *Reports of the Factory Commissions of 1833*. See also Pollard, *Genesis of Management*, 213–25.

52 Pinchbeck, *Women Workers*, 186; see also, Cohen, *American Management*, 63.

53 Wastage was about 6 percent of unit costs. (Waste comprised 20 percent of cotton costs, which in turn represented about 30 percent of all costs in 1811.)

54 Fitton, *Arkwrights*, 165. Fitton's evidence is from HL 1819 (24) CX, 436.

55 HL 1818 (90) XCVI, 177.

56 This section is an extension of Michael Huberman, "The Economic Origins of Paternalism: Lancashire Cotton Spinning in the First Half of the Nineteenth Century," *SH* 12 (May 1987), 177–93. For a critical response, see Mary Rose, Peter Taylor, and Michael J. Winstanley, "The Economic Origins of Paternalism: Some Objections," *SH* 14 (January 1989), 89–99. My reply is in the same issue, pages 99–103. Throughout this book I use the record books of the Gregs' and Ashworth's mills. They were large mills and in this respect unrepresentative, but their isolation and dependence on family units were characteristics of all rural sites. Their records are the most complete available.

57 For a comparative analysis of rural labor markets, see George Grantham, "Economic History and the History of Labor Markets," in George Grantham and Mary MacKinnon, eds., *Labour Market Evolution: The Economic History of Market Integration, Wage Flexibility and the Employment Relation* (London: Routledge, 1994), 1–26.

58 Collier, *Family Economy*, 45.

59 Arthur Redford, *Labour Migration in England, 1800–1850*, 2nd edn. (Manchester: Manchester University Press, 1964), 24.

60 This assessment is Mary Rose's, in *The Gregs of Quarry Bank Mill: The Rise and Decline of a Family Firm, 1750–1914* (Cambridge: Cambridge University Press, 1986), 31–33.

61 The Gregs' mills were an exception in hiring parish apprentices until the 1840s.

62 Many of the original parish apprentices had maintained residences around the mills and either retained employment or sent their children there: Redford, *Labour Migration*, 22–30.

63 Crompton's survey of 1811 reported that the number of spindles at Ashworth's mill was below the average of forty-one Bolton mills. As late as 1850, the average mule at the firm had 410 spindles; mules at M&K had reached this length in the 1820s, if not earlier: Redford, *Labour Migration*, 8, 74. This refutes the claim of Mary Rose, *et al.* ("Some Objections," 91), that rural and urban mills had machinery of the same size. As for kin relations, in rural areas around Preston in 1816, 24.5 percent of spinners worked with their children, whereas in the town of Preston it was only 11.6 percent: Michael M. Edwards and Roger Lloyd-Jones, "N. J. Smelser and the Cotton Factory Family: A Reassessment," in N. B. Harte and K. G. Ponting, eds., *Textile History and Economic History* (Manchester: Manchester University Press, 1973), 317–19.

64 Where there was an excess supply of male spinners, to keep the family unit intact the Ashworths found men "odd jobs in the mills, on roads, or in walling done by their sons, and family wages were credited to the father": Rhodes Boyson, *The Ashworth Cotton Enterprise: The Rise and Fall of a Family Firm, 1818–1880* (Oxford: Clarendon Press, 1970), 113–14. Mary Rose, *et al.* ("Some Objections," 91), wrote the "Ashworths boasted that no women married to their employees worked in the mill," but this is only partially accurate. Boyson (*Ashworth*, 106) in his history of the firm observed that in the 1840s Ashworth employed married women at home in winding and repairing.

65 PP 1842 (31) XXII, 361.

66 For a selection of employment histories, see PP 1833 (519) XXI; PP 1834 (167) XIX; Mary Rose, *Gregs*, 78–79.

67 On labor-market integration, see John C. Brown, "The Condition of England and the Standard of Living: Cotton Textiles in the Northwest, 1806–1850," *JEH* 50 (March 1990), 591–614.

68 Keijoru Otsuka, Hiroyuki Chuma, and Yujiro Hayami, "Land and Labor Contracts in Agrarian Economies," *JEL* 30 (December 1992), 1976.

69 Boyson, *Ashworth*, 107.

70 "Stiff penalties for exit are among the main devices generating or reinforcing loyalty in such a way as to repress either exit or voice or both": Albert Hirschman, *Exit, Voice, Loyalty* (Cambridge, Mass.: Harvard University Press, 1970), 93.

71 Mary Rose, *Gregs*, 105, 117.

72 Boyson, *Ashworth*, 102.

73 Richard Bendix, *Work and Authority in Industry* (New York: MacMillan, 1956), 16. On the general failure of paternalism in urban Lancashire, see Walton, *Lancashire*, 133. See also H. I. Dutton and J. E. King, "The Limits of Paternalism," *SH* 7 (January 1982), 59–73; for a review, see Mary Rose, "Paternalism, Industrial Welfare, and Business Strategy: Britain to 1939," in Erik Aerts *et al.*, eds., *Liberalism and Paternalism in the Nineteenth Century* (Leuven, Belgium: Leuven University Press, 1990).

74 Mary Rose, *Gregs*, 103.

3 Principals and agents: the labor market into the second generation

1 Donald Roy, "Quota Restriction and Goldbricking in a Machine Shop," *American Journal of Sociology* 57 (March 1952), 427–42.
2 Joseph E. Stiglitz, "Incentives, Risk, and Information: Notes Toward a Theory of Hierarchy," *Bell Journal of Economics and Management Science* 6 (Autumn 1975), 552–79.
3 Armen Alchian and Harold Demsetz, "Production, Information Costs, and Economic Organization," *AER* 62 (December 1972), 177–95.
4 For a model of this type, see Robert Gibbons, "Piece Rate Incentive Schemes," *JOLE* 5 (October 1987), 413–29.
5 Oliver Williamson, *Economic Institutions of Capitalism*, 262.
6 J. M. Malcolmson, "Efficient Labour Organization: Incentives, Power, and the Transaction Cost Approach," in F. J. Stephen, ed., *Firms, Organization, and Labour* (London: MacMillan, 1984), 120.
7 This section relies on Huberman, "Industrial Relations."
8 In the 1820s mules were built with 600 spindles, and by the late 1830s, 1,200: M&K Inventory Book.
9 Thomas Ellison, *The Cotton Trade of Great Britain* (London, 1886), 32.
10 HL 1818 (90) XCVI, Appendix 6; M&K Deeds and Documents.
11 On unions, see Turner, *Trade Union Growth*, 114, 128; and Sonya O. Rose, "Gender Antagonism and Class Conflict: Exclusionary Strategies of Male Trade Unionists in Nineteenth-Century Britain," *SH* 13 (January 1988), 191–208. On ideology, see Marianna Valverde, "Giving the Female a Domestic Turn: The Social, Legal, and Moral Regulation of Women's Work in British Cotton Mills, 1820–1850," *Journal of Social History* 21 (Summer 1988), 619–34. On physical abilities, see Lazonick, *Competitive Advantage*, 82–84; and S. J. Chapman, *The Lancashire Cotton Industry: A Study in Economic Development* (Manchester: Manchester University Press, 1904), 59. On supervision, see Lazonick, *Competitive Advantage*, 84–93; and Isaac Cohen, "Workers' Control in the Cotton Industry: A Comparative Study of British and American Mule Spinning," *Labor History* 26 (Winter 1985), 72. For a survey of different views, see Mary Freifeld, "Technological Change and the Self-Acting Mule: A Study of Skill and Sexual Division of Labour," *SH* 11 (October 1986), 319–43. Freifeld is concerned with the transition from common-mule to self-actor spinning, but her argument that there was a failure to transfer skills across generations of women has been criticized by Lazonick, *Competitive Advantage*, 90–93, and Cohen, *American Management*, 187–88.
12 Between 1818 and 1838 the proportion of young males aged thirteen to twenty at M&K rose from 14 percent to 24.3 percent: M&K Deeds and Documents.
13 Wayne Lewchuk, "Men and Monotony: Fraternalism as a Managerial Strategy in the Ford Motor Company," *JEH* 53 (December 1993), 824–25.
14 Contemporary definitions of skill were highly variable. While some authorities maintained that a worker needed three to seven years of training, others claimed that it could take as little as three months: cited in David Jeremy, *Transatlantic Industrial Revolution: The Diffusion of Textile Technologies*

Between Britain and America, 1790–1830s (Cambridge, Mass.: MIT Press, 1981), 30; Cohen, *American Management*, 32. On the endogeneity of skill in spinning, the classic statement is Turner, *Trade Union Growth*, 114.

15 Lazonick, *Competitive Advantage*, 84.

16 Quoted in Lazonick, *Competitive Advantage*, 86.

17 Sonya O. Rose, *Limited Livelihoods: Gender and Class in Nineteenth-Century England* (Berkeley: University of California Press, 1992), 27.

18 With the introduction of longer mules, spinners preferred to hire boys as piecers, because they would have to occasionally push the heavy carriages: Cohen, *American Management*, 67. The hiring of more male piecers limited women's access to spinning skills, thereby reducing further employers' incentives to hire them as spinners. Cf. Freifeld, "Technological Change."

19 Webb Collection, vol. XXXIV, 60.

20 Observing this restriction on internal mobility, M'Connel reported that the most valuable workers in his mill were those between eleven and eighteen years of age, although those over fifteen were most easily "disposed" of. M'Connel also concluded that there was a great abundance of workers over eighteen: PP 1833 (450) XX, E7.

21 John S. Lyons, "The Lancashire Textile Factory Sector and Occupational Mobility in the 1840s" (mimeograph, Miami University, Ohio, October 1991), 4.

22 For implicit contract models with observable states of the world, the standard works include Costas Azariadis, "Implicit Contracts with Underemployment Equilibria," *Journal of Political Economy* 83 (December 1975), 1183–1202, and D. F. Gordon, "A Neo-Classical Theory of Keynesian Unemployment," *Economic Inquiry* 12 (October 1974), 431–59.

23 For a discussion of these issues, see Jon Elster, *The Cement of Society: Studies in Rationality and Social Change* (New York: Cambridge University Press, 1989), 80–81.

24 For an implicit contract model where workers cannot observe whether managers are telling the truth about the state of the world, see Sanford Grossman and Oliver Hart, "Implicit Contracts, Moral Hazard, and Unemployment," *AER* 71 (March 1981), 301–07.

25 Cited in Neville Kirk, *The Growth of Working-Class Reformism in Mid-Victorian England* (Champaign: University of Illinois Press, 1985), 253.

26 For evidence of maltreatment, see PP 1833 (450) XX, D1, 688; PP 1833 (519) XXI, D2, 191, 194; Cohen, *American Management*, 64. Shuttleworth's survey recorded the percentage of spinners who inflicted punishment. At M&K 63 percent of spinners maltreated their piecers, but the average at nineteen spinning firms surveyed was 48 percent: John Shuttleworth, "Vital Statistics of Piecers and Spinners Employed in the Fine-Spinning Mills of Manchester," *Journal of the Royal Statistical Society* 5 (1842), 273.

27 Eric Seiler, "Piece Rate vs. Time Rate: The Effect of Incentives on Earnings," *Review of Economics and Statistics* 66 (August 1984), 363–75.

28 Note that in 1822 and 1824 high wastage rates were offset by high levels of productivity.

29 Lee, *Cotton Enterprise*, 133–45.
30 Landes, "What Do Bosses Really Do?," 586–96.
31 "The maximization of production and also of productive capacity represented the appropriate business strategy": C. H. Lee, "The Cotton-Textile Industry," in Roy Church, ed., *The Dynamics of Victorian Business* (London: Allen and Unwin, 1980), 170–71.
32 An examination of local newspapers and other contemporary accounts confirmed that there were no protracted stoppages at M&K or at neighborhood firms.
33 See chapter 5 and Thorstein Veblen, *The Engineers and the Price System* (New York: Huebsch, 1922).
34 Gibbons, "Piece Rate Incentive Schemes."
35 David M. Kreps and Robert Wilson, "Sequential Equilibria," *Econometrica* 50 (July 1982), 863. This framework is used in Wayne Lewchuk, *American Technology and the British Vehicle Industry* (Cambridge: Cambridge University Press, 1987), 30–32.
36 Robert Wilson, "Reputations in Games and Markets," in Alvin E. Roth, ed., *Game Theoretic Models of Bargaining* (Cambridge: Cambridge University Press, 1985), 27–63. Also, Robert Gibbons, *Game Theory for Applied Economists* (Princeton: Princeton University Press, 1992), 224–31; Eric Rasmusen, *Games and Information: An Introduction to Game Theory* (Oxford: Basil Blackwell, 1989), 118–20.
37 Craig Calhoun, *The Question of Class Struggle: Social Foundations of Popular Radicalism During the Industrial Revolution* (Chicago: University of Chicago Press, 1982); John Foster, *Class Struggle and the Industrial Revolution* (London: Methuen, 1974).
38 Wadsworth and Mann, *Cotton Trade*, 277. On the social origins of the first factory masters, see Katrina Honeyman, *Origins of Enterprise: Business Leadership in the Industrial Revolution* (Manchester: Manchester University Press, 1982).
39 This is known as the ratchet effect. See Yoshitsugu Kanemoto and W. Bentley MacLeod, "The Ratchet Effect and the Market for Secondhand Workers," *JOLE* 10 (January 1992), 85–98.
40 PP 1833 (450) XX, D2, 6; see also, HL 1818 (90) XCVI, 187.
41 Wilson, "Reputations in Games," 37.
42 After his death it was discovered that Picasso had kept much of his art in his attic.
43 This paragraph relies on the model of David I. Levine, "Piece Rates, Output Restriction, and Conformism," *Journal of Economic Psychology* 13 (September 1992), 473–89. Levine models the stigma of breaking rank. For a model of conformism in which workers dislike being different, see Stephen R. G. Jones, *The Economics of Conformism* (Oxford: Oxford University Press, 1984). In contrast to Levine, Jones ignored the effects of an individual's decision on the effort chosen by co-workers. See also Wayne Lewchuk, "Giving and Getting the Wrong Signals: Institutions, Technical Change, and the Decline of British Productivity Since 1850," *Business and Economic History* 20 (1991), 77–89.

44 Melville Dalton, "The Industrial 'Rate-Buster': A Characterization," *Applied Anthropology* 7 (Winter 1948), 5–18; Roy, "Quota Restriction."

45 See Levine, "Piece Rates." Dalton found that ratebusters had a low responsiveness to group pressures. Most of the ratebusters in his study came from different backgrounds than the average worker, and they were engaged in few common social activities.

46 Quoted in H. I. Dutton and J. E. King, *Ten Percent and No Surrender: The Preston Strike, 1853–54* (Cambridge: Cambridge University Press, 1981), 204; see also selections in the newspaper *Voice of the People*, 1831–32.

47 Douglas D. Heckathorn, "Collective Action and the Second-Order Free-Rider Problem," *Rationality and Society* 1 (July 1989), 78–101; Gary J. Miller, *The Political Economy of Hierarchy* (Cambridge: Cambridge University Press, 1992), 204–06.

48 The phrase is Veblen's, in *Engineers and the Price System*. This section differs in approach from Michael Huberman, "Testing for the 'Conscientious Withdrawal of Efficiency': Evidence from the Industrial Revolution," *Historical Methods* 26 (Summer 1993), 119–25.

49 Dalton studied skilled machinists in a large mid-western US manufacturing plant during 1942–45; Roy reported on machine-shop workers in the same region in 1944.

50 For evidence on the retention of mules by spinners, see Ure, *Philosophy*, 366; Harold J. Catling, *The Self-Acting Mule* (Newton Abbot: David and Charles, 1970), 149. The turnover assumption is not restrictive. The norm would be upheld even if individual spinners were replaced.

51 Other specifications of the dependent variable were estimated but the results did not differ greatly.

52 Hobsbawm, *Labouring Men*, 347–50.

4 Who's minding the mill? The supervision problem

1 Anonymous, *Lectures on Cotton Spinning* (Bolton, 1901), 60–61.

2 Thomas E. Weisskopf, David M. Gordon, and Samuel Bowles, "Hearts and Minds: A Social Model of US Productivity Growth," *Brookings Paper on Economic Activity*, no. 2 (1983), 381–450.

3 The quote is from PP 1833 (519) XXI, D1, 53. The other references are from HL 1818 (90) XCVI, 160, 192; HL 1819 (24) CX, 353; PP 1831–32 (706) XV, 75; PP 1833 (450) XX, 52–53; PP 1840 (218) XXIII, 11.

4 Boulton and Watt also attempted to design work studies, but their experiments were not pursued and applied in cotton: Pollard, *Genesis of Management*, 225.

5 Maxine Berg, *The Machinery Question and the Making of Political Economy* (Cambridge: Cambridge University Press, 1980), 179–202.

6 The manuals have been previously examined by Hobsbawm, *Labouring Men*, 366; S. D. Chapman, "The Textile Industries," in G. Roderock and M. Stephens, eds., *Where Did We Go Wrong? Industrial Performance, Education, and the Economy in Victorian Britain* (Lewes, Sussex: Falconer Press, 1981), 125–38; Jeremy, *Transatlantic Industrial Revolution*, 1981), 72. A list of techni-

cal manuals is included in a separate section of the bibliography; it is not intended to be exhaustive.

7 Before the 1820s technical details published on spinning machinery were found only in Abraham Rees' *The Cyclopedia; or Universal Dictionary of Arts, Science, and Literature* (Newton Abbott: David and Charles, reprint of selected articles, 1972); Jeremy, *Transatlantic Industrial Revolution*, 68.

8 J. Holland, *Cotton Spinner's and Manager's Assistant* (Bolton, 1847), 2.

9 J. Montgomery, *Carding and Spinner Master's Assistant* (Glasgow, 1832), 219–20. Montgomery revised and enlarged this volume in 1836 under a new title, *The Theory and Practice of Cotton Spinning*.

10 These terms are S. D. Chapman's, "Textile Industries," 130.

11 R. Scott, *Scott's Practical Cotton Spinner and Manufacturer* (Manchester, 1851), iv.

12 J. Montgomery, *Cotton Spinners' Manual* (Glasgow, 1850), v.

13 W. S. Taggart, *Cotton Spinning* (London, 1907), xi.

14 Pollard, *Genesis of Management*, 10. The relation between scale and monitoring was a prominent theme in Charles Babbage's *On the Economy of Machinery and Manufactures* (London, 1835). Gatrell ("Labour, Power," 96–97, 106) also observed the managerial constraint. Although he did not give the size of firm affected, based on the persistence of small and medium-sized establishments it can be inferred that the constraint took hold where 300 or more workers were employed. For modern treatments of the relation between size of establishment and monitoring, see George Stigler, "Information in the Labor Market," *Journal of Political Economy* 70 (October 1962), 94s–105s; Walter Oi, "Heterogeneous Firms and the Organization of Production," *Economic Inquiry* 21 (April 1983), 147–72; William A. Sundstrom, "Internal Labor Markets Before World War I: On-the-Job Training and Employee Promotion," *EEH* 25 (October 1988), 424–45.

15 The quote is from Sutcliffe, *Treatise on Canals*, 10. For other references on the association between size and monitoring, see HL 1819 (24) CX, 435; PP 1833 (519) XXI, D1, 76.

16 Quoted in S. D. Chapman, *Cotton Industry in the Industrial Revolution*, 48.

17 Cited in Clive Behagg, "Controlling the Product: Work, Time, and the Early Industrial Workforce in Britain, 1800–1850," in Cross, *Worktime and Industrialization*, 46–47.

18 Technical progress was more rapid in fine than in coarse spinning because mule speeds were slower and the weight of the carriage significantly less: PP 1834 (167) XIX, 383.

19 G. N. von Tunzelmann, *Steam Power and British Industrialization to 1860* (Oxford: Oxford University Press, 1978), 184.

20 Between 1815 and 1841 the median firm size in Manchester was between 351 to 400 workers. Firm sizes for Manchester can be found in Lloyd-Jones and LeRoux, "Size of Firms"; for Bolton, see James Longworth, *The Cotton Mills of Bolton* (Bolton: Bolton Museum and Art Gallery, 1987), 31; for the 1841 average, see PP 1842 (31) XXII.

21 John Pencavel, "Work Effort, On-the-Job Screening, and Alternative Methods

of Remuneration," in Ronald G. Ehrenberg, ed., *Research in Labor Economics*, vol. I (Greenwich, Conn.: Jai Press, 1977), 233.

22 For 1811 figures, see G. W. Daniels, "Samuel Crompton's Census of the Cotton Industry in 1811," *Economic Journal* (*Economic History Supplement*) 2 (1930), 12–18; for 1841 figures, see PP 1842 (31) XXII.

23 Dutton and King, *Ten Percent*, 10.

24 I wish to thank an anonymous referee for providing me with this information.

25 Dutton and King, *Ten Percent*, 77.

26 Anthony Howe, *The Cotton Masters, 1830–1860* (Oxford: Clarendon Press, 1984), 27; see also S. D. Chapman, "Financial Restraints on the Growth of Firms in the Cotton Industry, 1790–1850," *EHR* 32 (February 1979), 50–70.

27 Dutton and King, "Limits of Paternalism," 62, 66.

28 Joyce, *Work, Society, Politics*, 13. See also Howe, *Cotton Masters*, 91–92.

29 Dutton and King, *Ten Percent*, 86.

30 Quoted in Dutton and King, *Ten Percent*, 21.

31 For 1816 figures, see PP 1816 (397) III, 499; for 1841 figures, see PP 1842 (31) XXII. Unless noted otherwise, all references to 1816 and 1841 in this section are from these sources.

32 Horner's 1841 survey reported that 41 percent of Preston spinning firms also wove yarn; the figure for Bolton was 27 percent; Manchester, 38 percent; and Oldham, 32 percent.

33 The *Preston Chronicle* (28 January 1854) wrote that "Preston has always had a larger agricultural district in its immediate neighbourhood than either Bolton, Blackburn or Manchester, from which to import labour." The article in which this quote appeared is found in the Horrockses Papers, Lancashire Record Office, Preston, DDH 75.

34 James Lowe, "Account of the Strike and Lock-Out in the Cotton Trade at Preston in 1853," in National Association for the Promotion of Social Science, *Trades' Societies and Strikes* (London: National Association for the Promotion of Social Science, 1860), 207.

35 See chapter 2, note 23.

36 Michael Savage, *The Dynamics of Working-Class Politics: The Labour Movement in Preston* (Cambridge: Cambridge University Press, 1987), 69.

37 Population movements are discussed in chapter 8.

38 Anderson, *Family Structure*, 25.

39 The 1816 sample includes eleven mills from the neighborhood outside Preston.

40 The phrase is from Douglas A. Farnie, *The English Cotton Industry in the World Market* (Oxford: Oxford University Press, 1979), 246.

41 In 1811, the five largest mills (N = 33) housed 43 percent of all spindles (N = 306,770) in the town (Daniels, "Crompton's Census").

42 Gatrell, "Labour, Power," 96.

43 Howe, *Cotton Masters*, 165. On the Masters' Association, see Dutton and King, *Ten Percent*, 77–93. More general histories are Arthur J. McIvor, "Cotton Employers' Organisations and Labour Relations, 1890–1939," in J. A. Jowitt and A. J. McIvor, eds., *Employers and Labour in the English Textile Industries, 1850–1939* (London: Routledge, 1988); and Andrew Bullen,

"Pragmatism vs Principle: Cotton Employers and the Origins of an Industrial Relations System," in Jowitt and McIvor, *Employers and Labour*.

44 There were two significant exceptions: even though he was a fierce opponent of trade unions, John Goodair, whose mill ranked second in size to the Horrockses, did not join the association; another exception is Robert Gardner, who pioneered the short-time experiment described in chapter 7.

45 Dutton and King, *Ten Percent*, 180.

46 Howe, *Cotton Masters*, 166.

47 Bolin-Hort, *Work, Family*, 54. Bolin-Hort's account is based on his reading of the *Cotton Factory Times*.

48 Calculations based on disaggregated output for 1825. See chapter 6.

49 The industry total includes integrated (spinning and weaving) concerns but excludes specialized weaving firms: PP 1842 (31) XXII.

50 Ibid.

51 On the self-actor, see G. N. von Tunzelmann, "Time-Saving Technical Change: The Cotton Industry in the English Industrial Revolution," *EEH* 32 (January 1995), 1–28.

52 S. D. Chapman, *Cotton Industry in the Industrial Revolution*, 31; on energy prices, see von Tunzelmann, *Steam Power*.

53 Lazonick, *Competitive Advantage*, 88.

54 Joyce, *Work, Society, Politics*, 96–97. In the United States overlookers were used upon the introduction of the self-actor: Cohen, *American Management*, 127.

55 Lazonick, *Competitive Advantage*, 96–98; Cohen, *American Management*, 76–78.

56 Lazonick, *Competitive Advantage*, 98.

57 Anonymous, *Lectures on Cotton Spinning*, 60–61.

58 Peter Doeringer and Michael Piore, *Internal Labor Markets and Manpower Analysis* (Boston: D. C. Heath, 1971), 84.

59 Catling, *Self-Acting Mule*, 149.

60 Otsuka, Chuma, and Hayami, "Land and Labor Contracts," 1976.

61 For other examples of this response, see Yujiro Hayami and Masao Kikuchi, *Asian Village Economy at the Crossroads* (Baltimore: Johns Hopkins University Press, 1982), 218; Lee J. Alston and Joseph P. Ferrie, "Social Control and Labor Relations in the American South Before the Mechanization of the Cotton Harvest in the 1950s," *Journal of Institutional and Theoretical Economics* 145 (March 1989), 133–57.

62 Joyce, *Work, Society, Politics*, 121.

5   The fair wage model

1 Alfred Marshall, "A Fair Rate of Wages," in A. C. Pigou, ed., *Memorials of Alfred Marshall* (London: MacMillan, 1925), 213; quoted in Robert M. Solow, *The Labor Market as a Social Institution* (Oxford: Basil Blackwell, 1990), 16–17.

2 Otsuka, Chuma, and Hayami, "Land and Labor Contracts." For the macro-

economic implications of different payment schemes, see Martin Weitzman, *The Share Economy: Conquering Stagflation* (Cambridge, Mass.: Harvard University Press, 1984).

3 Edward Lazear, "Salaries and Piece Rates," *Journal of Business* 59, no. 3 (1986), 405–31; Eugene Fama, "Time, Salary, and Incentive Payoffs in Labor Contracts," *JOLE* 9 (January 1991), 25–44. For an earlier statement, see Stiglitz, "Incentives, Risk, and Information."

4 Charles Brown, "Firms' Choice of Method of Pay," *Industrial and Labor Relations Review* 43 (February 1990), 165s–82s; Seiler, "Piece Rate vs. Time Rate"; Pencavel, "Work Effort," 225–58.

5 Karl Marx, *Capital: Volume One* (New York: Vintage Books, 1977), 698.

6 Babbage, *Machinery and Manufactures*, 295.

7 There is a vast literature on Taylor. An excellent study is Daniel Nelson, *Frederick W. Taylor and the Rise of Scientific Management* (Madison: University of Wisconsin Press, 1980).

8 On the failure of scientific management in the textile industry, see John Singleton, *Lancashire on the Scrapheap: The Cotton Industry, 1945–1970* (Oxford: Oxford University Press, 1991), 66–88; for more general studies, see L. Urwick and E. F. L. Beach, *The Making of Scientific Management* (London: Pitman, 1963); Craig Littler, *The Development of the Labor Process in Capitalist Societies* (London: Heinemann, 1982).

9 This summary is based on Lewchuk, *American Technology*, 91.

10 Pencavel, "Work Effort," 233; Stiglitz, "Incentives, Risk, and Information," 558; Brown, "Firms' Choice of Method of Pay," 171s.

11 Richard Edwards, *Contested Terrain* (New York: Basic Books, 1979), 98–99.

12 For an excellent comparison and a bibliography of the two approaches, see Francis Green, "Neoclassical and Marxian Conceptions of Production," *Cambridge Journal of Economics* 12 (September 1988), 299–312.

13 H. Lorne Carmichael and W. Bentley MacLeod, "Worker Cooperation and the Ratchet Effect," paper prepared for a symposium at Osaka University, Japan, 1992.

14 David F. Schloss, *Methods of Industrial Remuneration* (Oxford: Williams and Norgate, 1898), 71–73. "Ca'canny" has been translated as "go easy"; "nibbling" refers to arbitrary rate changes and "the insidious process of continual petty reductions"; "chasing" denotes the practice of fixing the rate at a level set by exceptionally fast workers.

15 My emphasis. Mathewson recorded 223 instances of restriction in 105 establishments in 47 different locations: Stanley B. Mathewson, *Restriction of Output Among Unorganized Workers*, 2nd edn. (Carbondale: Southern Illinois University Press, 1969).

16 Richard Lansburg and William Spiegel, *Industrial Management*, 3rd edn. (New York: John Wiley, 1940); T. Lupton, *On the Shop Floor* (Oxford: Pergamon Press, 1963).

17 C. S. Myers, *Mind and Work* (London: University of London Press, 1920).

18 According to one authority, "deliberate restrictionism is still quite common in industry and rate cutting is often regarded as the greatest single cause of it":

R. P. Lynton, *Incentives and Management in British Industry* (London: Routledge & Kegan Paul, 1949); R. Marriot, *Incentive Payment Systems* (London: Staples Press, 1957).

19 S. J. Chapman observed the phenomenon of switching between piece and time payoffs in the 1880s: *Lancashire Cotton Industry*, 270.

20 Hicks wrote: "Different men cause all sorts of varying amounts of trouble to their employers; some are very 'reliable,' they are never very ill, never want a day off, are always content, and on good terms with the management. Others are always causing expensive temporary adjustments for such reasons. In all these ways there may be variations in efficiency, of which piece rates take no account, and indeed may make it more difficult to take account, since it is more difficult to pay more or less than standard piece rates than to vary from standard time-rates. The more obvious and easily accepted excuses are absent": *A Theory of Wages* (New York: St. Martin's Press, 1963), 40.

21 Pollard, *Genesis of Management*.

22 Gregory Clark, "Factory Discipline," *JEH* 54 (March 1994), 135.

23 PP 1833 (450) XX, 63–64; PP 1834 (167) XX, 168. Horner observed in 1851 that the proportion of piece work to fixed wages was "daily on the increase": cited in Geoff Brown, *Sabotage: A Study in Industrial Conflict* (Bristol: Spokesman Books, 1977), 83.

24 Carroll D. Wright, *Regulation and Restriction of Output: Eleventh Special Report of the Commissioner of Labor* (Washington, D. C.: Government Printing Office, 1904), 897.

25 Implicit contracting is discussed in chapter 3.

26 A variant of this approach is Lazear's solution (in "Salaries"), which models output restriction as a type of intertemporal strategic behavior. If workers know that tomorrow's rate is a function of today's output, it would seem that too little effort would be exerted in the current period. Assuming that there is some bonding mechanism that locks in workers, then there exists a two-period schedule with an inflated piece rate in the first period that offsets any deliberate attempts to restrict effort. Bonding is achieved and wages are freed to be used as a means to allocate labor. As in the auction model, they are set so that there are no unexploited wage bargains between the unemployed and firms. Lazear concluded: "All is efficient in equilibrium." The problem with this approach is that it assumes that workers will not or cannot quit.

27 Andrew Weiss, *Efficiency Wages: Models of Unemployment, Layoffs, and Wage Dispersion* (Princeton, N. J.: Princeton University Press, 1990), 8.

28 Webb Collection, vol. XXXIV, 60.

29 An extension of the apprenticeship-type bonding model was proposed by Kanemoto and MacLeod ("Ratchet Effect"). They argued that piece-rate contracts will be efficient if there exists an active market for second-hand workers. Competition will guarantee that workers' alternatives depend on their abilities. This approach assumes that firm-specific investments are low; their examples are agricultural work and retail sales.

30 Human capital and tournament models are discussed further in chapter 6. On tournaments, see Edward Lazear and Sherwin Rosen, "Rank Order

Tournaments as Optimum Labor Contracts," *Journal of Political Economy* 89 (1981), 841–64.
31 A. W. Coats, "Changing Attitudes to Labour in the Mid-Eighteenth Century," *EHR* 11 (January 1958), 35–51.
32 Cited in Stephen A. Marglin, "Understanding Capitalism: Control Versus Efficiency," in Gustafsson, ed., *Power and Institutions*, 236.
33 Berg, *Machinery Question*, 122.
34 Harvey Leibenstein, *Economic Backwardness and Economic Growth* (New York: Wiley, 1957).
35 For evaluations of efficiency wage theory, see George A. Akerlof and Janet L. Yellen, *Efficiency Wage Models of the Labor Market* (Cambridge: Cambridge University Press, 1986); Lawrence F. Katz, "Efficiency Wage Theories: A Partial Evaluation," in *NBER Macroeconomics Annual 1986* (Cambridge: MIT Press, 1986); Weiss, *Efficiency Wages.*
36 Jeremy I. Bulow and Lawrence H. Summers, "A Theory of Dual Labor Markets with Application to Industrial Policy, Discrimination, and Keynesian Unemployment," *JOLE* 4 (July 1986), 376–414; Alan B. Kreuger and Lawrence H. Summers, "Efficiency Wages and the Interindustry Wage Structure," *Econometrica* 56 (March 1988), 259–93; James B. Rebitzer and Lowell J. Taylor, "A Model of Dual Labor Markets when Product Demand is Uncertain," *Quarterly Journal of Economics* 106 (November 1991), 1373–83.
37 This paragraph relies on Katz, "Efficiency Wage Theories," 238–39; Robert J. Gordon, "What is New-Keynesian Economics," *JEL* 28 (September 1990), 1157.
38 More precisely the solution is:

$$e'(w^*)w^*/e(w^*) = 1$$
$$\text{and } e(w^*)F'(e(w^*)L) = w^*.$$

39 This point is also made by Charles W. Calomiris and Christopher Hanes, "Historical Macroeconomics and American Macroeconomic History," National Bureau of Economic Research, Working Paper No. 4935, November 1994.
40 George A. Akerlof, "Labor Contracts as Partial Gift Exchange," *Quarterly Journal of Economics* 97 (November 1982), 543–69; Akerlof and Janet L. Yellen, "Fair Wage–Effort Hypothesis and Unemployment," *Quarterly Journal of Economics* 105 (May 1990), 255–83 (the citation in this paragraph is from 260–61); Akerlof and Yellen, "Fairness and Unemployment," *AER* 78 (May 1988), 44–49; for an assessment of other types of efficiency wage models for Lancashire, see Huberman, "How Did Labor Markets Work."
41 This section relies on Michael Huberman, "Piece Rates Reconsidered: The Case of Cotton," *Journal of Interdisciplinary History* 26 (Winter 1996), 393–417. The approach here follows Miller, *Economy of Hierarchy*, 111–14. The figure is from 114. For more general models in the same spirit, see Gibbons, *Game Theory*, 173–224; Rasmusen, *Games and Information*, 107–21.
42 Miller, *Economy of Hierarchy*, 186–87.
43 "Cooperative behavior in the finitely repeated prisoners' dilemma game

depends in a fragile way on the small chance that one player is committed to cooperation, in which case he will imitate this behavior even if he is not committed, and the other player will reciprocate": Wilson, "Reputations in Games," 59; on related issues, see David Kreps, *Game Theory and Economic Modelling* (Oxford: Clarendon Press, 1990).

44 Schloss, *Industrial Remuneration*, 73.

45 Charles W. Lytle, *Wage Incentive Methods: Their Selection, Installation, and Operation* (New York: Ronald Press, 1938), 166.

46 Miller, *Economy of Hierarchy*, 195.

47 William R. Leiserson, "The Workers' Reaction to Scientific Management," in Edward E. Hint, ed., *Scientific Management Since Taylor* (Easton, Penn.: Hive, 1972), 224.

48 The indifference and isoprofit curves have standard features. Workers dislike giving effort; revenue increases with effort but at declining rate. The diagram is from H. Lorne Carmichael, "Efficiency Wage Models of Unemployment – One View," *Economic Inquiry* 27 (April 1990), 275–76.

49 If wages are set higher than w^*, workers would prefer to give back some of the money or ask for a wage cut rather than provide more effort.

50 For a model of this type, see Nicholas Rowe, *Rules and Institutions* (Ann Arbor: University of Michigan Press, 1989), 103–36; Jules L. Coleman, Steven Maser, and Douglas Heckathorn, "Bargaining and Contract," in Kenneth J. Koford and Jeffrey B. Miller, eds., *Social Norms and Economic Institutions* (Ann Arbor: University of Michigan Press, 1991), 227–57.

51 Solow, *Labor Market as a Social Institution*.

52 For a treatment of these issues, see Paul R. Milgrom, Douglass C. North, and Barry W. Weingast, "The Role of Institutions in the Revival of Trade: The Law Merchant, Private Judges, and the Champagne Fairs," *Economics and Politics* 2 (1990), 1–23.

53 Robert Sugden, *The Economics of Rights, Co-operation, and Welfare* (Oxford: Basil Blackwell, 1986), 173.

54 Solow, *Labor Market as a Social Institution*, 43. See also Andrew Schotter, *The Economic Theory of Social Institutions* (New York: Cambridge University Press, 1981); Schotter, "The Evolution of Rules," in Richard N. Langlois, ed., *Economics as a Process: Essays in the New Institutional Economics* (Cambridge: Cambridge University Press, 1986). In Schotter's view social institutions are optimal, a topic which is beyond the scope of this book. I have no evidence to suggest one set of institutions in Lancashire was superior to another. On norms and cooperation, see as well Cristina Bicherri, "Norms of Cooperation," *Ethics* 100 (July 1990), 838–61; Thrainn Eggerston, *Economic Behavior and Institutions* (New York: Cambridge University Press, 1990); Jack Knight, *Institutions and Social Conflict* (New York: Cambridge University Press, 1992). For a critical assessment of the new institutional economics and the optimality of social norms, see Elster, *Cement of Society*.

55 Ramana Ramaswamy and Robert E. Rowthorn, "Efficiency Wages and Wage Dispersion," *Economica* 58 (November 1991), 501–14.

56 This point is developed in Carl Shapiro and Joseph E. Stiglitz, "Equilibrium

Unemployment as a Worker Discipline Device," *AER* 74 (June 1984), 433–44; for an alternative bargaining model that generates a fixed wage based on a fair division of the surplus, see Ian M. McDonald and Robert M. Solow, "Wage Bargaining and Employment," *AER* 71 (December 1981), 896–908.

57 Equilibrium is thus achieved when unemployed workers are indifferent to accepting jobs at secondary firms, while workers at secondary firms are indifferent to unemployment. For an elaboration, see Huberman, "How Did Labor Markets Work," 96.

6 Fair and unfair wages: 1825–1850

1 Hicks, *Theory of Wages*, 318.
2 For empirical tests of efficiency wages, see Alan B. Kreuger and Lawrence H. Summers, "Reflections on the Inter-Industry Wage Structure," in Kevin Lang and Jonathan S. Leonard, eds., *Unemployment and the Structure of Labor Markets* (New York: Basil Blackwell, 1987); Jonathan S. Leonard, "Carrots and Sticks: Pay, Supervision, and Turnover," *JOLE* 5 (October 1987), 136s–53s; Peter Cappelli and Keith Chauvin, "An Interplant Test of the Efficiency Wage Hypothesis," *Quarterly Journal of Economics* 106 (August 1991), 769–87.
3 A good example is Daniel M. G. Raff and Lawrence H. Summers, "Did Henry Ford Pay Efficiency Wages?," *JOLE* 5 (October 1987), 57s–86s. See also Joel Mokyr, "Dear Labor, Cheap Labor, and the Industrial Revolution," in Patrice Higonnet *et al.*, eds., *Favorites of Fortune: Technology, Growth, and Economic Development Since the Industrial Revolution* (Cambridge, Mass.: Harvard University Press, 1991), 177–200.
4 Proceedings of the Manchester Chamber of Commerce, February 1826 and 1827.
5 There were twenty firms in the association. For a detailed study of the 1829 dispute, see Kirby and Musson, *Voice of the People*, 59–85.
6 M&K Letter Books, 17 October 1829.
7 The Bolton list is described in detail in chapter 8.
8 More exactly, discounts were applied of 1.5 percent for every twelve spindles over 300.
9 On the relation between the lists and customary or fair rates of pay, see J. W. F. Rowe, *Wages in Practice and Theory* (London: George Routledge, 1928), 153–57.
10 In his study of Lancashire firms, Anthony Howe observed that by 1830 large employers formed a cohesive group. "The economic and social mobility of 'from clogs to clogs' had given way to relatively stable family firms, the nucleus of the industry. Small firms remained economically viable and small men could rise, but the distinctive 'cotton lords' were the owners and inheritors of sizable family firms": Howe, *Cotton Masters*, 31.
11 See chapter 3.
12 PP 1833 (519) XXI, 165; see also *MG*, 29 February 1831.

13 M&K Letter Books, 28 October 1830.
14 Lee, *Cotton Enterprise*, 133–44.
15 John S. Lyons, "Vertical Integration in the British Cotton Industry, 1825–1850: A Revision," *JEH* 45 (March 1985), 421.
16 Ure, *Philosophy*, 366.
17 Joyce, *Visions of the People*, 110; the quote is from PP 1833 (450) XX, D177.
18 Quoted in Cohen, *American Management*, 190. Nor was the honorable employer confined to textiles. See Joyce, *Visions of the People*, 117.
19 Earnings declined in the 1840s but this was a result of short-time work. See chapter 7.
20 PP 1833 (519) XXI, 165; *MG*, 29 February 1831.
21 *MG*, 6 February 1830; *Poor Man's Advocate*, January and February 1832.
22 Kirby and Musson, *Voice of the People*, 109.
23 Joyce, *Visions of the People*, 111.
24 H. M. Boot, "How Skilled Were Lancashire Cotton Factory Workers in 1833?," *EHR* 48 (May 1995), 283–303.
25 PP 1833 (450) XX, E8. Tenure is discussed in more detail in chapter 7.
26 This account is from *The Economist*, 4 March 1848, 257.
27 Kirby and Musson (*Voice of the People*) reported a similar phenomenon in the 1830s in Manchester where earnings kept rising despite falling or constant piece rates.
28 PP 1833 (690) VI, 315. For an almost identical statement, see Okun, *Prices and Quantities*, 74.
29 The standard works on handloom weavers are Duncan Bythell, *The Handloom Weavers* (Cambridge: Cambridge University Press, 1969), and Lyons, "Family Response," 45–91.
30 For detailed records of piece rates in handloom weaving, see John S. Lyons, "The Lancashire Cotton Industry and the Introduction of the Powerloom, 1815–50," Ph.D. dissertation, University of California, Berkeley, 1977, 239–49.
31 Throughout, all d refer to old pence.
32 Nominal earnings of mule spinners are from Mary Rose, *Gregs*, 116. To find the real wage gap, I have added to rural wages a 10 percent premium for cost of living and a 25 percent premium for urban disamenities. (Figures are from Jeffrey G. Williamson, *Coping with City Growth During the British Industrial Revolution* [Cambridge: Cambridge University Press, 1990] 189, 191.) Corrected rural earnings were, therefore, about 189d per week, or 39d less than Manchester earnings. The gap was adjusted for rents which were on average 21d per week at Styal (Mary Rose, *Gregs*, 117) and 35d in Manchester (Williamson, *City Growth*, 241), leaving an unexplained gap of 25d.
33 Ibid., 194.
34 The mill was only stopped once, in 1842, by industrial action: Mary Rose, *Gregs*, 117–19.
35 W. R. Greg, "The Relation Between Employers and Employed," in Greg, *Essays on Political and Social Science* (Manchester, 1853), 287. The quote at the end of the section is from the same page.

36 Boyson, *Ashworth*, 103.
37 Since Ashworth's spun fine yarn, the appropriate benchmark is the upper wage of Bolton spinners: Wood, *History of Wages*, 58.
38 According to the wage books of the firm, fines and deductions often amounted to 13 percent of wages paid: ibid., 112. Fines of this magnitude were rare at urban mills.
39 Boyson, *Ashworth*, 109.
40 Ibid., 148–49.
41 Joyce referred to the relation between employers and workers as "paternalistic." He did not distinguish between urban and rural sites. I have argued that Joyce underestimated the economic aspects of paternalism, and there were substantive differences in relationships between workers and firms in urban and rural regions (see Huberman, "Economic Origins of Paternalism: Lancashire Cotton Spinning"). For another critical statement, see Mary Rose, "Paternalism."
42 Joyce, *Work, Society, Politics*, 161; for similar statements, see Farnie, *English Cotton Industry*, 211; Robert Gray, "The Languages of Factory Reform in Britain, c. 1830–1860," in Patrick Joyce, ed., *The Historical Meanings of Work* (Cambridge: Cambridge University Press, 1987), 142–43; Howard P. Marvel, "Factory Regulation: A Reinterpretation of Early English Experience," *Journal of Law and Economics* 20 (October 1977), 402; Clark Nardinelli, "The Successful Prosecution of the Factory Acts," *EHR* 38 (August 1985), 429.
43 D. A. Farnie, "The Emergence of Victorian Oldham as the Centre of the Cotton-Spinning Industry," *Bulletin of the Saddleworth Historical Society* 12 (Autumn 1982), 45; D. S. Gadian, "Class Consciousness in Oldham and Other North-West Industrial Towns," *Historical Journal* 21 (March 1978), 161–72.
44 Calhoun, *Question of Class Struggle*, 198.
45 Foster, *Class Struggle*, 49. To some analysts, Foster exaggerated the militancy of trade unions in Oldham. Mason ("Mule Spinner Societies") reported that Oldham unions were more volatile than those found in Bolton. The presence of unions in Oldham, combined with the town's lower wages, weakens the claim that wage levels across Lancashire were related primarily to trade union organization.
46 For a description of this survey, see Peter Temin, "Product Quality and Vertical Integration in the Early Cotton-Textile Industry," *JEH* 48 (December 1988), 891–907; Michael Huberman, "Vertical Disintegration in Lancashire: A Comment on Temin," *JEH* 50 (September 1990), 683–90.
47 Because some cells in table 6.5 have fewer than five firms, the test was conducted dividing the data into two groups: firms employing fewer than or exactly 150 workers and those above 150 (3 x 2 contingency table). The calculated statistic was $16.6 > X^2$ with 2 df (at the 0.005 level) = 10.6.
48 The result is (*t* statistics in parenthesis):

$$ln\ (wage) = 3.25 \ + \ .0233\ ln\ (size) + .0012\ ln\ (count)$$
$$(2.451)\ (4.511) \qquad\qquad (1.110)$$
$$N = 159\ R^2 = 0.12\ F\ test = 5.35\ DW = 1.87.$$

49 Overlookers' earnings in table 6.5 are for supervising women and young children in preparatory departments. In Oldham the average piecer wages in 1833 were 6s 2d, and in 1841, 7s; the corresponding figures for Bolton are 4s 8d and 9s. Source: Wood, *History of Wages*, 46, 58.

50 Akerlof and Yellen, "Fairness," 44–49. Not only were wages higher, but some of Wood's evidence points to a narrower wage dispersion in large firms. Cohesiveness of this type can also generate additional increases in individual output: David I. Levine, "Cohesiveness, Productivity, and Wage Dispersion," *Journal of Economic Behavior and Organization* 15 (1991), 237–57.

51 Maxine Berg, Pat Hudson, and Michael Sonenscher, "Introduction," in Berg, Hudson, and Sonenscher, eds., *Manufacture in Town and Country Before the Factory, 1750–1900* (Cambridge: Cambridge University Press, 1983), 6.

52 Wood's working papers and personal library are collected at the University of Huddersfield (formerly the Huddersfield Polytechnic) Library. There are more than 6,000 items in the collection, most of which deal with earnings and methods of remuneration. Volumes CB 76–84 contain the notes and sources consulted in preparation for his *History of Wages*. Wood frequently commented on the poor quality of the data, but they remain the best available.

53 I also assume the standard practice of quick conversion of cotton into yarn: Farnie, *English Cotton Industry*, 59. This section relies on Huberman, "How Did Labor Markets Work."

54 For marketing and technical reasons most firms did not substantially alter their production ranges, at least over the business cycle. The average coarse spinner produced a range of twenty to thirty counts: R. H. Baird, *The American Cotton Spinner and Managers' and Carders' Guide* (Philadelphia, 1851), 171; A. Kennedy, *Practical Cotton Spinner* (Glasgow, 1845), 98. Fine spinners produced a wider range, nos. 80–200 in the case of M&K, but these were all extremely fine counts which used the same inputs and were sold in the same markets.

55 Peter Gaskell, *Artisans and Machinery* (London: Parker, 1836), 394.

56 I use Ellison's aggregate series corrected by Lyons, "Lancashire Cotton," 143.

57 R. C. O. Matthews, *A Study in Trade Cycle History: Economic Fluctuations in Great Britain, 1833–42* (Cambridge: Cambridge University Press, 1954), 138–39.

58 J. R. T. Hughes, *Fluctuations in Trade, Industry, and Finance* (Oxford: Clarendon Press, 1960), 90; Turner, *Trade Union Growth*, 372.

59 Ellison, *Cotton Trade*, 179; S. J. Chapman, *Lancashire Cotton Industry*, 133–34.

60 Bolton spinners generally bought cotton a week before they needed it: Boyson, *Ashworth*, 49. M&K (Letter Books, 31 December 1811) could fill orders within fourteen days.

61 *Economist*, 23 December 1848, 1455.

62 Henry Ashworth, *An Inquiry into the Strike of Cotton Spinners of Preston* (Manchester, 1837), 85; *MG*, 2 January 1847.

63 S. J. Chapman, *Lancashire Cotton Industry*, 133–34; S. D. Chapman, "British Marketing Enterprise: The Changing Roles of Merchants, Manufacturers, and

Financiers, 1700–1860," *Business History Review* 53 (Summer 1979), 205–35; Douglas A. Farnie, "An Index of Commercial Activity: The Membership of the Manchester Royal Exchange, 1809–1948," *Business History* 21 (January 1979), 97–106.

64 For 1822–52, the estimates of trend values are (*t* statistics in parentheses):

$$\ln \ (ratio\ of\ cotton\ stocks\ to\ output \times 100) = 2.45 \ - \ 0.014 \ time$$
$$(22.837)\ (-2.231)$$
$$N = 31 \ R^2 = 0.146 \ F \ test = 4.997 \ DW = 1.472;$$
$$\ln \ (ratio\ of\ yarn\ inventories\ to\ output \times 100) = 3.265 \ - \ 0.002 \ time$$
$$(42.778)\ (-0.471)$$
$$N = 31 \ R^2 = 0.008 \ F \ test = 0.222 \ DW = 1.942.$$

65 The procedure of comparing levels of inventories and changes of output follows Robert Hall and John B. Taylor, *Macroeconomics: Theory, Performance, and Policy* (New York: Norton, 1986), 226.

66 This approach follows Robert J. Gordon, "US Wage and Employment Behaviour."

67 The procedure used to correct for growth follows James N. Brown, "How Close to an Auction is the Labor Market," in Ronald G. Ehrenberg, ed., *Research in Labor Economics*, vol. VI (Greenwich, Conn.: JAI, 1983), 189–237.

68 The bad years in coarse spinning were after 1835.

69 Shuttleworth's survey of Manchester in 1832 ("Vital Statistics") reported nineteen fine-spinning mills; for 1833, Stanway's survey (PP 1833 [450] XX) of the city recorded eighteen mills; in 1841 Horner (PP 1842 [31] XXII) found eighteen mills working.

70 R. S. Burn, *Statistics of the Cotton Trade* (London: Simpkin, 1847), 26.

71 Roger Lloyd-Jones and A. A. LeRoux, "Factory Utilization and the Firm: The Manchester Cotton Industry, c. 1825–1840," *Textile History* 15 (1984), 120.

72 Lyons, "Vertical Integration," 421.

73 S. D. Chapman, *Cotton Industry in the Industrial Revolution*, 60.

74 Cited in Gatrell, "Labour, Power," 138.

75 PP 1845 (639) XXV, 445.

76 S. D. Chapman, *Cotton Industry in the Industrial Revolution*, 60.

77 Horner reported that about 200 firms made investments in plant and equipment, of which 51 were investments in new mills. The vast majority of investments were minor improvements in machinery and horsepower. About 6 horsepower was added to each existing mill. (The average firm for the period housed between 20 and 50 horsepower.) Undoubtedly, the addition of machinery and power to existing mills biases the calculations, but the assumption that all fifty-one new mills had the capacity to produce 430,000 pounds of yarn provides an equal if not stronger bias in the other direction.

78 Charles Brown and James L. Medoff, "The Employer Size Wage Effect," *Journal of Political Economy* 97 (October 1989), 1027–59. For recent reviews of the empirical literature, see William T. Dickens and Kevin Lang, "The Reemergence of Segmented Labor Market Theory," *AER* 78 (May 1988),

129–34; Kevin Lang and Shulamit Kahn, "Efficiency Wage Models of Unemployment: A Second View," *Economic Inquiry* 28 (April 1990), 296–306; Solow, *Labor Market as a Social Institution*, 1–28.

79 Mark Blaug, "The Productivity of Capital in the Lancashire Cotton Industry During the Nineteenth Century," *EHR* 13 (March 1961), 359–91.

80 J. A. Mann, *The Cotton Trade of Great Britain* (Manchester: Thomson, 1860), 114.

81 Baines, *History of Cotton Manufacture*, 297–312; Kennedy, *Cotton Spinner*, 140; Baird, *American Cotton Spinner*, 244.

82 Blaug, "Productivity of Capital," 357.

7 Short hours and seniority in the "hungry 'forties"

1 Hicks, *Theory of Wages*, 55–56.

2 Ure, *Philosophy*, 366.

3 Martha E. Shiells and Gavin Wright, "Night Work as a Labor-Market Phenomenon: Southern Textiles in the Interwar Period," *EEH* 20 (July 1983), 331–50.

4 Hobsbawm, *Labouring Men*, 74.

5 MK Letter Books, 28 October 1830. Contemporaries used "short hours" or "short time" to describe cuts in production that kept workers intact. "Worksharing" was rarely used.

6 Richard Freeman and James L. Medoff, *What Do Unions Do?* (New York: Basic Books, 1984), 115. Freeman and Medoff also observe that worksharing has declined in popularity since 1945. They attribute this drop to the rise in unemployment insurance benefits and the increase in start-up costs, such as traveling to work.

7 Mark Lowenstein, "Worker Heterogeneity, Hours Restrictions, and Temporary Layoffs," *Econometrica* 51 (January 1983), 69–78.

8 For a theoretical treatment, see Sherwin Rosen, "The Theory of Equalizing Differences," in Orley Ashenfelter and Richard Layard, eds., *Handbook of Labor Economics* (Amsterdam: North Holland, 1986), 683.

9 PP 1842 (31) XXII, 417. Similar evidence is found in the testimony of millowners before the commissions on factory conditions: PP 1833 (450) XX, 34–38, 95–100.

10 Lee, "Cotton-Textile Industry," 170–71. Lee does recognize short-time work in the 1841–42 recession.

11 Mary Rose, "The Role of the Family in the Provision of Capital and Managerial Talent in Samuel Greg and Company 1750–1840," *Business History* 19 (January 1977), 42–43.

12 Bradford J. De Long, "Senior's Last Hour: A Suggested Explanation of a Famous Blunder," *History of Political Economy* 18 (Summer 1986), 325–33.

13 Marion Bowley, *Nassau Senior and Classical Economics* (Manchester: Manchester University Press, 1967), 256; for a more recent assessment of the relationship between the working day and productivity, see Chris Nyland,

Reduced Worktime and the Management of Production (New York: Cambridge University Press, 1989).

14 Matthews, *Trade Cycle History*, 142–43. Like Lee, Matthews did recognize some short-time work in 1841–42, but concluded that "under-employment resulting from short-time working was probably not very great": ibid., 142.

15 Lloyd-Jones and LeRoux, "Factory Utilization," 119–24.

16 This section relies on Michael Huberman, "Some Early Evidence of Worksharing: Lancashire Before 1850," *Business History* 37 (October 1995), 1–25.

17 Matthews, *Trade Cycle History*, 143; Mary Rose *et al.*, "Some Objections," 96. Gatrell ("Labour, Power") used the survey to describe the persistence of small and middle-sized firms in the industry. He broke down the survey by horse-power in estimating economies of scale, but he gave less emphasis to the response of firms in different locations and sectors to the downturn of 1841.

18 Thomas Ellison, "The Great Crises in the History of the Cotton Trade: A Retrospect of Prices and Supply, 1790–1862," *The Exchange* 1 (1862), 45–53.

19 Following Gatrell ("Labour, Power," 126), the retabulated figures exclude data on parishes in Horner's district outside Lancashire, and include all of Lancashire except the parishes of Todmorden and Warrington, which fell to other inspectors. Gatrell recorded 975 firms; the total number of firms analyzed in this chapter is lower. I have excluded firms which were closed for more than one year because in all likelihood they would have had to recruit a completely new workforce; I have labeled firms that spun both coarse and fine yarn as fine spinners as these firms used the same technology and required the same labor input as firms that specialized in fine spinning.

20 The median duration of short time was four weeks. The choice between cutting hours and closing one or two days appears to have been influenced by offsetting seasonal and technical factors. On the one hand, it was costly to fire up steam engines and firms would have preferred to close for the day; on the other hand, lighting expenses in the late afternoon in winter months in Lancashire were not insubstantial, and firms would have preferred to work six days a week at shorter hours.

21 PP 1842 (31) XXII, 343.

22 Burn (*Statistics*, 21) gave these figures for the weekly average number of cotton bales bought in Liverpool:

	Quarter				
Year	1	2	3	4	Yearly Average
1840	21365	24101	20934	21239	21910
1841	21881	15922	20937	21842	20146
1842	20241	22981	20820	22500	21636

23 *Stockport Advertiser*, 27 May, 5 August 1841; *Bolton Free Press*, 19 June, 4 September 1841; *Manchester Times*, 2 October 1841; *MG*, 7 April, 11 May, 15 August 1841; *Marriott and Co. Trade Circular*, 1 January 1842.

24 PP 1842 (31) XXII, 341; Ellison, "Great Crises," 46.

25 While fine yarn margins declined by 13 percent between 1840 and 1841, coarse margins fell by about 18 percent. The fine-spinning branch had suffered from a decline in trade from the late 1830s and stocks at firms were already at a low level by 1841.

26 *Marriott and Co. Trade Circular*, 1 January 1842. On the prospects of improvement in November and December, see *MG*, 15 September, 9 October, 13 October 1841.

27 Matthews (*Trade Cycle History*, 142–43 n. 2) speculated that a higher proportion of large firms worked short time because the demand for their products was "perhaps less elastic than for the products of other firms." The retabulated survey reveals, however, that large firms cut hours regardless of specialization.

28 See Horner's own report of the state of trade for the first half of 1842: PP 1842 (31) XXII, 446; *MG*, 1 December, 12 December 1841. The Chamber of Commerce statement is from the *MG*, 16 February 1842.

29 *MG*, 9 March 1842.

30 PP 1842 (31) XXII, 357.

31 M. A. Bienefeld, *Working Hours in British Industry: An Economic History* (London: Weidenfeld and Nicolson, 1972); Cross, *Quest for Time*; Cross, *Worktime and Industrialization*, including his own introduction.

32 Boot, "Unemployment."

33 Boyer, *History of Poor Law*, 233–64.

34 The regional variation of short time is discussed below, pp. 125–26.

35 Samuel Andrew, *Fifty Years of Work and Wages in the Cotton Trade* (Oldham, 1887), 10. On related themes, see Cross, *Quest for Time*; and the collection of articles edited by Cross, *Worktime and Industrialization*, including his introduction; Clive Behagg, "Controlling the Product"; and Stuart Weaver, "The Political Ideology of Short-Time: England, 1820–1850." See also J. E. King, "Perish Consumption! Free Trade and Underconsumption in Early British Radical Economics," *Australian Economic Papers* 20 (December 1981), 235–57.

36 For examples, see *MG*, 6 February 1830; Webb, vol. XXXV, 50.

37 *MG*, 1 November 1848.

38 Cross, *Quest for Time*, 27.

39 William Mass and William Lazonick, "The British Cotton Industry and International Competitive Advantage: The State of the Debates," in Mary Rose, ed., *International Competition and Strategic Response in the Textile Industries Since 1870* (London: Frank Cass, 1991), 11.

40 Ibid., 13.

41 Robert S. Gardner, *Letter to His Workpeople* (Manchester, 1845); Webb, vol. XXXIV, 238; John Ward, *The Factory Movement, 1830–1855* (London: MacMillan, 1962), 307.

42 PP 1849 (1017) XXII, 204, 206.

43 Wood, *History of Wages*, 133. This argument about the relation between effort and pay is consistent with the contemporary view of distinguishing between negotiated short-hour arrangements during downturns and a legislated

reduced workweek. As befitting their ideological position many large firms, including M&K, were hostile to any type of legislated intervention for adults, even though they may have recognized the benefits of reduced workweek on effort. Summarizing these arguments, Robert Gardner wrote: "I am satisfied [that] those mills that work short hours will have a choice of hands, and [that] individual interest will accomplish what is necessary without the intervention of the legislature": Gardner, *Letter*. See also Lee, *Cotton Enterprise*, 129; Gray, "Languages of Reform"; John Seed, "Unitarianism, Political Economy, and the Antinomies of Liberal Culture in Manchester, 1830–50," *SH* 7 (January 1982), 1–26.

44 See note 6 in this chapter; Joseph E. Stiglitz, "The Causes and Consequences of the Dependence of Quality on Price," *Journal of Economic Literature* 25 (March 1987), 33.

45 Rebitzer and Taylor, "Dual Labor Markets when Product Demand Is Uncertain."

46 Dutton and King, "Limits of Paternalism," 62; Letter Book of Thomas Miller, DDHs, Horrockses Papers, Lancashire Record Office, Preston.

47 S. J. Chapman and H. M. Hallsworth, *Unemployment: The Results of an Investigation Made in Lancashire* (Manchester: Manchester University Press, 1909); Noel Whiteside and James A. Gillespie, "Deconstructing Unemployment: Developments in Britain in the Interwar Years," *EHR* 44 (November 1991), 665–82. Some histories observe that short time was initiated after 1850 only to control speculation and smooth supply-side shocks. See chapter 6 and H. A. Clegg, Alan Fox, and A. F. Thompson, *A History of British Trade Unions, vol. I: 1889–1910* (Oxford: Clarendon Press, 1964), 112–13.

48 PP 1842 (31) XXII.

49 The argument is similar to that proposed by Martha E. Shiells, "Collective Choice of Working Conditions: Hours in Britain and US Steel, 1890–1923," *JEH* 50 (June 1990), 379–92; Shiells, "Hours of Work and Shiftwork in the Early Industrial Labor Markets of Great Britain, the United States, and Japan," (Ph.D. dissertation, University of Michigan, 1985). Hicks, in his classic, *The Theory of Wages* (107–09), expanded on this point in his explanation of why legislation or some other mechanism of enforcement is necessary to regulate hours of work. Competitive forces alone could not assure that all firms worked the same hours, because there is a "transitional period," between when hours are reduced and when employees' productivity increases; after this transitional period, "an employer has no guarantee that those men whose efficiency he has improved will stay with him. An individual worker's tastes for income and leisure may change; or because his improved efficiency allows him to claim a higher wage, he might want to substitute work for leisure by moving to a firm that still works longer hours. Thus, unless all firms reduce their hours at once, the enlightened employer may fail to capture the return from his investment in reducing hours."

50 Joyce, *Visions of the People*, 133. See, as well, the papers *Voice of the People*, 1831–32, and *Ten Hours' Advocate*, 1846–47.

51 *MG*, 13 October 1847.

52 Joyce, *Visions of the People*, 118.

53 Emphasis in original. Alexander J. Field, "Microeconomics, Norms, and Rationality," *Economic Development and Cultural Change* 32 (July 1984), 700–01. On informal and formal rules, see Douglass C. North, *Institutions, Institutional Change, and Economic Performance* (New York: Cambridge University Press, 1990), 36–54; Knight, *Institutions and Social Conflict*, 66–73.

54 Pat Hudson, "The Regional Perspective," in Hudson, ed., *Regions and Industries: A Perspective on the Industrial Revolution in Britain* (Cambridge: Cambridge University Press, 1989), 31.

55 For sources, see Huberman, "Economic Origins of Paternalism: Lancashire Cotton Spinning," and "Reply to Rose."

56 Mary Rose, *Gregs*, 117.

57 This section relies on Huberman, "Invisible Handshakes."

58 One employer observed that a spinner between forty and fifty years old would not find employment unless "he is a man of steady character": PP 1834 (167) XIX, D1, 471.

59 N = 3,770 male operatives. PP 1834 (167) XIX, 279; see also HL 1819 (24) CX, 110, 111; PP 1834 (44) XXVII, 53.

60 Assume that there is a positive correlation between attributes that are unobserved by the firm, like effort, and the worker's best alternative opportunity. If the more productive workers have better alternatives, then the cost of being fired is greatest for the lower ability types. As a result, firms would fire older or low productivity workers to sort and improve the distribution of their labor forces: Weiss, *Efficiency Wages*, 12, 80–81. Older workers might have had a higher value of leisure relative to their productivity, thus raising the premium required to prevent them from withholding effort.

61 Savage, *Working-Class Politics*, 84–87.

62 This optimism may have diminished after the middle of the century. By the 1880s, the oversupply of twenty-year-old big piecers waiting to become minders was in the order of three to five times the number vacancies for minders. Employers tried to exploit the imbalance and initiated a policy of "joining" whereby the status and earnings of minders were downgraded and the big piecer upgraded. The policy met with resistance and, by the 1930s, only 12 percent of mule spinners were joiner-minders: Savage, *Working-Class Politics*, 84–87.

63 Recall that Anderson in *Family Structure* referred to kinship bonds in periods of distress as "short-run" instrumentalism.

64 Webb, vol. XXXV, 43.

65 Joyce gives examples of comparable behavior that provided family and community members with their fair shares during economic crises: *Visions of the People*, 130.

66 The crisis of the 1840s came to an end in November 1848, but as of 1850 Horner reported that many mills remained on short time: PP 1850 (1140) XXIII, 23. It was not until 1853 that Horner observed a "scarcity of hands": PP 1852–53 (461) XL, 40, 551.

67 The sampling method is based on Roger S. Schofield, "Sampling in Historical Research," in E. A. Wrigley, ed., *Nineteenth-Century Society: Essays in the Use of Quantitative Methods for the Study of Social Data* (Cambridge: Cambridge University Press, 1972), 147–84.

68 Some estimates of the number of cotton spinners in Manchester are, for 1829, 2,400 (*MG*, 20 June 1829); for 1836, 2,000 (George Dodd, *The Textile Manufacturer of Great Britain* [London, 1844], 113); for 1837, 1,660 (Kirby and Musson, *Voice of the People*, 101). For Bolton, the 1833 estimate is 792 (James C. Scholes, *History of Bolton* [Bolton, 1842], 521). Anderson used a sample of 10 percent in *Family Structure*.

69 E. A. Wrigley and R. S. Schofield, *The Population History of England: A Reconstruction* (Cambridge: Cambridge University Press, 1989), 217.

70 P. M. Tillot, "Sources of Inaccuracy in the 1851 and 1861 Censuses," in E. A. Wrigley ed., *Nineteenth-Century Society: Essays in the Use of Quantitative Methods for the Study of Social Data* (Cambridge: Cambridge University Press, 1972), 105–07.

71 N = 837 fine spinners; Shuttleworth, "Vital Statistics." There is no significant difference between the average ages in Shuttleworth's survey (32.70) and the averages of the samples for Manchester and Bolton.

72 The overall results are consistent with the ages reported by R. Burr Litchfield for Stockport in "The Family and the Mill: Cotton Mill Work, Family Work Patterns, and Fertility in Mid-Victorian Stockport," in Anthony S. Wohl, ed., *The Victorian Family: Structure and Stresses* (London: Croom Helm, 1978), 184–85. In his sample the age of male spinners in 1841 was thirty-three years; in 1861, thirty. Litchfield does not report ages for spinners in 1851, but for the larger group of "Lower Factory" workers in which they are included, the proportion of workers under thirty falls between 1841 and 1851, and increases in the next decade. Using samples from the 1841 and 1851 census for mostly northern Lancashire towns, Lyons ("Lancashire Textile Factory Sector," 3) also found that the share of older adults was rising over the period.

73 Huberman, "Economic Origins of Paternalism: Lancashire Cotton Spinning," 188.

74 Greg Papers, C5/1/7/1–2, C5/1/15, Manchester Central Library.

75 Boyson, *Ashworth*, 102; Mary Rose, *Gregs*, 76. This pattern of occupational shifting as opposed to permanent layoffs was also common at rural mills in the American South: Gary Saxonhouse and Gavin Wright, "Two Forms of Cheap Labor in Textile History," in Saxonhouse and Wright, eds., *Technique, Spirit, and Form in the Making of Modern Economies: Essays in Honor of William N. Parker* (Greenwich, Conn.: JAI Press, 1984).

76 M&K Deeds and Documents; PP 1816 (397) III, 479; Boyson, *Ashworth*, 102–03; Collier, *Family Economy*, 44. This type of data on job spells underestimates the length of a completed tenure. In a steady state, where a survey is equally likely to occur at any point during a job in progress, tenure to date is on average half as long as a completed spell. See Susan B. Carter and Elizabeth Savoca, "Labor Mobility and Lengthy Jobs in Nineteenth-Century America," *JEH* 50 (March 1990), 5.

77 For the sub-period 1856–73, hour changes were responsible for 65 percent of improvements in labor quality and 24 percent of overall productivity: R. C. O. Matthews, C. H. Feinstein, and J. C. Odling-Smee, *British Economic Growth 1856–1973* (Oxford: Clarendon Press, 1982), 113, 500.

78 The success of short-time working during downturns helped pave the way for a legislated reduced workweek. For example, the 1833 legislation that reduced the hours of work of children below thirteen years to nine hours per day was sponsored mainly by large firms in urban centers. The opposition consisted of small and rural mills who could not compete with their larger rivals, but by the 1840s their numbers were growing smaller. The historian of the factory movement observed that the passage of the first ten hours' bill in 1848 coincided with a slump in trade when many manufacturers were already working short time; the experiments at Gardner's and at other mills on the effects of a reduced workday were widely reported and used as evidence in support of the ten hours' struggle: Marvel, "Factory Regulation"; Howe, *Cotton Masters*; Ward, *Factory Movement*, 419; PP 1845 (639) XXV, 449; PP 1850 (1140) XXIII, 183.

8 Rules and standards: wage lists in Lancashire

1 J. W. F. Rowe, *Wages in Practice*, 156.

2 Knight, *Institutions and Social Conflict*, 69.

3 Joyce, *Visions of the People*, 87–141.

4 Dutton and King, *Ten Percent*, 1; Mason, "Mule Spinner Societies," 48–52.

5 For the standard account, see Clegg, et al., *History of British Unions*, vol. I, 28.

6 William Taggart, *Cotton Mill Management: A Practical Guide for Managers, Carders, and Overlookers* (London: MacMillan, 1932), 19–20.

7 Sidney Webb and Beatrice Webb, *The History of Trade Unionism* (London: Longmans, Green, 1894), 308.

8 The most comprehensive account of these issues is found in Fowler and Wyke, *Barefoot Aristocrats*.

9 The following two sections rely on Huberman, "Piece Rates Reconsidered." The quote is from the British Association for the Advancement of Science, *On the Regulation of Wages by Means of Lists in the Cotton Industry* (Manchester, 1887), 11. The Webbs prepared the most comprehensive history of the lists. Their unpublished monograph, copies of the lists themselves, and interviews with representatives of worker and employer groups, are in the Webb Collection at the London School of Economics. Lazonick (*Competitive Advantage*) offers a more recent history. He finds that the lists were in place only after 1850. My account of the early history of the lists is similar to Cohen's in *American Management*, 83–87. However, Cohen did not explain the original makeup of the lists, nor was he concerned about labor-market adjustment.

10 S. J. Chapman, "The Regulation of Wages by Lists in the Spinning Industry," *Economic Journal* 9 (March 1899), 593–94.

11 "A General List of Prices of Spinning," ZZ/220, Bolton Public Library.

12 *MG*, 22 February 1823; PP 1834 (167) XIX, D1, 466; Ashworth, *Inquiry into Preston*.

13 E. P. Thompson, *The Making of the English Working Class* (Harmondsworth: Penguin, 1968), 531.

14 In 1841 in Bolton, 16 percent of firms employed fewer than fifty workers; 31 percent between 50 and 149; 53 percent over 150. The corresponding figures for Oldham are 40, 37, and 23 percent (PP 1842 [31] XXII). Crompton's study of 1811 (reprinted in Honeyman, *Origins of Enterprise*) presents a similar picture in terms of spindles per firm. In that year in Bolton, 28 percent of firms had fewer than 5,000 spindles; in Oldham, the figure was 42 percent.

15 For a description of the strike, see Mason, "Mule Spinner Societies," 23–24. Along with the 1829 Manchester dispute, long-wheel strikes were also waged in Ashton-under-Lyne in 1830, and in Preston in 1836–37. See also chapter 4 on firm size.

16 PP 1824 (51) V, 559.

17 John Jewkes and E. M. Gray, *Wages and Labour in the Lancashire Cotton-Spinning Industry* (Manchester: Manchester University Press, 1935), 110.

18 Gavin Wright, "Labor History," 320–21.

19 Webb, vol. XXXVI, 12; Edwin Butterworth, "Registrar of Trivial Events, 1829–43," 22 September 1835, 16 November 1836, 19 May 1841, Oldham Local Interest Centre, Oldham.

20 Farnie, *English Cotton Industry*, 246.

21 Ibid., 247–51.

22 The disputes are described in Andrew Bullen, "The Founding of the Amalgamation," in Fowler and Wyke, *Barefoot Aristocrats*, 67–68.

23 Farnie, "Emergence of Victorian Oldham," 264.

24 Fama, "Time, Salary," 25–44.

25 An indicator of labor pressures is that between 1874 and 1906 the average wages of Oldham cotton operatives in all stages of production (which includes spinners and workers in preparatory departments) rose more rapidly than in Bolton: Wood, *History of Wages*, 116.

26 According to John Dunlop, contours share three dimensions: (1) particular occupations and clusters; (2) a sector of industry; (3) a geographic location. The lists appear to satisfy these criteria. They were specific to spinners or minders; fine and coarse sectors; and geographic regions: John Dunlop, "Wage Contours," in Michael J. Piore, ed., *Unemployment and Inflation: Institutionalist and Structuralist Views* (White Plains, N. Y.: M. E. Sharpe, 1979), 63–74.

27 PP 1824 (51) V, 556–57.

28 Dutton and King, *Ten Percent*, 212–13.

29 This paragraph is based on Jewkes and Gray, *Wages and Labour*, 96–99.

30 *Bolton Chronicle*, 15 and 29 October 1836; Webb, vol. XXXIV, 56, 148–50, 231; vol. XXXVI, 54.

31 Jewkes and Gray, *Wages and Labour*, 108.

32 *Cotton Factory Times*, 25 May 1894.

33 Joyce, *Work, Society, Politics*, 110; Joyce, *Visions of the People*.

34 Walton, *Lancashire*, 249.

35 McIvor, "Cotton Employers' Organisations," 7.

36 Joyce, *Work, Society, Politics*, 134.

37 Webb, vol. XCIII, no. 3. The revised Oldham list of 1876 specified that piecers were prohibited from sharing in payments to minders for the extra work involved in such things as tubing, putting extra twist into the yarn, and faster carriage speeds, even though the piecers expended as much, if not more, of the extra labor power.

38 In Oldham the piecer–spinner pay ratios were 39, 40, 39 and 40 percent in 1860, 1880, 1890, and 1900; for the same years in Bolton the ratios were 26, 31, 30 and 29 percent: Wood, *History of Wages*, 54, 58–61.

39 For a discussion of related issues, see Lazonick, *Competitive Advantage*, 106–08.

40 *Minute Books of the Operative Cotton Spinners' Provincial Association*, Bolton District, Half Year Ending 7 June 1890, 57.

41 "It cannot be altogether fortuitous that the districts most favorable to the employer [like Oldham] were increasing in relative importance throughout the period, whilst other districts with unfavorable lists were falling back": Jewkes and Gray, *Wages and Labour*, 115. The evidence on spindles and unit costs are taken from pages 42 and 48. (This contrasts with Cohen's finding in *American Management*, 88.) There is a large and growing literature on changes in counts of yarn spun at the end of the nineteenth century. The point I want to emphasize is that if there was any increase in counts, this increase still fell within the range of the Oldham list.

42 Lazonick, *Competitive Advantage*, 158; Wood, *History of Wages*, 54. Figures are for coarse spinning.

43 Wood, *History of Wages*, 139. Other estimates of increased effort or "speed-up" range from 15 to 20 percent between 1865 and 1885: Lazonick, *Competitive Advantage*, 121; and Cohen, *American Management*, 88.

44 Jewkes and Gray, *Wages and Labour*, 205.

45 When corrected for the 1875 decline in hours worked, from 60 to 56.5, minders' pay in Oldham increased by 32 percent between 1870 and 1900. The piece rate as set by the list increased by 5 percent in the period, and workers' gain from productivity increases rose by about 15 percent, leaving 12 percent of the increase in earnings to be accounted for by increased effort. Conditions were different in Bolton: earnings of spinners rose by about 29 percent when adjusted for hours; the list was unaltered; and technical change was slower than in Oldham. With 15 percent as an upper estimate of the contribution of technical improvements, increased effort was responsible for at least 14 percent of the rise in earnings in Bolton. Note that the use of inferior cotton required even greater effort to maintain levels of earnings. Hence, my calculation underestimates the gross contribution of effort, at least for coarse spinning.

46 Matthews, *et al.*, *British Economic Growth*, 104, 503.

47 Quoted in G. von Schulze-Gaevernitz, *The Cotton Trade in England and on the Continent* (London: Simpkin, Marshall, 1895), 130.

48 Cited in J. W. F. Rowe, *Wages in Practice*, 164.

49 See, for example, J. H. Porter, "Industrial Peace in the Cotton Trade,

1875–1913," *Yorkshire Bulletin of Economic and Social Research* 19 (May 1967), 49–62; Cohen, *American Management*, 85–87.
50 For models of this type, see Oliver D. Hart, "Optimal Labour Contracts Under Asymmetric Information: An Introduction," *Review of Economic Studies* 50 (January 1983), 3–35.
51 Dutton and King, *Ten Percent*, 45, 179.
52 Mason, "Mule Spinners' Societies," 54.
53 Quoted in Cohen, *American Management*, 86.
54 Andrew Bullen, "A Modern Spinners' Union," in Fowler and Wyke, *Barefoot Aristocrats*, 76.
55 The agreement also set up an elaborate grievance procedure to settle disputes. The quote is from Porter, "Industrial Peace," 49.
56 My emphasis. The source is British Association for the Advancement of Science, *Regulation of Wages by Means of Lists*, 12. For similar statements, see Webb, vol. XXXIV, 171–72; and sources quoted by Cohen, *American Management*, 86.
57 Note that flexible wages by themselves are not sufficient to produce Weitzman-like results. If workers' share of revenue is 100 percent, the firm would have no incentive to hire more workers. The standard work is Weitzman, *Share Economy*; see also Daniel J. B. Mitchell, "Explanations of Wage Inflexibility: Institutions and Incentives," in Wilfred Beckerman, ed., *Wage Rigidity and Unemployment* (Baltimore: Johns Hopkins University Press, 1986), 64–65. For length of tenure after 1850, see Joyce, *Work, Society, Politics*, 119–20.
58 Lee, *Cotton Enterprise*, 152–53; S. J. Chapman and Hallsworth, *Unemployment*, 38; Whiteside and Gillespie, "Deconstructing Unemployment."
59 Note that the price series for the two periods is from the same source.
60 Grantham, "Economic History of Labor Markets."
61 Gregory Clark, "Why Isn't the Whole World Developed: Lessons from the Cotton Mills," *JEH* 47 (March 1987), 134–67.

9 More lessons from the cotton mills

1 Arthur M. Okun, "Inflation: Its Mechanics and Welfare Costs," *Brookings Papers on Economic Activity*, no. 2 (1975), 369.
2 "[Wage] rigidity would have been irrational before World War II, especially in periods when the gold standard was being followed": Allen, "Changes in Cyclical Sensitivity," 123.
3 See, among others, Raphael Samuel, "The Workshop of the World," *History Workshop* 3 (1977), 6–72; Joyce, *Historical Meanings of Work*; and Clive Behagg, *Politics and Production in Nineteenth-Century England* (London: Routledge, 1991). For a more complete bibliography and analysis, see Maxine Berg and Pat Hudson, "Rehabilitating the Industrial Revolution," *EHR* 45 (February 1992), 24–50.
4 Eric Hobsbawm, *Industry and Empire* (Harmondsworth: Penguin, 1969), 2.
5 Randall, *Before the Luddites*. The quotes in this section are from pages 285 and 255.

6 Grantham, "Economic History of Labor Markets," 64.

7 This paragraph is based on Jeffrey Williamson, *Did British Capitalism*, 20. Much of this work was originally published in articles with Peter H. Lindert; see also Jeffrey Williamson, *City Growth*; Joel Mokyr, "Is There Still Life in the Pessimist Case? Consumption During the Industrial Revolution, 1790–1850," *JEH* 48 (March 1988), 69–92; Stephen Nicholas and Richard H. Steckel, "Heights and Living Standards During the Early Years of Industrialization, 1770–1815," *JEH* 51 (December 1991), 937–57. For a more exhaustive bibliography and summary of issues, see Peter H. Lindert, "Unequal Living Standards," in Roderick Floud and Donald McCloskey, eds., *The Economic History of Britain Since 1700*, 2nd edn., vol. I (Cambridge: Cambridge University Press, 1992).

8 For an explicit statement, see R. M. Hartwell and Stanley Engerman, "Models of Immiseration: The Theoretical Basis of Pessimism," in Arthur J. Taylor, ed., *The Standard of Living in Britain in the Industrial Revolution* (London: Methuen, 1975).

9 Jeffrey Williamson (*Did British Capitalism*) uses a two-sector model, but he distinguishes between skill groups, and not within them.

10 Jeffrey Williamson, *Did British Capitalism*, 21; Hobsbawm, *Labouring Men*, 74; on the negative effects of short time on income and welfare, see R. S. Neale, *Writing Marxist History: British Society, Economy, and Culture Since 1700* (Oxford: Basil Blackwell, 1985), 109–41; Sara Horrell and Jane Humphries, "Old Questions, New Data, and Alternative Perspectives: The Standard of Living in the British Industrial Revolution," *JEH* 52 (December 1992), 849–81.

11 Sidney Pollard, "Labour in Great Britain," in Peter Mathias and Michael M. Postan, eds., *The Cambridge Economic History of Europe, Volume VII. The Industrial Economies: Capital, Labour, and Enterprise* (Cambridge University Press, 1978), 902–03.

12 Cited in Jeffrey Williamson, *City Growth*, 104–05.

13 Ibid., 102–29.

14 Gavin Wright, "Labor History," 320–21.

15 See the collection of essays in Bernard Elbaum and William Lazonick, *The Decline of the British Economy* (Oxford: Clarendon Press, 1986).

16 John Maynard Keynes, "Industrial Reorganisation: Cotton," in Donald E. Moggridge, ed., *The Collected Writings of John Maynard Keynes, Vol. XIX, Part ii. Activities, 1922–1929: The Return to the Gold Standard and Industrial Policy* (Cambridge: Cambridge University Press, 1981), 578.

17 Henry Clay, *Report on the Position of the British Cotton Industry* (Confidential Report for Securities Management Trust, Ltd., London, 20 October 1931).

18 However, J. H. Porter showed that the lists reduced industrial conflict and, more recently, Lazonick argued that they were integral to the successful performance of the textile industry, eliciting effort from spinners and thereby raising productivity and reducing unit fixed costs: Porter, "Industrial Peace"; Lazonick, *Competitive Advantage*.

19 See Douglass C. North, *Structure and Change in Economic History* (New York: Norton, 1981); and North, *Institutions, Institutional Change*; for a critical

assessment, see Alexander J. Field, "The Problem with Neoclassical Institutional Economics: A Critique with Special Reference to the North/Thomas Model of Pre-1500 Europe," *EEH* 18 (April 1981), 174–98.

20 Field, "Microeconomics, Norms."

21 The lists codified the standard wages firms paid spinners and minders using mules; with the introduction of ring-spinning technology, a new set of arrangements developed. Using rings, workers were paid by a list that was based on a time payoff and which was more flexible than the mule-wage lists. Ring-spinning operatives were mainly women, who neither supervised operations nor controlled the speed of the machine which was nearly fully automatic. Unlike mule spinners, ring operatives were unable to exercise control over production. They were paid by time, because employers had full information about how much output could normally be produced in a specified period: Jewkes and Gray, *Wages and Labour*, 116–30.

22 Walton, *Lancashire*, 259.

23 This point was made by Solow, *Labor Market as a Social Institution*; on persistence, see also Kaushik Basu, Eric Jones, and Ekkehart Schlicht, "The Growth and Decay of Custom: The Role of the New Institutional Economics," *EEH* 24 (January 1987), 1–21.

Bibliography

Primary sources

Business records

Ashworth Papers. John Rylands Library, Manchester.
Greg Papers. Manchester Central Library, Manchester.
Horrockses Papers. Lancashire Record Office, Preston.
M'Connel and Kennedy Papers. John Rylands Library, Manchester.

Diaries, trade union papers, and miscellaneous

Butterworth, Edwin. "Registrar of Trivial Events, 1829–43." Oldham Local Interest Centre, Oldham.
Census Papers. Enumerators' Schedules for 1841, 1851, and 1861. Public Record Office, London.
"A General List of Prices of Spinning," ZZ/220, Bolton Public Library.
Liverpool Cotton Association. Trade Circular Reports. Liverpool Record Office, Liverpool.
Manchester Chamber of Commerce. Proceedings of the Manchester Chamber of Commerce, 1821–49. Manchester Central Library, Manchester.
Minute Books of the Operative Cotton Spinners' Provincial Association, Bolton District, Half Year Ending 7 June 1890.
Rowbottom, James. The Annals of Oldham, 1815–30. Oldham Local Interest Centre, Oldham.
Webb Trade Union Collection. Library of the London School of Economics and Political Science, London.
Wood Collection. University of Huddersfield (formerly Huddersfield Polytechnic) Library, Huddersfield, Yorkshire.

Newspapers and periodicals

Bolton Chronicle, 1827–46.
Bolton Free Press, 1837–42.
Cotton Factory Times, 1894–14.

The Economist, 1845–56.
Liverpool Mercury, 1822–52.
Manchester Guardian, 1825–53.
Manchester Times, 1841–42.
Poor Man's Advocate, 1832.
Stockport Advertiser, 1823–52.
Ten Hours' Advocate, 1846–47.
Voice of the People, 1831–32.

Parliamentary papers

1816 (397) III. *Report from the Select Committee on the State of Children Employed in the Manufactories of the United Kingdom.*
1824 (51) V. *Report from the Select Committee on Artisans and Machinery.*
1831–32 (706) XV. *Report from the Committee on the Bill to Regulate the Labour of Children.*
1833 (690) VI. *Report from the Select Committee on Manufactures, Commerce, and Shipping.*
1833 (450) XX. *First Report of the Commissioners on the Employment of Children.*
1833 (519) XXI. *Second Report of the Commissioners on the Employment of Children.*
1834 (167) XIX. *Supplementary Report on the Employment of Children.*
1834 (167) XX. *Supplementary Report on the Employment of Children.*
1834 (44) XXVII. *Report from the Commissioners on the Poor Laws.*
1840 (218) XXIII. *Report of the Inspectors of Factories.*
1842 (31) XXII. *Report of the Inspectors of Factories.*
1843 (342) XXII. *Population Tables for 1841.*
1843 (496) XXII. *England and Wales Enumeration Abstract.*
1843 (429) XXVII. *Report of the Inspectors of Factories.*
1845 (639) XXV. *Report of the Inspectors of Factories.*
1847 (828) XV. *Report of the Inspectors of Factories.*
1849 (1017) XXII. *Report of the Inspectors of Factories.*
1850 (1140) XXIII. *Report of the Inspectors of Factories.*
1852–53 (461) XL. *Report of the Inspectors of Factories.*
1852–53 (1691) LXXXVIII. *Ages and Civil Condition of Population in 1851.*

Lords sessional papers

1818 (90) XCVI. *Minutes of Evidence of the Committee on Cotton Factories.*
1819 (24) CX. *Minutes of Evidence on Children Employed in the Cotton Manufactories.*

Technical spinning manuals

Baird, R. 1851. *American Cotton Spinner and Carders' Guide*. Philadelphia.
Cotton Spinner's Ready Reckoner and Pay List. 1798. Glasgow.
Etchells, W. 1812. *Cotton Spinner's Companion*. Manchester.

Galbraith, G. 1834. *Cotton Spinner's Companion.* Glasgow.

Hargreaves, J. 1853. *New Pocket Companion.* Bolton.

Holland, J. 1847. *Cotton Spinner's and Manager's Assistant.* Bolton.

Holme, J. E. 1889. *Handbook on Cotton Spinning.* Manchester.

Jones, T. 1798. *Ready Numberer or Cotton Spinner's Calculator.* Glasgow.

Kennedy, A. 1845. *Practical Cotton Spinner.* Glasgow.

Leigh, E. 1877. *Science of Modern Cotton Spinning.* London.

McFarlane, D. 1811. *Cotton Spinner And Manufacturer's Calculator, Showing the Prices of Cotton.* Glasgow.

Manufacturers' Assistant. 1798. Glasgow.

Marsden, R. 1884. *Cotton Spinning.* London.

Milne, J. 1837. *Manufacturer's Assistant for Calculating the Wages of Operatives.* London.

Montgomery, J. 1832. *Carding and Spinning Master's Assistant.* Glasgow.

1836. *Theory and Practice of Cotton Spinning.* Glasgow.

1850. *Cotton Spinners' Manual.* Glasgow.

Moss, J. 1848. *Cotton Manufacturers', Managers' and Spinners' New Pocket Guide.* Manchester.

Nasmith, J. 1896. *Student's Cotton Spinning.* Manchester.

Neste, K. 1865. *Mule Spinning Process.* Manchester.

Pearson, H. 1866. *Pearson's Work on Cotton Spinning.* Manchester.

Scott, R. 1851. *Scott's Practical Cotton Spinner and Manufacturer* or *Managers', Over-Lookers, and Mechanics' Companion.* Manchester.

Speakman, C. 1855. *Cotton Tables.* Manchester.

Taggart, W. S. 1907. *Cotton Spinning.* London.

Thornley, T. 1893. *Self-Acting Mules.* Manchester.

1899a. *Practical Treatise on Mule Spinning.* Manchester.

1899b. *Practical Treatise Upon Self-Acting.* Manchester.

Walter, P. 1809. *Cotton Yarn Tables for Cotton Spinners and Manufacturers.* Glasgow.

Secondary sources

Akerlof, George A. "Labor Contracts as Partial Gift Exchange," *Quarterly Journal of Economics* 97 (November 1982), 543–69.

"The Market for 'Lemons': Quality Uncertainty and the Market Mechanism," *Quarterly Journal of Economics* 84 (August 1970), 488–500.

Akerlof, George A., and Janet L. Yellen. *Efficiency Wage Models of the Labor Market.* Cambridge: Cambridge University Press, 1986.

"The Fair Wage–Effort Hypothesis and Unemployment," *Quarterly Journal of Economics* 105 (May 1990), 255–83.

"Fairness and Unemployment," *American Economic Review* 78 (May 1988), 44–49.

Alchian, Armen, and Harold Demsetz. "Production, Information Costs, and Economic Organization," *American Economic Review* 62 (December 1972), 177–95.

Allen, Steve G. "Changes in the Cyclical Sensitivity of Wages in the United States, 1891–1987," *American Economic Review* 82 (March 1992), 122–40.

Alston, Lee J., and Joseph P. Ferrie. "Social Control and Labor Relations in the American South Before the Mechanization of the Cotton Harvest in the 1950s," *Journal of Institutional and Theoretical Economics* 145 (March 1989), 133–57.

Anderson, Michael. *Family Structure in Nineteenth-Century Lancashire.* Cambridge: Cambridge University Press, 1971.

"Sociological History and the Working-Class Family: Smelser Revisited," *Social History* 1 (October 1976), 317–34.

Andrew, Samuel. *Fifty Years of Work and Wages in the Cotton Trade.* Oldham, 1887.

Anonymous. *Lectures on Cotton Spinning.* Bolton, 1901.

Ashton, T. S. *The Industrial Revolution, 1760–1830.* London: Oxford University Press, 1948.

Ashworth, Henry. *An Inquiry into the Strike of Cotton Spinners of Preston.* Manchester, 1837.

Azariadis, Costas. "Implicit Contracts with Underemployment Equilibria," *Journal of Political Economy* 83 (December 1975), 1183–1202.

Babbage, Charles. *On the Economy of Machinery and Manufactures.* London, 1835.

Baines, Edward. *History of the Cotton Manufacture of Great Britain.* London: Cass, 1835 (reprinted in 1966).

Baird, R. H. *The American Cotton Spinner and Managers' and Carders' Guide.* Philadelphia, 1851.

Basu, Kaushik, Eric Jones, and Ekkehart Schlicht, "The Growth and Decay of Custom: The Role of the New Institutional Economics," *Explorations in Economic History* 24 (January 1987), 1–21.

Behagg, Clive. "Controlling the Product: Work, Time, and the Early Industrial Workforce in Britain, 1800–1850," in Cross, *Worktime and Industrialization. Politics and Production in Nineteenth-Century England.* London: Routledge, 1991.

Bendix, Richard. *Work and Authority in Industry.* New York: MacMillan, 1956.

Berg, Maxine. *The Age of Manufactures: Industry, Innovation, and Work in Britain, 1700–1820.* Oxford: Basil Blackwell, 1985.

The Machinery Question and the Making of Political Economy. Cambridge: Cambridge University Press, 1980.

"On the Origins of Capitalist Hierarchy," in Bo Gustafsson, ed., *Power and Economic Institutions: Reinterpretations in Economic History.* London: Edward Elgar, 1991.

Berg, Maxine, and Pat Hudson. "Rehabilitating the Industrial Revolution," *Economic History Review* 45 (February 1992), 24–50.

Berg, Maxine, Pat Hudson, and Michael Sonenscher. "Introduction," in Berg, Hudson, and Sonenscher, eds., *Manufacture in Town and Country Before the Factory, 1750–1900.* Cambridge: Cambridge University Press, 1983.

Bicherri, Cristina. "Norms of Cooperation," *Ethics* 100 (July 1990), 838–61.

Bienefeld, M. A. *Working Hours in British Industry: An Economic History.* London: Weidenfeld and Nicolson, 1972.

Blaug, Mark. "The Productivity of Capital in the Lancashire Cotton Industry During the Nineteenth Century," *Economic History Review* 13 (March 1961), 359–91.

Bolin-Hort, Per. *Work, Family, and the State: Child Labour and the Organization of Production in the British Cotton Industry.* Lund, Sweden: Lund University Press, 1989.

Boot, H. M. "How Skilled Were Lancashire Cotton Factory Workers in 1833?," *Economic History Review* 48 (May 1995), 283–303.

"Unemployment and Poor Law Relief in Manchester, 1845–50," *Social History* 15 (May 1990), 217–29.

Bowles, Samuel, and Herbert Gintis, "The Revenge of Homo Economicus: Contested Exchange and the Revival of Political Economy," *Journal of Economic Perspectives* 7 (Winter 1993), 83–102.

Bowley, Marion. *Nassau Senior and Classical Economics.* Manchester: Manchester University Press, 1967.

Boyer, George. *An Economic History of the English Poor Law, 1750–1850.* Cambridge: Cambridge University Press, 1990.

Boyson, Rhodes. *The Ashworth Cotton Enterprise: The Rise and Fall of a Family Firm, 1818–1880.* Oxford: Clarendon Press, 1970.

British Association for the Advancement of Science. *On the Regulation of Wages by Means of Lists in the Cotton Industry.* Manchester, 1887.

Brown, Charles. "Firms' Choice of Method of Pay," *Industrial and Labor Relations Review* 43 (February 1990), 165s–82s.

Brown, Charles, and James L. Medoff. "The Employer Size Wage Effect," *Journal of Political Economy* 97 (October 1989), 1027–59.

Brown, Geoff. *Sabotage: A Study in Industrial Conflict.* Bristol: Spokesman Books, 1977.

Brown, James N. "How Close to an Auction is the Labor Market," in Ronald G. Ehrenberg, ed., *Research in Labor Economics*, vol. VI. Greenwich, Conn.: Jai Press, 1983.

Brown, John C. "The Condition of England and the Standard of Living: Cotton Textiles in the Northwest, 1806–1850," *Journal of Economic History* 50 (March 1990), 591–614.

Brown, William, and Keith Sisson, "The Use of Comparisons in Workplace Wage Determination," *British Journal of Industrial Relations* 13, no. 1 (1975), 23–51.

Bullen, Andrew. "The Founding of the Amalgamation," in Fowler and Wyke, *Barefoot Aristocrats.*

"A Modern Spinners' Union," in Fowler and Wyke, *Barefoot Aristocrats.*

"Pragmatism vs Principle: Cotton Employers and the Origins of an Industrial Relations System," in J. A. Jowitt and A. J. McIvor, eds., *Employers and Labour in the English Textile Industries, 1850–1939.* London: Routledge, 1988.

Bulow, Jeremy I., and Lawrence H. Summers. "A Theory of Dual Labor Markets with Application to Industrial Policy, Discrimination, and Keynesian Unemployment," *Journal of Labor Economics* 4 (July 1986), 376–414.

Burn, R. S. *Statistics of the Cotton Trade.* London: Simpkin, 1847.

Bushaway, Bob. *By Rite: Custom, Ceremony, and Community in England.* London: Junction Books, 1982.

Bythell, Duncan. *The Handloom Weavers.* Cambridge: Cambridge University Press, 1969.

Calhoun, Craig. *The Question of Class Struggle: Social Foundations of Popular Radicalism During the Industrial Revolution.* Chicago: University of Chicago Press, 1982.

Calomiris, Charles W., and Christopher Hanes. "Historical Macroeconomics and American Macroeconomic History," National Bureau of Economic Research, Working Paper No. 4935, November 1994.

Cappelli, Peter, and Keith Chauvin, "An Interplant Test of the Efficiency Wage Hypothesis," *Quarterly Journal of Economics* 106 (August 1991), 769–87.

Carmichael, H. Lorne. "Efficiency Wage Models of Unemployment – One View," *Economic Inquiry* 27 (April 1990), 275–76.

Carmichael, H. Lorne, and W. Bentley MacLeod. "Worker Cooperation and the Ratchet Effect," paper prepared for a symposium at Osaka University, Japan, 1992.

Carter, Susan B., and Elizabeth Savoca. "Labor Mobility and Lengthy Jobs in Nineteenth-Century America," *Journal of Economic History* 50 (March 1990), 1–16.

Carter, Susan B., and Richard Sutch. "Sticky Wages, Short Weeks, and Fairness: The Response of Connecticut Manufacturing Firms to the Depression of 1893–94," University of California Historical Labor Statistics Project, Working Paper no. 2, 1992.

Catling, Harold J. *The Self-Acting Mule.* Newton Abbot: David and Charles, 1970.

Chapman, S. D. "British Marketing Enterprise: The Changing Roles of Merchants, Manufacturers, and Financiers, 1700–1860," *Business History Review* 53 (Summer 1979), 205–35.

The Cotton Industry in the Industrial Revolution, 2nd edn. London: MacMillan, 1987.

"Financial Restraints on the Growth of Firms in the Cotton Industry, 1790–1850," *Economic History Review* 32 (February 1979), 50–70.

"Introduction," in Gilbert French, *The Life and Times of Samuel Crompton.* Bath: Redwood Press, 1970.

"The Textile Industries," in G. Roderock and M. Stephens, eds., *Where Did We Go Wrong? Industrial Performance, Education, and the Economy in Victorian Britain.* Lewes, Sussex: Falconer Press, 1981.

Chapman, S. D., and S. Chassagne. *European Textile Printers in the Eighteenth Century.* London: Heinemann, 1981.

Chapman, S. J. *The Lancashire Cotton Industry: A Study in Economic Development.* Manchester: Manchester University Press, 1904.

"The Regulation of Wages by Lists in the Spinning Industry," *Economic Journal* 9 (March 1899), 593–94.

Chapman, S. J. and H. M. Hallsworth. *Unemployment: The Results of an Investigation Made in Lancashire*. Manchester: Manchester University Press, 1909.

Clark, Gregory. "Factory Discipline," *Journal of Economic History* 54 (March 1994), 128–64.

"Why Isn't the Whole World Developed: Lessons from the Cotton Mills," *Journal of Economic History* 47 (March 1987), 134–67.

Clay, Henry. *Report on the Position of the British Cotton Industry*. Confidential Report for Securities Management Trust, Ltd., London, 20 October 1931.

Clegg, H. A., Alan Fox, and A. F. Thompson. *A History of British Trade Unions, vol. I: 1889–1910*. Oxford: Clarendon Press, 1964.

Coats, A. W. "Changing Attitudes to Labour in the Mid-Eighteenth Century," *Economic History Review* 11 (January 1958), 35–51.

Cohen, Isaac. *American Management and British Labor: A Comparative Study of the Cotton-Spinning Industry*. New York: Greenwood Press, 1990.

"Workers' Control in the Cotton Industry: A Comparative Study of British and American Mule Spinning," *Labor History* 26 (Winter 1985), 53–85.

Coleman, Jules L., Steven Maser, and Douglas Heckathorn. "Bargaining and Contract," in Kenneth J. Koford and Jeffrey B. Miller, eds., *Social Norms and Economic Institutions*. Ann Arbor: University of Michigan Press, 1991.

Collier, Frances. *The Family Economy of the Working Classes in the Cotton Industry, 1784–1833*. Manchester: Manchester University Press, 1964.

Cross, Gary. *A Quest for Time: The Reduction of Work in Britain and France, 1840–1940*. Berkeley: University of California Press, 1989.

Cross, Gary, ed. *Worktime and Industrialization: An International History*. Philadelphia: Temple University Press, 1988.

Dalton, Melville. "The Industrial 'Rate-Buster': A Characterization," *Applied Anthropology* 7 (Winter 1948), 5–18.

Daniels, G. W. *The Early English Cotton Industry*. Manchester: Manchester University Press, 1920.

"The Early Records of a Great Manchester Cotton-Spinning Firm," *Economic Journal* 25 (June 1915), 175–88.

"Samuel Crompton's Census of the Cotton Industry in 1811," *Economic Journal (Economic History Supplement)* 2 (1930), 107–10.

De Long, Bradford J. "Senior's Last Hour: A Suggested Explanation of a Famous Blunder," *History of Political Economy* 18 (Summer 1986), 325–33.

Deane, Phyllis. *The First Industrial Revolution*. Cambridge: Cambridge University Press, 1962.

Dickens, William T., and Kevin Lang. "The Reemergence of Segmented Labor Market Theory," *American Economic Review* 78 (May 1988), 129–34.

Dodd, George. *The Textile Manufacturer of Great Britain*. London, 1844.

Doeringer, Peter, and Michael Piore. *Internal Labor Markets and Manpower Analysis*. Boston: D. C. Heath, 1971.

Dunlop, John. "Wage Contours," in Michael J. Piore, ed., *Unemployment and Inflation: Institutionalist and Structuralist Views*. White Plains, N. Y.: M. E. Sharpe, 1979.

Dutton, H. I., and J. E. King. "The Limits of Paternalism," *Social History* 7 (January 1982), 59–73.

Ten Percent and No Surrender: The Preston Strike, 1853–54. Cambridge: Cambridge University Press, 1981.

Edwards, Michael M., and Roger Lloyd-Jones. "N. J. Smelser and the Cotton Factory Family: A Reassessment," in N. B. Harte and K. G. Ponting, eds., *Textile History and Economic History.* Manchester: Manchester University Press, 1973.

Edwards, Richard. *Contested Terrain.* New York: Basic Books, 1979.

Eggerston, Thrainn. *Economic Behavior and Institutions.* New York: Cambridge University Press, 1990.

Elbaum, Bernard, and William Lazonick. *The Decline of the British Economy.* Oxford: Clarendon Press, 1986.

Ellison, Thomas. *The Cotton Trade of Great Britain.* London, 1886.

"The Great Crises in the History of the Cotton Trade: A Retrospect of Prices and Supply, 1790–1862," *The Exchange* 1 (1862), 45–53.

Elster, Jon. *The Cement of Society: Studies in Rationality and Social Change.* New York: Cambridge University Press, 1989.

Fama, Eugene. "Time, Salary, and Incentive Payoffs in Labor Contracts," *Journal of Labor Economics* 9 (January 1991), 25–44.

Farnie, Douglas A. "The Emergence of Victorian Oldham as a Centre of the Cotton-Spinning Industry," *Bulletin of the Saddleworth Historical Society* 12 (Autumn 1982), 41–54.

The English Cotton Industry in the World Market. Oxford: Oxford University Press, 1979.

"An Index of Commercial Activity: The Membership of the Manchester Royal Exchange, 1809–1948," *Business History* 21 (January 1979), 97–106.

Field, Alexander J. "Microeconomics, Norms, and Rationality," *Economic Development and Cultural Change* 32 (July 1984), 683–711.

"The Problem with Neoclassical Institutional Economics: A Critique with Special Reference to the North/Thomas Model of Pre-1500 Europe," *Explorations in Economic History* 18 (April 1981), 174–98.

Fitton, R. S. *The Arkwrights: Spinners of Fortune.* Manchester: Manchester University Press, 1989.

Fitton, R. S., and A. P. Wadsworth. *The Strutts and the Arkwrights, 1758–1830: A Study in the Early Factory System.* Manchester: Manchester University Press, 1958.

Foster, John. *Class Struggle and the Industrial Revolution.* London: Methuen, 1974.

Fowler, Alan, and Terry Wyke, eds. *The Barefoot Aristocrats: A History of the Amalgamated Association of Operative Cotton Spinners.* Littleborough: George Kelsall, 1987.

Freeman, Richard, and James L. Medoff. *What Do Unions Do?* New York: Basic Books, 1984.

Freifeld, Mary. "Technological Change and the Self-Acting Mule: A Study of Skill and Sexual Division of Labour," *Social History* 11 (October 1986), 319–43.

Freudenberger, Herman, Frances J. Mather, and Clark Nardinelli. "A New Look at the Early Factory Labor Force," *Journal of Economic History* 44 (December 1984), 1085–91.

Gadian, D. S. "Class Consciousness in Oldham and Other North-West Industrial Towns," *Historical Journal* 21 (March 1978), 161–72.

Gardner, Robert S. *Letter to His Workpeople.* Manchester, 1845.

Gaskell, Peter. *Artisans and Machinery.* London: Parker, 1836.

Gatrell, V. A. C. "Labour, Power, and the Size of Firms in Lancashire Cotton in the Second Quarter of the Nineteenth Century," *Economic History Review* 30 (February 1977), 95–139.

Gayer, A. D., W. R. Rostow, and A. J. Schwartz. *The Growth and Fluctuations of the British Economy, 1790–1850.* Oxford: Oxford University Press, 1952.

Gibbons, Robert. *Game Theory for Applied Economists.* Princeton: Princeton University Press, 1992.

"Piece Rate Incentive Schemes," *Journal of Labor Economics* 5 (October 1987), 413–29.

Gordon, D. F. "A Neo-Classical Theory of Keynesian Unemployment," *Economic Inquiry* 12 (October 1974), 431–59.

Gordon, Robert J. "What is New-Keynesian Economics," *Journal of Economic Literature* 28 (September 1990), 1115–71.

"Why US Wage and Employment Behaviour Differs from that in Britain and Japan," *Economic Journal* 92 (March 1982), 13–41.

Grantham, George. "Economic History and the History of Labor Markets," in George Grantham and Mary MacKinnon, eds., *Labour Market Evolution: The Economic History of Market Integration, Wage Flexibility, and the Employment Relation.* London: Routledge, 1994.

Gray, Robert. "The Languages of Factory Reform in Britain, c. 1830–1860," in Joyce, *Historical Meanings of Work.*

Green, Francis. "Neoclassical and Marxian Conceptions of Production," *Cambridge Journal of Economics* 12 (September 1988), 299–312.

Greg, W. R. "The Relation Between Employers and Employed," in W. R. Greg, *Essays on Political and Social Science.* Manchester, 1853.

Grossman, Sanford, and Oliver Hart. "Implicit Contracts, Moral Hazard, and Unemployment," *American Economic Review* 71 (March 1981), 301–07.

Habakkuk, H. J. *American and British Technology in the Nineteenth Century: The Search for Labor-Saving Inventions.* Cambridge: Cambridge University Press, 1962.

Hall, Robert G. "Tyranny, Work, and Politics: The 1818 Strike Wave in the English Cotton District," *International Review of Social History* 34, no. 3 (1989), 433–70.

Hall, Robert, and John B. Taylor. *Macroeconomics: Theory, Performance, and Policy.* New York: Norton, 1986.

Hammond, John L., and Barbara Hammond. *The Town Labourer, 1760–1830.* London: Longmans Green, 1917.

Hanes, Christopher. "The Development of Nominal Wage Rigidity in the Late

Nineteenth Century," *American Economic Review* 83 (September 1993), 732–56.

Harrison, Mark. "The Ordering of the Urban Environment: Time, Work, and the Occurrence of Crowds, 1790–1835," *Past and Present* 110 (February 1986), 134–68.

"A Rejoinder to David Landes," *Past and Present* 116 (August 1987), 199–206.

Hart, Oliver D. "Optimal Labour Contracts Under Asymmetric Information: An Introduction," *Review of Economic Studies* 50 (January 1983), 3–35.

Hartwell, R. M., and Stanley Engerman. "Models of Immiseration: The Theoretical Basis of Pessimism," in Arthur J. Taylor, ed., *The Standard of Living in Britain in the Industrial Revolution*. London: Methuen, 1975.

Hayami, Yujiro, and Masao Kikuchi. *Asian Village Economy at the Crossroads*. Baltimore: Johns Hopkins University Press, 1982.

Heckathorn, Douglas D. "Collective Action and the Second-Order Free-Rider Problem," *Rationality and Society* 1 (July 1989), 78–101.

Hicks, J. R. *A Theory of Wages*. New York: St. Martin's Press, 1963.

Hirschman, Albert. *Exit, Voice, Loyalty*. Cambridge, Mass.: Harvard University Press, 1970.

Hobsbawm, Eric J. *Industry and Empire*. Harmondsworth: Penguin, 1969.

Labouring Men. London: Weidenfeld and Nicolson, 1968.

Honeyman, Katrina. *Origins of Enterprise: Business Leadership in the Industrial Revolution*. Manchester: Manchester University Press, 1982.

Horrell, Sara, and Jane Humphries. "Old Questions, New Data, and Alternative Perspectives: The Standard of Living in the British Industrial Revolution," *Journal of Economic History* 52 (December 1992), 849–81.

Howe, Anthony. *The Cotton Masters, 1830–1860*. Oxford: Clarendon Press, 1984.

Huberman, Michael. "The Economic Origins of Paternalism: Lancashire Cotton Spinning in the First Half of the Nineteenth Century," *Social History* 12 (May 1987), 177–93.

"The Economic Origins of Paternalism: A Reply to Rose, Taylor, Winstanley," *Social History* 14 (1989), 99–103.

"How Did Labor Markets Work in Lancashire? More Evidence on Prices and Quantities, 122–52," *Explorations in Economic History* 28 (January 1991), 87–120.

"Industrial Relations and the Industrial Revolution: Evidence from M'Connel and Kennedy," *Business History Review* 65 (Summer 1991), 345–78.

"Invisible Handshakes in Lancashire: Cotton Spinning in the First Half of the Nineteenth Century," *Journal of Economic History* 46 (December 1986), 980–91.

"Piece Rates Reconsidered: The Case of Cotton," *Journal of Interdisciplinary History* 26 (Winter 1996), 393–417.

"Some Early Evidence of Worksharing: Lancashire Before 1850," *Business History* 37 (October 1995), 1–25.

"Testing for the 'Conscientious Withdrawal of Efficiency': Evidence from the Industrial Revolution," *Historical Methods* 26 (Summer 1993), 119–25.

"Vertical Disintegration in Lancashire: A Comment on Temin," *Journal of Economic History* 50 (September 1990), 683–90.

Hudson, Pat. "The Regional Perspective," in Hudson, ed., *Regions and Industries: A Perspective on the Industrial Revolution in Britain.* Cambridge: Cambridge University Press, 1989.

Hughes, J. R. T. *Fluctuations in Trade, Industry, and Finance.* Oxford: Clarendon Press, 1960.

Jaffe, James A. *The Struggle for Market Power: Industrial Relations in the British Coal Industry, 1800–1840.* Cambridge: Cambridge University Press, 1991.

Jeremy, David. *Transatlantic Industrial Revolution: The Diffusion of Textile Technologies Between Britain and America, 1790–1830s.* Cambridge, Mass.: MIT Press, 1981.

Jewkes, John, and E. M. Gray. *Wages and Labour in the Lancashire Cotton-Spinning Industry.* Manchester: Manchester University Press, 1935.

Jones, Steven R. G. *The Economics of Conformism.* Oxford: Oxford University Press, 1984.

Joyce, Patrick. "Labour, Capital, and Compromise: A Response to Richard Price," *Social History* 9 (January 1984), 67–76.

Visions of the People: Industrial England and the Question of Class, 1848–1914. Cambridge: Cambridge University Press, 1991.

Work, Society, and Politics: The Culture of the Factory in Later Victorian England. Brighton: University of Sussex Press, 1980.

Joyce, Patrick, ed. *The Historical Meanings of Work.* Cambridge: Cambridge University Press, 1987.

Kanemoto, Yoshitsugu, and W. Bentley MacLeod. "The Ratchet Effect and the Market for Secondhand Workers," *Journal of Labor Economics* 10 (January 1992), 85–98.

Katz, Lawrence F. "Efficiency Wage Theories: A Partial Evaluation," in *NBER Macroeconomics Annual 1986.* Cambridge: MIT Press, 1986.

Kennedy, John. "A Brief Memoir of Samuel Crompton, with a Description of His Machine Called the Mule and the Subsequent Improvement of the Machine by Others," *Memoirs of the Literary and Philosophical Society of Manchester* 5 (1831), 335–43.

Keynes, John Maynard. "Industrial Reorganisation: Cotton," in Donald E. Moggridge, ed., *The Collected Writings of John Maynard Keynes, Vol. XIX, Part ii. Activities, 1922–1929: The Return to the Gold Standard and Industrial Policy.* Cambridge: Cambridge University Press, 1981.

Kiesling, L. Lynne. "Institutional Choice Matters: The Poor Law and Implicit Labor Contracts in Victorian Lancashire," *Explorations in Economic History* 33 (January 1996), 65–85.

King, J. E. "Perish Consumption! Free Trade and Underconsumption in Early British Radical Economics," *Australian Economic Papers* 20 (December 1981), 235–57.

Kirby, R. G., and A. E. Musson. *The Voice of the People. John Doherty, 1789–1854: Trade Unionist, Radical, and Factory Reformer.* Manchester: Manchester University Press, 1975.

Kirk, Neville. *The Growth of Working-Class Reformism in Mid-Victorian England.* Champaign: University of Illinois Press, 1985.

Knight, Jack. *Institutions and Social Conflict.* New York: Cambridge University Press, 1992.

Kreps, David. *Game Theory and Economic Modelling.* Oxford: Clarendon Press, 1990.

Kreps, David M., and Robert Wilson. "Sequential Equilibria," *Econometrica* 50 (July 1982), 863–94.

Kreuger, Alan B., and Lawrence H. Summers. "Efficiency Wages and the Interindustry Wage Structure," *Econometrica* 56 (March 1988), 259–93.

"Reflections on the Inter-Industry Wage Structure," in Kevin Lang and Jonathan S. Leonard, eds., *Unemployment and the Structure of Labor Markets.* New York: Basil Blackwell, 1987.

Landes, David S. "The Ordering of the Urban Environment: Time, Work, and the Occurrence of Crowds, 1790–1835," *Past and Present* 116 (August 1987), 192–99.

The Unbound Prometheus: Technological Change and Industrial Development in Western Europe from 1750 to the Present. Cambridge: Cambridge University Press, 1969.

"What Do Bosses Really Do?," *Journal of Economic History* 46 (September 1986), 585–624.

Lang, Kevin, and Shulamit Kahn. "Efficiency Wage Models of Unemployment: A Second View," *Economic Inquiry* 28 (April 1990), 296–306.

Lang, Kevin, Jonathan S. Leonard, and David Lilien. "Labor Market Structure, Wages, and Unemployment," in Kevin Lang and Jonathan S. Leonard, eds., *Unemployment and the Structure of Labor Markets.* New York: Basil Blackwell, 1987.

Lansburg, Richard, and William Spiegel. *Industrial Management,* 3rd edn. New York: John Wiley, 1940.

Lazear, Edward. "Salaries and Piece Rates," *Journal of Business* 59, no. 3 (1986), 405–31.

Lazear, Edward, and Sherwin Rosen. "Rank Order Tournaments as Optimum Labor Contracts," *Journal of Political Economy* 89 (1981), 841–64.

Lazonick, William. *Competitive Advantage on the Shop Floor.* Cambridge, Mass.: Harvard University Press, 1990.

Lee, C. H. *A Cotton Enterprise, 1795–1840: A History of M'Connel and Kennedy, Fine Cotton Spinners.* Manchester: Manchester University Press, 1972.

"The Cotton-Textile Industry," in Roy Church, ed., *The Dynamics of Victorian Business.* London: Allen and Unwin, 1980.

Leibenstein, Harvey. *Economic Backwardness and Economic Growth.* New York: Wiley, 1957.

Leiserson, William R. "The Workers' Reaction to Scientific Management," in Edward E. Hint, ed., *Scientific Management Since Taylor.* Easton, Penn.: Hive, 1972.

Leonard, Jonathan S. "Carrots and Sticks: Pay, Supervision, and Turnover," *Journal of Labor Economics* 5 (October 1987), 136s–53s.

Levine, David I. "Cohesiveness, Productivity, and Wage Dispersion," *Journal of Economic Behavior and Organization* 15 (1991), 237–57.

"Piece Rates, Output Restriction, and Conformism," *Journal of Economic Psychology* 13 (September 1992), 473–89.

Lewchuk, Wayne. *American Technology and the British Vehicle Industry.* Cambridge: Cambridge University Press, 1987.

"Giving and Getting the Wrong Signals: Institutions, Technical Change, and the Decline of British Productivity Since 1850," *Business and Economic History* 20 (1991), 77–89.

"Men and Monotony: Fraternalism as a Managerial Strategy in the Ford Motor Company," *Journal of Economic History* 53 (December 1993), 824–75.

Lindert, Peter H. "Unequal Living Standards," in Roderick Floud and Donald McCloskey, eds., *The Economic History of Britain Since 1700*, 2nd edn., vol. I. Cambridge: Cambridge University Press, 1992.

Litchfield, R. Burr. "The Family and the Mill: Cotton Mill Work, Family Work Patterns, and Fertility in Mid-Victorian Stockport," in Anthony S. Wohl, ed., *The Victorian Family: Structure and Stresses.* London: Croom Helm, 1978.

Littler, Craig. *The Development of the Labor Process in Capitalist Societies.* London: Heinemann, 1982.

Lloyd-Jones, Roger, and A. A. LeRoux. "Factory Utilization and the Firm: The Manchester Cotton Industry, c. 1825–1840," *Textile History* 15 (1984), 119–27.

"The Size of Firms in the Cotton Industry: Manchester, 1815–41," *Economic History Review* 33 (February 1980), 72–82.

Longworth, James. *The Cotton Mills of Bolton.* Bolton: Bolton Museum and Art Gallery, 1987.

Lowe, James. "Account of the Strike and Lock-Out in the Cotton Trade at Preston in 1853," in National Association for the Promotion of Social Science, *Trades' Societies and Strikes.* London: National Association for the Promotion of Social Science, 1860.

Lowenstein, Mark. "Worker Heterogeneity, Hours Restrictions, and Temporary Layoffs," *Econometrica* 51 (January 1983), 69–78.

Lupton, T. *On the Shop Floor.* Oxford: Pergamon Press, 1963.

Lynton, R. P. *Incentives and Management in British Industry.* London: Routledge & Kegan Paul, 1949.

Lyons, John S. "Family Response to Economic Decline: Handloom Weavers in Early Nineteenth-Century Lancashire," *Research in Economic History* 12 (1989), 45–91.

"The Lancashire Cotton Industry and the Introduction of the Powerloom, 1815–50," Ph.D. dissertation, University of California, Berkeley, 1977.

"The Lancashire Textile Factory Sector and Occupational Mobility in the 1840s," mimeograph, Miami University, Ohio, October 1991.

"Vertical Integration in the British Cotton Industry, 1825–1850: A Revision," *Journal of Economic History* 45 (March 1985), 419–27.

Lytle, Charles W. *Wage Incentive Methods: Their Selection, Installation, and Operation.* New York: Ronald Press, 1938.

M'Connel, J. W. *A Century of Fine Spinning*. Manchester, 1906.

McDonald, Ian M., and Robert M. Solow. "Wage Bargaining and Employment," *American Economic Review* 71 (December 1981), 896–908.

McIvor, Arthur J. "Cotton Employers' Organisations and Labour Relations, 1890–1939," in J. A. Jowitt and A. J. McIvor, eds., *Employers and Labour in the English Textile Industries, 1850–1939*. London: Routledge, 1988.

Magnusson, Lars. "From Verlag to Factory: The Contest for Efficient Property Rights," in Bo Gustafsson, ed., *Power and Economic Institutions: Reinterpretations in Economic History*. London: Edward Elgar, 1991.

Malcolmson, J. M. "Efficient Labour Organization: Incentives, Power, and the Transaction Cost Approach," in F. J. Stephen, ed., *Firms, Organization, and Labour*. London: MacMillan, 1984.

Mankiw, N. Gregory. "A Quick Refresher Course in Macroeconomics," *Journal of Economic Literature* 28 (December 1990), 1645–60.

Mann, J. A. *The Cotton Trade of Great Britain*. Manchester: Thomson, 1860.

Marglin, Stephen A. "Understanding Capitalism: Control Versus Efficiency," in Bo Gustafsson, ed., *Power and Economic Institutions: Reinterpretations in Economic History*. London: Edward Elgar, 1991.

"What Do Bosses Do? The Origins and Functions of Hierarchy in Capitalist Production," *Review of Radical Political Economics* 6 (Summer 1974), 33–60.

Marriot, R. *Incentive Payment Systems*. London: Staples Press, 1957.

Marshall, Alfred. "A Fair Rate of Wages," in A. C. Pigou, ed., *Memorials of Alfred Marshall*. London: MacMillan, 1925.

Marvel, Howard P. "Factory Regulation: A Reinterpretation of Early English Experience," *Journal of Law and Economics* 20 (October 1977), 379–402.

Marx, Karl. *Capital: Volume One*. New York: Vintage Books, 1977.

Mason, John. "Mule Spinner Societies and the Early Federations," in Fowler and Wyke, *Barefoot Aristocrats*.

Mass, William, and William Lazonick. "The British Cotton Industry and International Competitive Advantage: The State of the Debates," in Mary Rose, ed., *International Competition and Strategic Response in the Textile Industries Since 1870*. London: Frank Cass, 1991.

Mathewson, Stanley B. *Restriction of Output Among Unorganized Workers*, 2nd edn. Carbondale: Southern Illinois University Press, 1969.

Matthews, R. C. O. *A Study in Trade Cycle History: Economic Fluctuations in Great Britain, 1833–42*. Cambridge: Cambridge University Press, 1954.

Matthews, R. C. O., C. H. Feinstein, and J. C. Odling-Smee. *British Economic Growth 1856–1973*. Oxford: Clarendon Press, 1982.

Milgrom, Paul R., Douglass C. North, and Barry W. Weingast. "The Role of Institutions in the Revival of Trade: The Law Merchant, Private Judges, and the Champagne Fairs," *Economics and Politics* 2 (1990), 1–23.

Miller, Gary J. *The Political Economy of Hierarchy*. Cambridge: Cambridge University Press, 1992.

Mitchell, Daniel J. B. "Explanations of Wage Inflexibility: Institutions and Incentives," in Wilfred Beckerman, ed., *Wage Rigidity and Unemployment*. Baltimore: Johns Hopkins University Press, 1986.

Mokyr, Joel. "Dear Labor, Cheap Labor, and the Industrial Revolution," in Patrice Higonnet *et al.*, eds., *Favorites of Fortune: Technology, Growth, and Economic Development Since the Industrial Revolution*. Cambridge, Mass.: Harvard University Press, 1991.

    "Is There Still Life in the Pessimist Case? Consumption During the Industrial Revolution, 1790–1850," *Journal of Economic History* 48 (March 1988), 69–92.

Morris, Robert J. *Class and Class Consciousness in the Industrial Revolution, 1780–1850*. London: MacMillan, 1979.

Myers, C. S. *Mind and Work*. London: University of London Press, 1920.

Nardinelli, Clark. "The Successful Prosecution of the Factory Acts," *Economic History Review* 38 (August 1985), 428–30.

Neale, R. S. *Writing Marxist History: British Society, Economy, and Culture Since 1700*. Oxford: Basil Blackwell, 1985.

Nelson, Daniel. *Frederick W. Taylor and the Rise of Scientific Management*. Madison: University of Wisconsin Press, 1980.

Nicholas, Stephen, and Richard H. Steckel. "Heights and Living Standards During the Early Years of Industrialization, 1770–1815," *Journal of Economic History* 51 (December 1991), 937–57.

North, Douglass C. *Institutions, Institutional Change, and Economic Performance*. New York: Cambridge University Press, 1990.

    Structure and Change in Economic History. New York: Norton, 1981.

Nyland, Chris. *Reduced Worktime and the Management of Production*. New York: Cambridge University Press, 1989.

O'Brien, Anthony. "The Cyclical Sensitivity of Wages," *American Economic Review* 75 (December 1985), 1124–32.

Oddy, David J. "Urban Famine in Nineteenth-Century Britain: The Effect of the Lancashire Cotton Famine on Working-Class Diet and Health," *Economic History Review* 36 (February 1983), 68–86.

Oi, Walter. "Heterogeneous Firms and the Organization of Production," *Economic Inquiry* 21 (April 1983), 147–72.

Okun, Arthur M. "Inflation: Its Mechanics and Welfare Costs," *Brookings Papers on Economic Activity*, no. 2 (1975), 351–90.

    Prices and Quantities: A Macroeconomic Analysis. Washington, D. C.: Brookings Institution, 1981.

Otsuka, Keijoru, Hiroyuki Chuma, and Yujiro Hayami. "Land and Labor Contracts in Agrarian Economies," *Journal of Economic Literature* 30 (December 1992), 1965–2019.

Pencavel, John. "Work Effort, On-the-Job Screening, and Alternative Methods of Remuneration," in Ronald G. Ehrenberg, ed., *Research in Labor Economics*, vol. I. Greenwich, Conn.: JAI, 1977.

Phillips, A. W. "The Relation Between Unemployment and the Rate of Change of Money Wage Rates in the United Kingdom, 1861–1957," *Economica* 25 (May 1958), 283–300.

Pinchbeck, Ivy. *Women Workers and the Industrial Revolution*. London: Virago Press, 1980.

Polanyi, Karl. *The Great Transformation*. Boston: Beacon Press, 1944.

Pollard, Sidney. *The Genesis of Modern Management*. London: Edwin Arnold, 1965.

"Labour in Great Britain," in Peter Mathias and Michael M. Postan, eds., *The Cambridge Economic History of Europe, Volume VII. The Industrial Economies: Capital, Labour, and Enterprise*. Cambridge: Cambridge University Press, 1978.

Porter, J. H. "Industrial Peace in the Cotton Trade, 1875–1913," *Yorkshire Bulletin of Economic and Social Research* 19 (May 1967), 49–62.

Price, Richard. "The Labor Process and Labor History," *Social History* 8 (January 1983), 57–73.

Raff, Daniel M. G., and Lawrence H. Summers. "Did Henry Ford Pay Efficiency Wages?," *Journal of Labor Economics* 5 (October 1987), 57s–86s.

Ramaswamy, Ramana, and Robert E. Rowthorn. "Efficiency Wages and Wage Dispersion," *Economica* 58 (November 1991), 501–14.

Randall, Adrian. *Before the Luddites: Custom, Community, and Machinery in the English Woollen Industry 1776–1809*. Cambridge: Cambridge University Press, 1991.

Rasmusen, Eric. *Games and Information: An Introduction to Game Theory*. Oxford: Basil Blackwell, 1989.

Reach, Angus B. *Manchester and the Textile Districts in 1849*, ed. C. Aspin. Rossendale: Helmshore Local History Society, 1972.

Rebitzer, James B., and Lowell J. Taylor. "A Model of Dual Labor Markets when Product Demand Is Uncertain," *Quarterly Journal of Economics* 106 (November 1991), 1373–83.

Redford, Arthur. *Labour Migration in England, 1800–1850*, 2nd edn. Manchester: Manchester University Press, 1964.

Rees, Abraham. *The Cyclopedia; or Universal Dictionary of Arts, Science, and Literature*. Newton Abbott: David and Charles, reprint of selected articles, 1972.

Reid, D. A. "The Decline of Saint Monday 1766–1876," *Past and Present* 71 (January 1976), 76–102.

Richardson, Philip. "The Structure of Capital During the Industrial Revolution Revisited: Two Case Studies from the Cotton-Textile Industry," *Economic History Review* 42 (November 1989), 484–503.

Roberts, Bryan. "Agrarian Organization and Urban Development," in J. O. Wirth and R. L. Jones, eds., *Manchester and Sao Paulo: Problems of Rapid Urban Growth*. Stanford: Stanford University Press, 1978.

Rose, Mary. *The Gregs of Quarry Bank Mill: The Rise and Decline of a Family Firm, 1750–1914*. Cambridge: Cambridge University Press, 1986.

"Paternalism, Industrial Welfare, and Business Strategy: Britain to 1939," in Erik Aerts *et al.*, eds., *Liberalism and Paternalism in the Nineteenth Century*. Leuven, Belgium: Leuven University Press, 1990.

"The Role of the Family in the Provision of Capital and Managerial Talent in Samuel Greg and Company 1750–1840," *Business History* 19 (January 1977), 42–43.

Rose, Mary, Peter Taylor, and Michael J. Winstanley. "The Economic Origins of Paternalism: Some Objections," *Social History* 14 (January 1989), 89–99.

Rose, Sonya O. "Gender Antagonism and Class Conflict: Exclusionary Strategies of Male Trade Unionists in Nineteenth-Century Britain," *Social History* 13 (January 1988), 191–208.

Limited Livelihoods: Gender and Class in Nineteenth-Century England. Berkeley: University of California Press, 1992.

Rosen, Sherwin. "The Theory of Equalizing Differences," in Orley Ashenfelter and Richard Layard, eds., *Handbook of Labor Economics.* Amsterdam: North Holland, 1986.

Rousseaux, Paul. *Les mouvements de fond de l'economie anglaise: 1800-1903.* London, 1930.

Rowe, J. W. F. *Wages in Practice and Theory.* London: George Routledge, 1928.

Rowe, Nicholas. *Rules and Institutions.* Ann Arbor: University of Michigan Press, 1989.

Roy, Donald. "Quota Restriction and Goldbricking in a Machine Shop," *American Journal of Sociology* 57 (March 1952), 427–42.

Rule, John. *The Experience of Labour in Eighteenth-Century English Industry.* New York: St. Martin's Press, 1981.

Sachs, Jeffrey. "The Changing Cyclical Behavior of Wages and Prices: 1890–1976," *American Economic Review* 70 (March 1980), 78–90.

Samuel, Raphael. "The Workshop of the World," *History Workshop* 3 (1977), 6–72.

Samuelson, Paul, and Robert M. Solow. "Analytic Aspects of Anti-Inflation Policy," *American Economic Review* 50 (May 1960), 177–94.

Savage, Michael. *The Dynamics of Working-Class Politics: The Labour Movement in Preston.* Cambridge: Cambridge University Press, 1987.

Saxonhouse, Gary, and Gavin Wright. "Two Forms of Cheap Labor in Textile History," in Saxonhouse and Wright, eds., *Technique, Spirit, and Form in the Making of Modern Economies: Essays in the Honor of William N. Parker.* Greenwich, Conn.: JAI Press, 1984.

Schloss, David F. *Methods of Industrial Remuneration.* Oxford: Williams and Norgate, 1898.

Schofield, Roger S. "Sampling in Historical Research," in E. A. Wrigley, ed., *Nineteenth-Century Society: Essays in the Use of Quantitative Methods for the Study of Social Data.* Cambridge: Cambridge University Press, 1972.

Scholes, James C. *History of Bolton.* Bolton, 1842.

Schotter, Andrew. *The Economic Theory of Social Institutions.* New York: Cambridge University Press, 1981.

"The Evolution of Rules," in Richard N. Langlois, ed., *Economics as a Process: Essays in the New Institutional Economics.* Cambridge: Cambridge University Press, 1986.

Seed, John. "Unitarianism, Political Economy, and the Antinomies of Liberal Culture in Manchester, 1830–50," *Social History* 7 (January 1982), 1–26.

Seiler, Eric. "Piece Rate vs. Time Rate: The Effect of Incentives on Earnings," *Review of Economics and Statistics* 66 (August 1984), 363–76.

Shapiro, Carl, and Joseph E. Stiglitz. "Equilibrium Unemployment as a Worker Discipline Device," *American Economic Review* 74 (June 1984), 433–44.

Shiells, Martha E. "Collective Choice of Working Conditions: Hours in Britain and US Steel, 1890–1923," *Journal of Economic History* 50 (June 1990), 379–92.

"Hours of Work and Shiftwork in the Early Industrial Labor Markets of Great Britain, the United States, and Japan," Ph.D. dissertation, University of Michigan, 1985.

Shiells, Martha E., and Gavin Wright. "Night Work as a Labor-Market Phenomenon: Southern Textiles in the Interwar Period," *Explorations in Economic History* 20 (July 1983), 331–50.

Shuttleworth, John. "Vital Statistics of Piecers and Spinners Employed in the Fine-Spinning Mills of Manchester," *Journal of the Royal Statistical Society* 5 (1842), 268–73.

Singleton, John. *Lancashire on the Scrapheap: The Cotton Industry, 1945–1970.* Oxford: Oxford University Press, 1991.

Smelser, Neil J. *Social Change in the Industrial Revolution: An Application of Theory to the Lancashire Cotton Industry, 1770–1840.* London: Routledge and Kegan Paul, 1959.

Smith, Roland. "Manchester as a Centre for the Manufacture and Merchandising of Cotton Goods, 1820–30," *University of Birmingham Historical Journal* 4 (1953–54), 47–65.

Solow, Robert M. *The Labor Market as a Social Institution.* Oxford: Basil Blackwell, 1990.

"On Theories of Unemployment," *American Economic Review* 70 (March 1980), 1–12.

Stigler, George. "Information in the Labor Market," *Journal of Political Economy* 70 (October 1962), 94s–105s.

Stiglitz, Joseph E. "The Causes and Consequences of the Dependence of Quality on Price," *Journal of Economic Literature* 25 (March 1987), 1–49.

"Incentives, Risk, and Information: Notes Toward a Theory of Hierarchy," *Bell Journal of Economics and Management Science* 6 (Autumn 1975), 552–79.

Stiglitz, Joseph E., and Andrew Weiss. "Credit Rationing in Markets with Imperfect Information," *American Economic Review* 71 (June 1981), 393–411.

Styles, John. "Embezzlement, Industry, and the Law in England, 1500–1800," in Maxine Berg, Pat Hudson, and Michael Sonenscher, eds., *Manufacture in Town and Country Before the Factory, 1750–1900.* Cambridge: Cambridge University Press, 1983.

Sugden, Robert. *The Economics of Rights, Co-operation, and Welfare.* Oxford: Basil Blackwell, 1986.

Sundstrom, William A. "Internal Labor Markets Before World War I: On-the-Job Training and Employee Promotion," *Explorations in Economic History* 25 (October 1988), 424–45.

"Real Wages or Small Equilibrium Adjustments? Evidence from the Contraction of 1893," *Explorations in Economic History* 29 (October 1992), 430–56.

Sutch, Richard. "All Things Reconsidered: The Life-Cycle Perspective and the Third Task of Economic History," *Journal of Economic History* 51 (June 1991), 271–89.

Sutcliffe, John. *A Treatise on Canals and Reservoirs*. Rochdale, 1816.

Sykes, R. A. "Some Aspects of Working-Class Consciousness in Oldham, 1830–1842," *Historical Journal* 23 (March 1980), 167–80.

Taggart, William. *Cotton Mill Management: A Practical Guide for Managers, Carders, and Overlookers*. London: MacMillan, 1932.

Temin, Peter. "Product Quality and Vertical Integration in the Early Cotton-Textile Industry," *Journal of Economic History* 48 (December 1988), 891–907.

Thompson, Edward P. *The Making of the English Working Class*. Harmondsworth: Penguin, 1968.

"The Moral Economy of the English Crowd in the Eighteenth Century," *Past and Present* 50 (February 1971), 76–136.

"Time, Work-Discipline, and Industrial Capitalism," *Past and Present* 38 (December 1967), 56–97.

Tillot, P. M. "Sources of Inaccuracy in the 1851 and 1861 Censuses," in E. A. Wrigley, ed., *Nineteenth-Century Society: Essays in the Use of Quantitative Methods for the Study of Social Data*. Cambridge: Cambridge University Press, 1972.

Turner, H. A. *Trade Union Growth, Structure, and Policy: A Comparative Study of the Cotton Unions in England*. Toronto: University of Toronto Press, 1962.

Ure, Andrew. *The Philosophy of Manufacturers*. London: Charles Knight, 1835.

Urwick, L., and E. F. L. Beach. *The Making of Scientific Management*. London: Pitman, 1963.

Valverde, Marianna. "Giving the Female a Domestic Turn: The Social, Legal, and Moral Regulation of Women's Work in British Cotton Mills, 1820–1850," *Journal of Social History* 21 (Summer 1988), 619–34.

Veblen, Thorstein. *The Engineers and the Price System*. New York: Huebsch, 1922.

von Schulze-Gaevernitz, G. *The Cotton Trade in England and on the Continent*. London: Simpkin, Marshall, 1895.

von Tunzelmann, G. N. *Steam Power and British Industrialization to 1860*. Oxford: Oxford University Press, 1978.

"Time-Saving Technical Change: The Cotton Industry in the English Industrial Revolution," *Explorations in Economic History* 32 (January 1995), 1–28.

Wadsworth, A. P., and J. de L. Mann. *The Cotton Trade and Industrial Lancashire*. Manchester: Manchester University Press, 1931.

Walton, John K. *Lancashire: A Social History, 1558–1939*. Manchester: Manchester University Press, 1987.

"Proto-industrialization and the First Industrial Revolution," in Pat Hudson, ed., *Regions and Industries: A Perspective on the Industrial Revolution in Britain*. Cambridge: Cambridge University Press, 1989.

Ward, John. *The Factory Movement, 1830–1855*. London: MacMillan, 1962.

Weaver, Stuart. "The Political Ideology of Short-Time: England, 1820–1850," in Cross, *Worktime and Industrialization*.

Webb, Sidney, and Beatrice Webb. *The History of Trade Unionism*. London: Longmans, Green, 1894.

Weiss, Andrew. *Efficiency Wages: Models of Unemployment, Layoffs, and Wage Dispersion*. Princeton, N. J.: Princeton University Press, 1990.

Weisskopf, Thomas E., David M. Gordon, and Samuel Bowles. "Hearts and Minds: A Social Model of US Productivity Growth," *Brookings Paper on Economic Activity*, no. 2 (1983), 381–450.

Weitzman, Martin. *The Share Economy: Conquering Stagflation*. Cambridge, Mass.: Harvard University Press, 1984.

Whiteside, Noel, and James A. Gillespie. "Deconstructing Unemployment: Developments in Britain in the Interwar Years," *Economic History Review* 44 (November 1991), 665–82.

Williamson, Jeffrey G. *Coping with City Growth During the British Industrial Revolution*. Cambridge: Cambridge University Press, 1990.

Did British Capitalism Breed Inequality? Boston: Allen and Unwin, 1985.

Williamson, Oliver E. *The Economic Institutions of Capitalism: Firms, Markets, Relational Contracting*. New York: Free Press, 1985.

Wilson, Robert. "Reputations in Games and Markets," in Alvin E. Roth, ed., *Game Theoretic Models of Bargaining*. Cambridge: Cambridge University Press, 1985.

Wood, George H. *The History of Wages in the Cotton Trade During the Past Hundred Years*. Manchester: Hughes, 1910.

Wright, Carroll D. *Regulation and Restriction of Output: Eleventh Special Report of the Commissioner of Labor*. Washington, D. C.: Government Printing Office, 1904.

Wright, Gavin. "Cheap Labor and Southern Textiles Before 1880," *Journal of Economic History* 39 (September 1979), 655–80.

"Labor History and Labor Economics," in Alexander J. Field, ed., *The Future of Economic History*. Boston: Kluwer, 1987.

Wrigley, E. A., and R. S. Schofield. *The Population History of England: A Reconstruction*. Cambridge: Cambridge University Press, 1989.

Index